1

W9-BXD-574

A1290T 623029

The Social Studies Wars

Withdrawn

I.C.C. LIBRARY

The Social Studies Wars

WHAT SHOULD WE TEACH THE CHILDREN?

Ronald W. Evans

I.C.C. LIBRARY

Teachers College, Columbia University
New York and London

LB
1584
.E95
2004

Published by Teachers College Press, 1234 Amsterdam Avenue, New York, NY 10027

Copyright © 2004 by Teachers College, Columbia University

All rights reserved. No part of this publication may be reproduced or transmitted in any form or by any means, electronic or mechanical, including photocopy, or any information storage or retrieval system, without permission from the publisher.

Portions of Chapter 5 are adapted from "Communism v. Democracy: Anti-Communism as Citizenship Education in the Cold War Era," by R. W. Evans, 2002, *International Journal of Social Education, 17,* 107–137. Copyright 2002 by Ball State University. Adapted with permission.

Portions of Chapter 7 are adapted from "National Standards for United States History: The Storm of Controversy Continues," by R. W. Evans and V. O. Pang, 1995, *The Social Studies, 86,* 270–274. Copyright 1995 by Heldref Publications. Adapted with permission.

Library of Congress Cataloging-in-Publication Data

Evans, Ronald W.
    The social studies wars : what should we teach the children? / Ronald W. Evans.
        p.   cm.
    Includes bibliographical references and index.
    ISBN 0-8077-4419-0 (pbk. : alk. paper)—ISBN 0-8077-4420-4 (cl. : alk. paper)
    1. Social sciences—Study and teaching—United States—History. I. Title.

LB1584.E95 2004
300'.71—dc22
                                                                    2003060188

ISBN 0-8077-4419-0 (paper)
ISBN 0-8077-4420-4 (cloth)

Printed on acid-free paper
Manufactured in the United States of America

11   10   09   08   07   06   05   04   8   7   6   5   4   3   2   1

Amazon 24.95

To my children, Katie, Mira, and Kai. May they
experience meaningful social studies.

Contents

Acknowledgments

As I send this book to press, I wish to acknowledge the many persons who have helped make it possible. My partner, Mika, our children, Katie, Mira, and Kai, and my parents, Hugh and Dorothy, have all given their support and encouragement. I wish to express my deep sense of gratitude to my mentor, Richard E. Gross, who read the first lengthy draft and offered encouragement and thoughtful suggestions. A number of other scholars read portions of the work as conference papers and offered helpful insights and comments. Among these were Murry R. Nelson, Oliver Keels, Karen L. Riley, Greg Hamot, Bruce Fenn, and O. L. Davis. I would like to especially acknowledge three "diehards," my colleagues Mark Previte, Skip Chilcoat, and Jerry Ligon, for their continuing support and encouragement.

My colleagues at San Diego State University provided direct financial support for archival research and photocopying, and approved generous paid leaves that helped provide much needed time. I am especially indebted to Andrea Saltzman, a former student assistant who helped obtain many of the necessary materials, to the staff of the interlibrary loan office for enduring my many requests, and to technical assistance from the university support staff. Also, I would like to acknowledge my debt to David Ment and his colleagues at Special Collections, Milbank Memorial Library, Teachers College, Columbia University.

I am also indebted to the many scholars, teachers, and citizens who have contributed to the rich history of the social studies field both in writing about it and living it. I am especially indebted to a number of scholars who have closely influenced my thought and intellectual development. Among these are Dan Selakovich, Richard E. Gross, Shirley Engle, Anna Ochoa-Becker, Jim Shaver, Fred Newmann, Byron Massialas, Jack Nelson, David Tyack, Howard Zinn, and numerous others. Finally, I wish to express my gratitude to my editors at Teachers College Press, Brian Ellerbeck and Lyn Grossman, and to the anonymous reviewers who provided invaluable feedback. Though many others contributed to this work I assume full responsibility for the accounts, interpretations, and conclusions presented.

The Struggle for Social Studies

THE CENTRAL AIM OF THIS BOOK is to describe and interpret the history and continuing battles over the purposes, content, methods, and theoretical foundations of the social studies curriculum. In the book I focus on developments in the modern era, from the late 19th century to the present. To be sure, social studies is an enigma. The history of social studies is a story of turf wars among competing camps, each with its own leaders, philosophy, beliefs, and pedagogical practices. As I argue in the book, the major competing camps struggling at different times to either retain control of social studies or influence its direction include traditional historians, who support history as the core of social studies; mandarins, advocates of social studies as social science; social efficiency educators, who hope to create a smoothly controlled and more efficient society; social meliorists, Deweyan experimentalists who want to develop students' reflective thinking and contribute to social improvement; and social reconstructionists, who cast social studies in schools in a leading role in the transformation of American society. Finally, the consensus and eclectic camps include advocates of a general approach in which the term *social studies* serves as an umbrella—i.e., social studies is history and the social sciences simplified, integrated, and adapted for pedagogical purposes—as well as those who choose to meld major aspects of more than one tradition. My thesis is that what began as a struggle among interest groups gradually evolved into a war against progressive social studies that has strongly influenced the current and future direction of the curriculum.

Other camps may be identified as well. For example, the work of many social studies theorists and practitioners suggests a citizenship education camp. However, the terms *civics* and *citizenship education* can have multiple meanings. Usually, citizenship education advocates and projects have first allegiance to one camp or another, or have melded two or more traditions. Another difficulty is presented by the fact that each camp has evolved over the years and is far from static in its specific approach.

One danger with developing this kind of scheme is that it may lead to an oversimplification of a complex reality. Yet if such a rubric can be used to make social studies more comprehensible while still doing justice to the complexities and nuances of the many different proposals over the years, it may prove helpful. Another problem is that there are multiple theorists and groups of theorists within each camp. For instance, within the traditional history camp, some are inclined to support student inquiry into primary sources as a major part of the curriculum, while others support more traditional teaching with minor excursions into primary sources as an enhancement to build interest and provide additional insights.

Despite such difficulties, the camps outlined above seem to encompass most of the major social studies initiatives. Different camps, or combinations, have held prominent and less prominent positions in the struggle for control of the social studies curriculum at different times in the past. Moreover, each of these camps promotes not only an approach to curricular content and method, but also a particular conception of citizenship and of what it means to be a "good citizen." For example, advocates of traditional history recommend a textbook-centered approach with a focus on development of old-fashioned patriotism through filiopietistic history. Their approach emphasizes socialization. On the other hand, meliorist, issues-centered progressives recommend a curriculum focused on social issues, decision-making, and problems with the aim of developing a more critical version of patriotism. Their approach tends to emphasize counter-socialization, especially at the upper grade levels.

Proposals for change in the field of social studies often serve as a lightning rod for commentary and criticism regarding the nature of the field, the purposes of schooling, and competing visions of the worthy society. At the level of ideals, visions, and values, at certain times in the past social studies movements have challenged either American institutions or a segment of Americans' beliefs about the good way of life. These challenges have often provoked severe criticism from various groups interested in preserving their particular version of the American Way.

Of course, developments throughout the history of social studies have been influenced by many factors in the historical and educational context: the economy; war; perceived threats from abroad or within; the beliefs and ideas of educators and the public regarding the role of schooling and the purposes of social studies education; the monetary funding of commissions, committees, and school reform movements, which can strongly influence curriculum politics; the status anxiety of groups of educators as they seek a voice and influence over the curricular future; and the bureaucratic structure of schooling, which often deflects attempts at reform. An in-depth examination of this century-long struggle will help inform discussants in both current and future negotiations over social studies and may help to clarify the meaning, direction, and purposes of social studies instruction in schools.

Several perspectives are possible when thinking about educational reform and the history of social studies. One approach, that taken by the earliest historians of the field, is to situate the changes in thought and practice in internal developments within social studies. In contrast, another approach, as illustrated by more recent histories, is to locate the wellspring of social studies reform outside the field, portraying social studies as influenced by trends in education and society. A realistic interpretation of the history of the field would admit a complex and judicious mix of both internal trends, institutional realities, and profound external influences. Many earlier frameworks are too simplistic, from either the celebratory (internal) or revisionist (external) perspective. Kliebard's (1996) formulation of what we might call "interest groups theory," which he derived from historians of the Progressive Era, offers the possibility of a richly textured interpretation, in which competing camps within social studies engage in continuing turf wars, struggle over the shape and future direction of the curriculum, and are influenced by a wide array of institutional and historical factors from within and outside education. This approach offers several strengths: It allows for complexity and definition of camps; it may help clarify competing interests in the field; it allows use of multiple lenses to explain changes and trends; and it provides a structural framework around which a richly textured interpretation could be created.

So in developing a framework for understanding social studies I will describe five camps offering competing definitions of the field and engaging in continuing turf wars, with a sixth camp providing a consensus definition and offering itself as a compromise. It is the nature of the field that there have been competing visions of social studies from the 19th century to the present, with multiple ways of describing its purposes, contents, and methods.

It may be helpful to think of social studies curriculum development over time as a negotiation, if not a war, among competing camps, each with its own leaders, philosophy, beliefs, and pedagogical practices. During the hundred-year-long conversation on the nature of social studies in schools, one camp emerges as prominent for a time, only to recede a few years later. At any point in time one vision may be most visible, even dominant, while others are still present, as indicated by ongoing debates, turf wars among interest groups, continuing and repeating with each new significant trend or direction. Viewed from the perspective of the social studies insider, from at least the late 1930s, these conflicts might be seen as the relatively persistent symptoms of a war against social studies by philosophical opponents of the progressive versions of the field. This war on social studies has had a profound influence on the past, present, and future direction of the curriculum.

Through it all, although reforms have changed schooling, schools as institutions have inexorably muted or derailed reforms. The institutional momentum that Tyack and Cuban (1995) have called "the grammar of schooling"—the standard shapes and forms of schools as institutions—has frequently deflected attempts at reform. In fact, social studies may be the most handicapped of any school subject by these institutional barriers and by the persistence of traditional teaching.

This book is drawn from both primary and secondary sources, including literature pertaining to the teaching of history and social studies (books, journals, bulletins, etc.) from the time under study, primary source materials from the archives of the National Council for the Social Studies, previously published works on the history of social studies and curriculum, and numerous doctoral dissertations.

This history of social studies includes elements of several alternative genres. It contains aspects of the Western, with a full cast of heroes and villains, myth and legend. It also contains elements of the mystery, especially around key questions such as, What happened to the Problems of Democracy course, and to social reconstructionism? It also embodies elements of tragedy, in the struggle over the Rugg textbook series and in the failure of issues-centered reform to have a greater influence. On the whole, I have written this history largely as the story of a civil war, with competing armies of American educators clashing on the battlefield of curriculum development and their recommendations breaking over the anvil of classroom constancy.

Establishing Traditional History

OVER THE COURSE of the 20th century, traditional history, chronological and textbook-centered, has dominated the social studies curriculum. However, prior to 1861, what would later be called social studies was in a rather chaotic condition with a number of isolated subjects appearing in the curriculum. Indeed, there were "twenty-two fields of history, eleven of geography, six of civics, political economy, an array of mental and moral philosophy, and religious education" (Roorbach, 1937, p. 7). The foremost aim was to help students understand the sacred antiquities and to appreciate classical literature. Other purposes for offering history included "to entertain," to give students a connected idea of human affairs and time sequence, and to impart citizenship and precept training along with mental and moral discipline (pp. 229–230).

Underlying what was frequently stated, ideological aims were central, including the purposes of transmitting culture and myth, patriotism, and good citizenship. In *Guardians of Tradition,* Ruth Elson writes that 19th-century schoolbooks "take a firm and unanimous stand on matters of basic belief. The value judgement is their stock in trade: love of country, love of god, duty to parents, the necessity to develop habits of thrift, honesty, and hard work in order to accumulate property, the certainty of progress, the perfection of the United States. These are not to be questioned" (1964, p. 338).

From the 18th century to the 1890s, history in schools typically meant studying the myths and legends of ancient Greece and Rome, heroes of the American Revolution, the discovery of the New World, and "other stories designed to inspire patriotism and moral certitude" (Saxe, 1991, p. 30). However, in the early years the condition of history teaching was poor, texts were a hodgepodge of historical information and facts, and the general method of instruction in schools was formal recitation or question and answer.

By the late 19th century, dissatisfaction arose over the condition of historical study in schools. The early origins of what became the traditional history curriculum are traceable to historians such as Andrew White, Herbert Baxter Adams, Charles Kendall Adams, and others, who believed in "the value of historical knowledge to strengthen the individual, sharpen the mind, broaden the horizon, and give depth to the soul." They believed "that history had great pedagogical value for school students beyond simply standardizing courses for university admission." These historians sought to emphasize history's value "not only for its mental discipline but also as a source of useful facts. To its developers, the discipline of history was directed by a scientifically coherent method of inquiry that provided a . . . holistic view of the world. They believed that this new way to treat history had the ultimate civic and social values required by the modern age. To these pioneers, history was a window to the past and a door to the future, and anyone who studied it properly could apply its lessons to everyday life" (Saxe, 1991, p. 30). Thus, the movement toward promoting professional history began among university historians at about the time of the founding of the American Historical Association in 1884.

ENTER THE COMMITTEES

Given rising concerns about the curriculum, national committees set out to bring order to the reigning confusion over what ought to be taught. This was largely a struggle over defining the proper subject matter. Should it be drawn from university subjects or should it be more open, broad, and interdisciplinary? Should history or the child be at the center of the curriculum? Other areas of disagreement included the pattern of curricular organization, the role of subject matter, and the place of mental discipline in the curriculum. Beginning in the 1890s and continuing for at least 2 decades, the answers provided by historians strongly influenced the answers in schools.

By the 1880s, it had become increasingly apparent that school programs were chaotic and not uniform, predictable, or comparable. Academic programs were idiosyncratic and often whimsical. With this condition, transferring credits from one high school to another was not only difficult, but sometimes nearly impossible. In addition, it was difficult for colleges to evaluate candidates in their preparation for college (Boozer, 1960). Thus, the ostensible need for curricular standardization.

The Committee of Ten

The first national effort to suggest a high school curriculum for social studies came with the work of the Committee of Ten, appointed by the National Education Association (NEA) to examine the entire school curriculum. Appointment of the Committee of Ten grew out of ferment concerning the objectives and content of education, concerns over electives and college entrance requirements, and questions about the relative worth of various studies. Toward the end of the 1880s, the NEA called for a national commission to deal with the rational development of both high school and university curriculum together. Some viewed that development as part of an effort by universities to align the schools with their own needs, with entrants who would have some coherent pattern of preparation. Led by Charles W. Eliot, the Harvard University president and humanist, and William Torney Harris, of the U.S. Office of Education, the committee looked at all major curricular areas, both modern and classical, and appointed a subcommittee to examine each area of the curriculum. Each subcommittee, including the History Ten of the Madison Conference, was asked to consider the proper limits of the subject area, methods of instruction, methods of testing for pupil accomplishment, the most desirable time allotment for each subject, and college admission requirements (National Education Association [NEA], 1894). At its root, the impulse behind the Ten was an outgrowth of the industrial era desire for standardization and to create an authority to specify a curriculum.

The politics of the Committee of Ten were distinctly conservative and elitist in orientation as it sought to modernize the curriculum, to establish continuity between secondary schools and colleges, and attempted to develop a curricular compromise between individualism and social responsibility. The approach of the Ten was based on the "one education for all" theory. While such an education would aim at intellectual enlightenment for all, the impact in practice was to provide an education aimed at a rather select clientele, "those few who were going on to college" (Saxe, 1991, p. 41).

A subcommittee, also a committee of ten, and henceforth referred to as the Madison Conference or the History Ten, was appointed to examine curricula for the subjects of history, civil government, and political economy. Chaired by Charles Kendall Adams of the University of Wisconsin, the committee included university, college, and high school teachers, and such luminaries as Woodrow Wilson, James Harvey Robinson, and Albert Bushnell Hart.

Of the members of the History Ten, Hart was perhaps most influential. He was the most active historian in the 1890s debate over the secondary school curriculum. As secretary of the Madison Conference, he contributed profoundly to the shaping of the final report, which he authored (Whelan, 1997a). The report of the Madison Conference presented the framework for the modern-style history that swept into the curriculum. The committee established the formalization of history as a legitimate discipline for secondary schools, described the purposes and benefits of studying history, and laid out a program for schools.

The Committee's Recommendations. The Madison Conference of the Committee of Ten called for historical study in each school year from grades 5 to 12; an 8-year sequence, including American history in grades 7 and 11; Greek and Roman history; French and English history; and, in grade 12, study of a special period from history along with study of civil government. The report also called for an end to formal instruction in political economy, but suggested that economic subjects be treated in connection with other pertinent subjects. Likewise, civil government was to be included in the study of American history. It also recommended that the first 3 years of study be devoted to mythology and to biography based on general history and American history (NEA, 1894).

The report recommended an 8-year sequence, as follows:

> 1st year. Biography and mythology
> 2nd year. Biography and mythology.
> 3rd year. American history: and elements of civil government
> 4th year. Greek and Roman history, with their Oriental connections
> [At this point the pupil would naturally enter the high school.]
> 5th year. French history. (To be so taught as to elucidate the general movement
>   of mediaeval and modern history.)
> 6th year. English history. (To be so taught as to elucidate the general movement
>   of mediaeval and modern history.)
> 7th year. American history.
> 8th year. A special period, studied in an intensive manner; and civil govern-
>   ment (p. 162).

The conference also framed an alternative 6-year program for schools that were unable to adopt the longer program, deleting French history and the intense study of a special period, and combining American history and civil government in the 6th and final year.

On relations with colleges, the committee held that instruction should be precisely the same for all, whether college bound or not, and that college entrance exams in history ought to be framed as to require comparison and the use of judgment, rather than the mere use of memory. The conference report stressed that it would "suggest nothing that was not already being done by some good schools" and that could not reasonably be attained elsewhere. It also did not insist on a "uniform program," but held that the time devoted to history and allied subjects should be increased, that the subjects treated should not be confined to our own country, and that the "dry and lifeless system of instruction by text-book should give way to a more rational kind of work" (p. 167).

The report made several strong statements in support of historical study, arguing that its value lay in the "training of the mind" and in promoting the "mental powers" of judgment and comparison and in showing the relationship between cause and effect, as well as in encouraging the "acquirement of useful facts." Describing history as a philosophical and scientific subject, the report argued that history includes the study of mind, character, and motives, and requires skills of analysis comparable to those needed for a laboratory science. "Grappling with history is grappling with life. . . . It offers an opportunity for growth of discriminative judgement, for the weighing of evidence, for training in patriotism, and as a medium for literary expression. It provides a common vocabulary for metaphors and allusions, and abounds in literary material." The committee also cited the value of history for moral training; "It is a study in which the mistakes and failures of national life and private life become suggestive warnings" (pp. 169–170).

The History Ten argued that some historical study could begin profitably in the grammar school, as soon as children "begin to read at all." They suggested that the formal study of history could begin by ages 9 to 11. In addition they argued that the subject deserved a great deal of time in the curriculum and that it could best be taught by "offering a small number of subjects thoroughly taught," and they recommended "intensive study" of selected periods or topics (pp. 181–194).

The committee recommended improvement of teaching method and called for minimal use of set lectures; wise use of multiple textbooks; recitation as a supplement to the reading; comment through "open textbook recitations"; encouragement of impromptu discussions and debate; and parallel readings in historical literature, poems, historical novels, and biographies. It also called for written exercises ranging from the simple to the elaborate, frequently employing use of historical sources (pp. 181–197).

In its report, the Madison Conference provided a definition for a modern approach to history instruction. History was compared to science, and it was argued that the study of history would lead to "discrimination of judgement" and understanding of "cause and effect." The report made analogies to chemistry and geology and emphasized chronology and "development of the Anglo-Saxon race" (Keels, 1988, pp. 44–45).

Reactions to the Ten. The report of the Madison conference did stir comment. On one matter before each of the committees making up the NEA Ten, the conferees were united. That was the question of whether subject matter should be treated differently for college prep and non-college-bound students? The committees were unanimously against this idea, and numerous articles appeared shortly after the report approving this decision. The conferees had established an open-ended ladder of opportunity, or so it appeared, when their proposals were compared with the European systems (Boozer, 1960).

However, there were some objections to the report, based mostly on the makeup of the committee and its focus. Critics charged that elementary education needed more attention and that the committees were weighted disproportionately with college and university men. In a response to critics, Charles W. Eliot, president of Harvard and chair of the Committee of Ten, argued that "principles and methods of educational reform and construction have a common interest for all teachers," whether at the college, university, high school, or elementary school (1894, pp. 209–210).

In summary, the Madison Conference of the Committee of Ten had an important influence. It set the stage for later reports and studies, resulted in an elevated status for history, and hastened the demise of the more classical and less utilitarian subjects by giving support to the notion that it was not valid to set up hierarchies of subjects. Its work was considered the best curriculum effort up to that time to be aimed at secondary education, setting a precedent of cooperation in the study of educational matters and provided a structural framework for the introduction of history as a formal subject of study into the schools, particularly the high school. Nonetheless, vague language and generalities led to a call for more specific guidance and, ultimately, to the forming of the Committee of Seven. In this light, the Ten might be viewed as a first step toward the Seven and toward the creation of a viable program of traditional history for the schools.

The Committee of Seven

The American Historical Association (AHA), at the request of the NEA, appointed the Committee of Seven in 1896. At the time, college admission requirements were quite varied, with each college or university determining its own prerequisites. This had become a continuing emphasis of the NEA and AHA and was one of the motivating factors for appointing the Ten. The Committee of Seven was asked to consider the subject of history in the secondary schools and to draw up a scheme of college entrance requirements in history. The committee subsequently held five meetings, each lasting several days (American Historical Association [AHA], 1899).

Of the members of the Committee of Seven, Herbert Baxter Adams was especially important. Adams had been instrumental in the founding of the AHA. As a professor at Johns Hopkins, Adams promoted scientific history as a modern alternative to the popular view of history as "literary art, as cultural embellishment, as dry chronicle, or as simple chronological outline" (Keels, 1988, pp. 38–40).

In its proposals for a social studies curriculum emphasizing history, the report of the Committee of Seven differed little from the report of the Madison Conference. Its proposals were much more influential, however, if measured by extent of adoption (Hertzberg, 1981). The Committee of Seven carried the mounting inertia of the traditional history movement from the university into secondary schools, and its report came to be seen as the definitive statement on traditional history by both proponents and critics. The report of the Seven was based in part on an extensive survey of secondary schools. The survey found a curriculum in chaos and argued that history was equal to any other subject in the curriculum in the value and benefits derived from its study and in its focus on development of intellectual skills (Saxe, 1991, pp. 51–59). In its recommendations, the Seven promoted the "four blocks" of history instruction: ancient, medieval, modern, and American, and emphasized the training of pupils in the art of "thinking historically." The report of the Seven was more detailed and more comprehensive than the report of the Ten, but differed little in substance. In each report the main goal of historians was to promote general understanding of the nature of history (Keels, 1988, pp. 43–45).

The official, stated motive of the committee was to prepare students to meet the entrance requirements of colleges. Their proposed program, however, was in many ways a curriculum for conformity and social control. The report of the Seven represented an adjustment of the Ten's recommendations, broadened and closer to actual school practice, more clearly developmental, and with more emphasis on the value of history for citizenship. The report also cemented the connection between the history profession and schools and helped to ensure a leading place for history at the core of social studies (Hertzberg, 1981, pp. 15–16). In addition to reporting on conditions in schools and describing its proposed program, the report addressed methods of teaching, urging teachers to guide students to "think historically," to "tell a story," to "bring out dramatic aspects," and to "awaken interest and attention." Thus, in calling for traditional history as the bulwark of school social studies, historians ignored the suggestions of the new social sciences for schools to make a more relevant and meaningful contribution in attending to social problems. In essence, the historians of both the Ten and the Seven argued for development of intellect, rather than an individual sense of social awareness.

Contents of the Report. In addressing the value of historical study, the Committee of Seven discussed several aims. Its comments read, in part:

> The chief object of every experienced teacher is to get pupils to think properly. . . . not an accumulation of information, but the habit of correct think-

ing . . . the student who is taught to consider political subjects in school, who is led to look at matters historically, has some mental equipment for a comprehension of the political and social problems that will confront him in everyday life, and has received practical preparation for social adaptation and for forceful participation in civic activities. (AHA, 1899, p. 18)

Thus, the committee argued, first, for history as a preparation for civic competence, to "bring boys and girls to some knowledge of their environment and to fit them to become intelligent citizens." History directly "aids the pupil to think correctly, to be accurate and painstaking," and awakens students' interest in books and gives them resources within themselves to fit them "for good and useful citizenship" (pp. 20–21). Second, the committee argued, "history cultivates the judgement by leading the pupil to see the relation between cause and effect, as cause and effect appear in human affairs." Third, it argued, "the study of history gives training not only in acquiring facts, but in arranging and systematizing them" (pp. 21–23). "History is also helpful in developing what is sometimes called the scientific habit of mind and thought"; everybody is required to study and think and examine before he or she positively asserts a point, to approach every question without prejudice. "While we believe that power and not information must be the chief end of all school work, we must not underestimate the value of a store of historical material. By the study of history the pupil acquires a knowledge of facts" (pp. 23–30).

The Four Blocks. At the heart of the Committee's report was the recommendation that historical study in the secondary school consist of 4 years' work, composed of four blocks or periods to be studied in chronological order. These were to include (1) ancient history, (2) medieval and modern European history, (3) English history, and (4) American history and civil government. The committee argued that in-depth study of each of these periods was essential, and that none could be omitted without leaving serious gaps in student knowledge.

The committee also argued against the general history course, a common offering in many secondary schools, largely because of their advocacy of a four-block program. The conferees argued that either general history was too superficial in its presentation for students to gain understanding or insight into the discipline, or students were "led to deal with large and general ideas . . . beyond their comprehension," merely learning facts without seeing relationships (pp. 44–46).

Through study of ancient history, the first of the four blocks, the conferees hoped to give students an "inculcation of the sweep of time" and an understanding that the acts of individuals have great and grave influences on their own times and for the future and that the thread of life beginning in ancient times extends to the present. For some students, they argued, this may be the "only opportunity of coming in contact with ancient ideas" (pp. 44–46). The second block, medieval and modern European history, covered a period of a thousand years and the history of at least four or five important nations. The third block, English history, was to be studied because of the close connection between American political institutions and their historic roots in England, the "taproot" of democratic ideals (p. 67). The fourth block, American history, was to be studied for the "purpose of getting a clear idea of the course of events in the building of the American Republic and the development of its political ideas." It should foster fundamental knowledge of the society and lead to "an appreciation of [one's] duties as a citizen, and to an intelligent, tolerant patriotism" and to learning the "leading features of our constitutional system." Furthermore, "the greatest aim of education is to impress upon the learner a sense of duty and responsibility, and an acquaintance with his human obligations . . . to give the pupil a sense of duty as a responsible member" of society. Clearly, study of political history and the inculcation of political ideas were the chief aim (pp. 74–76).

Civil government was to be taught, if possible, in conjunction with American history, as "the two subjects are in some respects one," and civil government can be studied as a part of history. The conferees recommended that civil government be offered with American history in an "integrated fashion," and stated, "We must not distort the past in an effort to give meaning to the present, yet we can fully understand the present only by a study of the past" (pp. 81, 85).

The committee had quite a lot to say about methods of instruction, but thoughtfully emphasized, "More important . . . than method, is object; means are valueless to one who has no end to be attained." Further, "the accumulation of facts is not the sole, or perhaps not the leading, purpose of studying history. . . . The scientific spirit can be awakened and methods of scientific thinking cultivated." This included power in handling language and an ability for "grasping grammatical distinctions . . . the literary sense . . . the historical sense, the beginnings of historical thinking."

As for specific and concrete recommendations to teachers, the committee had several, and they would be viewed today as rather traditional, but basic. These included recommendations to use a textbook to help students maintain sight of the main current of the story and to use collateral material and outside reading. The committee also recommended use of written work in the form of reports "weaving together various narratives or opinions"; written recitations or tests; required notebooks, maps, and books for reference and reading, with the library as "the centre and soul" of all study in history and literature (pp. 86–92).

On the use of primary sources, the committee recommended they be used sparingly, and "in connection with a good textbook," to keep in mind a "clear outline view" of the whole subject studied. The conferees recommended "a limited contact with a limited body of materials" to show the child the nature of the historical process. They also recommended limited use of documents and the use of literature, objects, photos, and the "remains" of the past "as adjuncts to good textbook work" (pp. 104–105).

Thus, the approach to teaching history advocated by the Committee of Seven was textbook centered. Yet the committee hoped that teachers would impart "wide information," "accurate knowledge," and "a capacity to awaken enthusiasm and to bring out the inner meanings." The good teacher would lead students to accuracy and definiteness and help them to think carefully and soberly. Furthermore, under the tutelage of an able teacher, the student would be "tempted to range beyond the limits of the text and to give free reign to his imagination" (p. 114).

The committee also addressed college entrance requirements and argued that because of the limited numbers of students who went to college, it was "wrong to shape secondary courses primarily with a view to college needs." They called for elasticity in college requirements, and while advocating a four-block program optimally over 4 years, they recommended a minimum of one unit in history as a college entrance requirement (pp. 120, 123).

In short, the approach to teaching history advocated by the Committee of Seven was a refined version of the traditional history put forth by the Committee of Ten. The report of the Seven was more developed and detailed, but differed little in substance. It was an approach to social studies built around the study of a textbook in one discipline, history, and a storytelling approach to teaching that would, it was hoped, awaken the historical spirit and imagination in the young and assist in development of both memory and intellect. The report promoted a scientific approach to history, but with a subtle difference. Instead of seeing history as science, the Seven promoted the image of history as being "like" a science. Thus, the Seven refrained from the Ten's literal claim of history being a science, instead emphasizing that the methods of modern history are similarly empirical (Keels, 1988, p. 45). The reports of the Ten and the Seven led to two main benefits for the advocates of traditional history. They made a logical and persuasive case for the value of the study of history in schools, and they helped to clarify and organize the curriculum. To this point in time, no other group had done this with the schools in mind.

Reactions to the Seven. The Report of the AHA Committee of Seven was generally well received. However, there were some objections. The committee's recommendation to delete "general history" drew criticism as impractical in some schools (Boozer, 1960, p. 59). Others complained that the report gave too much attention to ancient history, too much time to cover during the first year, too little attention to methods appropriate for the schools, too much emphasis on methods more appropriate for the university, and insufficient time to study modern history.

Conferees at the 1904 meeting of the Association of History Teachers of the Middle States and Maryland found four "defects" in the report: too much work in ancient history, too much emphasis on "university" methods, too little reference to practical secondary methods, and insufficient time allowed for modern history (Association, 1904, p. 429). The 1909 meeting of the New England History Teachers Association called for more specificity, including a need for more "definite" recommendations for ancient history; for "more definite divisions and limitations of courses" on medieval, modern, and English history; and for the separation of civil government and American history (New England, 1909, pp. 89–90).

Others called for the use of history for the social goal of Americanizing immigrants (Addams, 1907; AHA, 1904). At the 1908 meeting of the American Historical Association, a "Conference on History" was held to discuss criticisms of the Seven's heavy emphasis on ancient history and its lack of attention to civil government. As conferees debated the value of ancient history and civil government, it was argued that ancient history was "too difficult for high school consumption." Conferees were also distressed over the lack of civics instruction in the schools to counter the growing problem of juvenile delinquency (AHA, 1908, pp. 65, 71).

There was also the question of what kind of history is most appropriate for "industrial" or vocational schools. This question created dissention and conflict among history teachers and led historian James Harvey Robinson, a member of the Ten, to modify his initial thoughts on traditional history and to reconceptualize history for schools with what he would label "the new history." Initially, Robinson proposed this "new" history as most appropriate for industrial education (vocational schools) but he and many other educators soon came to believe that the new history was most appropriate for all students in the secondary schools. It meant a focus not on learning about the past for its own sake, but on matters most relevant to present concerns and interests of society (1912).

Combined, the Ten and the Seven were the most influential committees to influence the traditional history curriculum. Together, they did a great deal to improve the quality of the teaching of history. Surveys established that the traditional history curriculum was dominant for some time and remained influential into the 1930s and beyond (Tryon, 1935). In short, the work of the Ten and the Seven had a profound impact on the social studies curriculum for at least a generation.

DEBATE OVER TRADITIONAL HISTORY

In the period after publication of the report of the Seven, new currents of change were emerging. The record shows that not everyone was in agreement with the traditional history curriculum as defined by the Ten and the Seven. A review of AHA "Proceedings" from the organization's annual report shows multiple competing views on the history and social science curriculum; attention to the "correlation" of history with geography, literature, politics, and the social sciences; a healthy debate over use of the "source method" in schools; and advocacy of more attention to European history.

The study of history for progressive purposes was also increasingly common, as shown in William Sloane's address to the AHA on the 25th anniversary of the founding of the organization in 1909. Sloane commented, "We are not now studying history so much for entertainment as for light upon to-day" (AHA, 1909a, p. 70). Sloane's comment contained the spirit of Robinson and represented a major shift from the study of history for its own sake, for knowledge and mental discipline.

During the same period, a developing crosscurrent was the increasing specialization and organization of the professoriate. The AHA had been established in 1884, and the American Economic Association in 1885. Shortly after the turn of the century, several other social sciences established professional organizations. These included the American Political Science Association (1903), the Association of American Geographers (1904), and the American Sociological Society (1905). Thus, the early near monopoly of history as a professional association of scholars was challenged, and demands for a place in the school curriculum were not far behind. Early in the first decade of the 20th century, there were growing proposals from the newly defined social sciences for a place in the curriculum. As one observer noted, "Each year we find that an increasing number of schools are introducing them into their programs" (Hill, 1901, p. 110).

It was perhaps natural for the AHA to give little attention to the teaching of allied subjects. Nonetheless, a demand was developing that high school pupils be more fully introduced to political and economic thought than they commonly were in history courses. This was combined with rising discontent with historical instruction because of its military and political character and its tendency to focus on isolated facts, meaningless dates, and biographical episodes. Moreover, advocates of the social sciences tended to draw together in opposition to the monopoly of history. Thus, the type of history being taught drew fire from advocates of the social sciences and contributed to a growing discontent among secondary school teachers and administrators during the 1910s. For their part, historians appeared to grudgingly acquiesce to an increasing emphasis on social and industrial history, though many, if not most, maintained a traditional focus. As one prominent observer put it a few years later, "While the historians were busy with politics, battles and diplomacy . . . our social and international life was being transformed by bewildering inventions, by significant legislation, by industrial activities" (Beard, 1929, p. 370).

Meanwhile, among historians, the generally positive reaction to the Seven led the AHA to appoint another committee a few years later to do for elementary teaching what the Seven had accomplished for the high school. A conference on the teaching of history in the elementary school was held at the 1904 AHA annual meeting. J. A. James, professor of history, Northwestern University, and chairman of the conference, noted at the outset that there was "no agreement in practice or in theory" and "few indications of any tendency to uniformity in the schools" (AHA, 1904, pp. 27–28). Henry W. Thurston of Chicago Normal School argued that the course of study should "begin with the child's problems in his social environment and carry on . . . examination of such contemporary social problems as are within the child's comprehension." In contrast, George O. Virtue argued against placing stress on the interests of the child and recommended a program of traditional history, with instruction "rich in possibilities for developing the imagination, rousing the enthusiasm, and building standards of personal and civic conduct" (p. 28).

After making a preliminary report in 1905, the Eight presented the general conclusions of the committee in 1909 in *The Study of History in the Elementary Schools.* In its recommendations, the committee sided with Virtue rather than Thurston, with traditional history rather than a progressive program, and called for the institutionalization of what would later serve as a framework for the "holiday curriculum" (AHA, 1909b).

The Report of the Eight became the standard for a generation. According to Henry Johnson, it "approached in influence a ruling document" in elementary schools (1940, p. 60). Tryon noted courses of study that were "almost verbatim duplicates" of the report and provided before-and-after evidence of the report's influence on the curriculum (1935, pp. 27–28). A survey conducted in the years immediately preceding showed that the committee induced most elementary schools in the nation to follow a pattern that many schools were already using.

Work on the secondary history curriculum by the Committee of Seven was followed by the work of the AHA Committee of Five, which met from 1907 to 1911 and was appointed to reexamine the efforts of the Ten and Seven. The AHA viewed criticisms of the Seven as sufficiently important to call for a reappraisal of the Seven's recommendations. The report of the Five, published in 1910, stated that an investigation by the committee found a general satisfaction with the recommendations of the Seven. In their recommendations, the Five "stuck to the four-block system" proposed by the Seven and offered an able defense and justification of the recommendations of the Seven, including a glowing assessment of its impact as a "wise and admirable" and "logically developed series of history courses." They found that general history had been abandoned by the majority of schools and that schools were "taking history more seriously" (AHA, 1910, pp. 212–216). The committee did recommend "more time for modern history," which it identified as a growth area, and some time for the "separate study" of government. Thus, the slightly revised four blocks included (1) ancient history to A.D. 800; (2) English history to 1760, including European history and colonial America; (3) modern European history from 1760; and (4) American history and government with some time for the separate study of government (pp. 234, 239–240).

So, with the reaffirmations and minor adjustments recommended by the Five, the foundation of the traditional history camp was complete. As a result, the traditional history curriculum as established by the series of reports brought greater standardization and uniformity, the four-block pattern became more pervasive, and history became a more fully developed part of the curriculum. The reports, and their subsequent influence, gave stability to history as a school subject. But the rumblings of alternative approaches to social studies and competing directions with an emphasis on the civic mind were beginning to be heard. These competing approaches would challenge the monopoly of history after only a few years, as traditional history would soon be under fire. Thus, stability was illusory. Given the fluidity of political, social, cultural, and intellectual affairs in the early 20th century, this is not surprising. Traditional history, it seemed, gave too little attention to the insistent present and provided too little linkage to forward-looking social purposes, and in the end, its dominance fell to modernism.

CONCLUSION

Early social studies in the United States was predominantly history as it developed during the 19th century, with some attention to geography and civil government. By 1915, most schools offered three or four courses in history, reflecting the recommendations of the Ten and Seven, and textbooks dominated the course (Koos, 1917; Gold, 1917). Curricular attention to social issues was, apparently, virtually nonexistent.

Several factors may account for the early dominance of history in the curriculum. History instruction, like civil government, was aimed at developing the good, patriotic, and obedient citizen. Likewise, history is frequently a conservative discipline, focused, by definition, on the past, and often imbued with explicitly patriotic purposes. In fact, it has been called "the conservative discipline par excellence" (White, 1978). The early professionalization of historians and their widespread interest in the teaching of history in the schools was a major factor in the early dominance of historical study. Historians' organizations and professional posts at universities created a power base through which historians, and to a lesser extent others, especially geographers and political scientists, could exert influence over the school curriculum. Traditional history won the day, becoming the dominant core, in its traditional, modern, and scientific version, as historians professionalized and sought status in the university and the society. The decline of general social science and the American Social Science Association was a significant part of the story, along with the shift toward discipline-based, segmented, "scientific," nonpartisan approaches to understanding the social world. The curriculum studied in schools was deeply influenced by the work of commissions and committees on behalf of traditional history, though classroom practice shifted only slightly, with the focus on recitation and on knowing for the sake of knowing still the dominant pattern.

While historians supported history in schools because of their belief in the power of the "scientific" and modernized discipline, and its value in educating both judgment and knowledge, their underlying motives included status politics and a conservative nation-building impulse. The history taught in the nation's schools in the era around and after the turn of the century was both traditional and conservative. It served to glorify the nation's past by instituting fact, myth, and legend for historical analysis, and asking few questions about the structure of society or the direction in which it was headed.

In general, the nation was headed in the direction of consolidation of industrial power, colonial expansion and imperialism, and heavy immigration to help perform much of the work. The traditional history curriculum was profoundly connected to the imposition of a glorified and Eurocentric history, which would compel allegiance to the elite of a growing nation, from new arrivals and older residents alike. It was no accident that the institution of laws requiring study of American history and the Constitution were enacted during this period and earlier (Tyack & James, 1985).

Considering the turmoil of the times, traditional history as defined by historians at the turn of the century was a conservative educational program focusing on memory, intellect, and patriotism and largely serving purposes congruent with the aim of national chauvinism. The intellectual emphasis was too often lost in translation to schools, and the focus too often became history for its own sake. The theory of society and the role of schooling underlying traditional history was something of a throwback, and that is not too surprising. After all, the founders of traditional history were academic historians, elites ensconced in an ivory tower, disconnected from the masses, not educators with a broad conception of social purpose.

The discipline of history that was held up as a model for education in schools was modern scientific history, but with emphasis on tradition. The curriculum that historians created did not do justice to their vision. Mired in the tradition of ancient history, linked to the classics of ancient Greece and Rome, it gave too little emphasis and made too little connection to the present society and to students' lives. As a discipline, history created distance, an artificial veil of objectivity on social issues—as if such objectivity was possible—and served largely to separate students from the community, to imbue them with a cultural birthmark, and to legitimate the state.

The 1916 Compromise:
The Report on Social Studies

THE 1916 REPORT of the Social Studies Committee of the NEA Commission on the Reorganization of Secondary Education is generally given credit for the creation of the national pattern of social studies courses that existed more or less unchanged for the greater part of a century. According to some, the work of the committee was the origin of social studies. However, as others have suggested, the committee had many precursors. Trends were well in motion prior to their work.

The 1916 report proposed a new synthesis of social studies subjects and suggested a pattern of courses that was different from what existed in most schools prior to that time. In its report, the committee recommended greater emphasis on current issues, social problems, and recent history and a greater emphasis on the needs and interests of students. This new synthesis represented a significant shift from the pattern of history, history, and more history, the pattern recommended by the AHA committees of preceding decades.

The shift in educational thinking and in curricular pattern represented by the report was several years in the making. The Committee on Social Studies grew out of the continuing effort to coordinate college admission requirements and school curricula. Clarence Kingsley, a Massachusetts schools administrator, circulated a report among New York City teachers on curriculum articulation between high schools and colleges that was distributed by the NEA in 1910. The NEA then established a Committee on Articulation and appointed Kingsley as chairman. The committee was later expanded to include subcommittees on each of the major subject fields, and, in 1913, was renamed the Committee on the Reorganization of Secondary Education (CRSE). One of the original subcommittees of the CRSE was the Committee on Social Science, appointed in 1912, with Thomas Jesse Jones designated to serve as its chair. Jones, apparently, renamed it the Committee on Social Studies (Drost, 1967; Kingsley, 1913).

By 1913, the traditional history curriculum fostered by the Committees of Ten and Seven had fallen into disrepute in NEA circles because it embodied an approach that held the individual at the center. The trend was toward "social centered education," an approach that grew out of psychology, the social sciences and philosophy (Saxe, 1991, p. 110). Previous interpretations of the report have suggested, variously, that its main influences were social efficiency, social welfare, and a progressive version of history teaching. To some extent, each of these was present in the development of the 1916 report on social studies. However, the work of the committee was a compromise, influenced by multiple camps, all of which were represented in the final report.

Commission reports are almost always an expression of change already under way. One major precursor was the "school efficiency" and school progress movement, a mania by 1912. Tests for teachers and preservice educators trumpeted the goals of school efficiency and addressing the needs of students. Edward L. Thorndike, in a statistical monograph, found that less than 10% of students were graduating under the current system, and attributed this to "incapacity and lack of interest in the sort of intellectual work demanded by present courses of study" (1907, p. 10). Others focused attention on making schools more efficient, eliminating waste, and reforming the teaching of subject matter that lacked practical value.

Other precursors were linked directly to members of the committee or scholars who strongly influenced its work. Probably the single most important influence on the committee was John Dewey. In his writings, Dewey synthesized progressive ideas that had been brewing for some time. He made no specific attacks against traditional history, but did offer critiques through euphemisms such as "our present instruction," and the "existing school system." The problem with the system, Dewey charged, was that it attacked the subject matter first and the student second. Dewey held that dogmatic faith in the educational value of the subject matter, in this case traditional history, ignored the primacy of student interests and needs. He wrote that educators should strive to make history functional "by relating the past to the present as if the past were a projected present in which all the elements are enlarged." And, he wrote, "past events cannot be separated from the living present and retain meaning. The true starting point of history is always some present situation with its problems" (Dewey, 1897, p. 22; Dewey, 1916, p. 251; Saxe, 1991, pp. 118–124).

If Dewey's influence was passive and behind the scenes, the influence of another scholar was direct and vociferous. David Snedden was the chief critic of traditional history and favored studies that would be strictly "functional." In Snedden's view, the main goals of education were social control and proper social conduct with the overarching aim of fitting the child to the needs of society. For Snedden, citizenship education was aimed at indoctrinating students in "social virtues, or moral worths." All this was made necessary, supposedly, by the demands of contemporary civilization. On this basis, Snedden favored the social sciences, which he saw as directly efficient, and opposed history as inefficient. In Snedden's view, this belief was based on scientifically derived data (Saxe, 1991, pp. 125–133; Snedden, 1914, p. 279).

Historians viewed Snedden as a gadfly, and were less than receptive to the idea of social studies. However, many educators had come to view traditional history instruction as it was practiced in schools as antiquated, out of step with the modern era. Yet there was little debate in the leading journal, which continued its focus on history. One shrill critic, as expected, was historian Henry Johnson, who argued that a curriculum designed by current events was an absurdity, because events are constantly changing. He argued that educators and the schools should stay with traditional history (Johnson, 1917).

By the mid-1910s the ground under traditional history and foundation for the curriculum established by the Committee of Seven was beginning to shift. Social studies insurgents were poorly organized and less respected than historians. Yet their criticisms of traditional history struck a nerve. Many historians, such as Johnson, stood firm, while others, such as the progressive historians, argued for a modernized and socially responsible approach to history. As we shall see, several important currents of the time lent direct and indirect support to the development of a new approach to the field.

THE REPORT ON SOCIAL STUDIES

In the 1913 preliminary report of the Committee on Social Studies, Thomas Jesse Jones, who authored the report, wrote that a curriculum based on history should be replaced by a broader form of social studies. "Good citizenship," the report declared, "should be the aim of social studies in the high school." Arguing that "facts, conditions, theories, and activities that do not contribute rather directly to the appreciation of methods of human betterment have no claim," the report attacked and dismissed traditional history and introduced a curriculum that specialized in attending to the present growth needs and interests of the learner (T. J. Jones, 1913, p. 1). This shift, the report noted, was largely supported by the notion of practical or functional history. It was apparent in the preliminary report that the committee had taken on a sociological outlook. The academic backgrounds of several committee members could be traced to sociologists Franklin Giddings,

George Vincent, and Albion Small. The preliminary report also included Robinson's view of history instruction, "organized, not on the traditional basis of chronology and politics, but on that of (students) own immediate interests," and rejected the four blocks (Jones, 1913, p. 1).

Early in its pages, the 1916 report offered a definition of social studies as "those whose subject matter relates directly to the organization and development of human society, and to man as a member of social groups" (U.S. Bureau of Education, 1916, p. 9). This was a broad definition, yet it failed to directly address the debate over social studies, because it did not mention history, the social sciences, or a fusionist alternative. The authors of the report discussed the purposes of social studies and stated, "The keynote of modern education is social efficiency. . . . Instruction in all subjects should contribute to this end" (p. 9). Social efficiency included the training of individuals as members of society in the broadest sense. In its use of the term *social efficiency,* the report combined social service and social control, and elements of both the meliorist and social efficiency camps.

Regardless of the course, the report advocated a shift "to immediate needs of social growth" and insisted that selection of topics and organization of subject matter should be determined by "immediate needs." Yet the report refrained from offering detailed outlines of courses, on the ground that they tend to fix instruction in "stereotyped forms inconsistent with a real socializing purpose" (p. 10).

The report also made a strong case for a focus on "present interests and needs of the pupil," but held that students were expected to follow the lead of the teacher. This was a Deweyan position. Dewey held that the child's needs and interests were vital, but that students were not to dictate curricula. In addressing needs, the report referred to needs of pupils, native-born Americans, immigrants, local communities, local conditions and requirements, and industry concerns, but offered no empirical support, instead basing its description of need on the basis of Deweyan philosophy.

The report also made clear that its authors were interested in development of both the individual and the group, but that individual interests and needs were secondary to the needs of society as a whole. This was a major difference with the AHA reports, which had created a traditional history curriculum. For those earlier reports, individual intellectual development was primary (Krug, 1964).

Curriculum Recommendations

The report recommended a two-cycle system for secondary social studies, with a complete course of study in each cycle. This was, at least in part, out of deference to the reality that many students would leave school after eighth grade. Thus, the majority would at least make it through the first cycle. The report focused almost exclusively on secondary education, grades 7–12. The first cycle was described as "elementary," with basic skills and knowledge; the second cycle would create a "broader horizon" with more intensive study (U.S. Bureau of Education, 1916, p. 12). For the junior high, the report recommended courses in geography, European history, American history, and the course Community Civics. For the high school, the report recommended European history, American history, and Problems of Democracy—social, economic, and political. Both Community Civics and Problems of Democracy were rather radical proposals when compared to the traditional history program created by the AHA.

The report focused at length on the teaching of Community Civics, repeating much of the material from the 1915 report, *The Teaching of Community Civics*. For the authors of the report, Community Civics included local, national, and international arenas. The central aim of Community Civics was to promote proper social behavior. Community Civics was the idealized version, the prototype, of education for social efficiency, and as such it represented the tentacles of the industrial machine in the curriculum more directly than most other social studies courses.

The authors of *The Teaching of Community Civics* described the aims of the course in a section titled "What Is Community Civics?" in which they wrote, "The aim of community civics is to help the child to know his community . . . what it does for him and how it does it, what the community has a right to expect from him, and how he may fulfill his obligation . . . cultivating in him the essential qualities and habits of good citizenship." They went on to suggest that Community Civics emphasized the local community because it is closest to the citizen, and because it is easier to feel a sense of responsibility for it. Nonetheless, the authors of the report argued, what is important is the implication of a "community of interests" that is equally applicable to the national community as well (Barnard et al., 1915, p. 11).

As for the history curriculum, the *Report on Social Studies* was critical of current programs in history because they contained too much emphasis on ancient and medieval history. The report recommended more attention to European history. It also recommended combining ancient, medieval, and Oriental civilizations to the end of the 17th century. A topical approach to history was urged, with selection of topics and time allotted depending on "the degree to which such topic can be related to the present life interests of the pupil, or can be used by him in his present processes of growth" (p. 44). The report combined the "new history" of James Harvey Robinson and other progressive historians with the pedagogy of John Dewey. Both were quoted liberally. The report also embraced social efficiency, not Snedden's version, but a form of social efficiency closer to the meliorist pedagogy of John Dewey. Unfortunately, the authors of the report failed to provide many practical examples, which led to little immediate change in actual teaching practice in most history courses.

According to the report, "history would aim to develop a vivid conception of American nationality," a "strong and intelligent patriotism," and a "keen sense of the responsibility of every citizen for national efficiency" (p. 39). Instead of advocating traditional, narrative history, the report argued for selection of aspects that met the qualification of "functioning in the present." Thus, within each history course, the committee recommended "(1) the adoption to the fullest extent possible of a 'topical' method, or a 'problem' method, as opposed to a method based on chronological sequence alone [and] (2) [t]he selection of topics or problems for study with reference to (a) the pupil's own immediate interest; [and] (b) general social significance" (p. 37).

The committee also recommended another new course, Problems of Democracy. This course was the apparent invention of the committee, an answer to the rival claims for the 12th year, and was an important development for a number of reasons. Problems of Democracy was one of the first conscious attempts at curricular fusion; it represented the revisionist plan for social studies, focused on developing curriculum centered around social problems; it was modernist in design and intent; it represented the purist position on social studies; and, at the time, at least, it seemed a workable compromise. The course answered the rival claims of the social sciences for a place in the curriculum, and resembled the ASSA model of a general social science offering. If the course represented the social efficiency strand of social studies, it was social efficiency of a liberal, softer, reconstructionist bent with the piecemeal examination of "actual problems, or issues, or conditions as they occur in life" rather than the direct inculcation of preferred citizen behaviors as exemplified by Community Civics (p. 53).

In the report's description of Problems of Democracy, no one social science was to be highlighted. Instead, the course would involve all social studies, including history, by centering the class on a study of problems or issues. This was a radical departure from standard practice. Course content would be selected on the grounds of student interest and importance to society. However, the report contained fewer than five pages of actual description or discussion of the course. Reflecting this lack of discourse, the course became a largely experimental one. As presented in textbooks, the course tended to fuse content from three main disciplines, government, economics, and sociology, with a smattering of historical backgrounds or other contents. Nonetheless, the new Problems of Democracy course represented the idealized version of education for social betterment. As such, it was the meliorist prototype for social studies in both form and content, addressing social issues and problems directly in the curriculum, fusing subject matter from several social science disciplines, and focusing at least some attention on the process of reflective thinking.

Philosophically, the vision of social studies as an integrated, issues-centered field of study was directly linked to the meliorist Progressive movement in education. Proponents of this definition for social studies envisioned a unitary field of study, fusing materials from the disciplines and organizing curricula around societal issues or problems. Historically, this vision embodied the highest hopes of progressive reformers and pedagogues and represented the flowering of the Progressive impulse for societal reform in the curriculum. The most influential progressive, John Dewey, viewed the school as a focal point in preparation for citizenship with the aim of guaranteeing a society "which is worthy, lovely, and harmonious." This cast the school as a lever for social change, for as soon as the goal of a "worthy, lovely, and harmonious" society is defined, educational theory becomes social theory, and the educator becomes an agent for social change, a social reconstructionist. Curricula devoted to the integrated study of societal issues developed within this context and became an institutional embodiment of the Protestant social gospel.

At its root, the reform impulse that led educators to propose a course such as Problems of Democracy, and to advocate a problem-centered approach to other courses, was rooted in the small-town pietist values held by members of the progressive "educational trust." Many of the leaders of the educational trust were sons of Protestant clergy. Others testified to the importance of their early evangelical training in their later careers. Their religious upbringing left them with the conventional stress on hard work, thrift in time and money, and a pietist imperative to set the world straight. Reformers made a partial transfer of redemptive power from religious to secular institutions, developing a view of social evolution that held that people could control and improve their world by conscious means. Thus, the reform vision underlying creation of the Problems of Democracy course, and the meliorist camp, owed its being to the social gospel of Protestant religion, which inspired faith in the crusade to redeem society through rational planning and piecemeal reform (Tyack & Hansot, 1982, pp. 114–117).

REFLECTIONS

Several strands of explanation may help us understand the contents and direction of the *Report on Social Studies*. These include its intellectual roots in progressive education, the influence of the protestant social gospel, the impact of the heavy wave of immigration into the United States during the period, perceived economic necessity, and the desire on the part of the Committee on Social Studies of the CRSE to create a practical and flexible document. One significant influence on the report was the vision for schooling of the NEA committee of which it was a part. Its intellectual roots may be traced from the statements contained in *Cardinal Principles* (NEA, 1918), drawn from Herbert Spencer. The social Darwinism of the report was of the reform strand, influenced by the work of early sociologists such as Lester Ward and Albion Small, Franklin Giddings, and George Vincent, and through the competing though related educational visions of John Dewey and David Snedden. Its disciplinary forbears included advocates of the New History, among them James Harvey Robinson, Carl Becker, Charles Beard and other Progressive historians. In the truest sense, the report was progressivism writ small, an application of Progressive ideas within the context of the early 20th century (Cremin, 1961).

A second major influence on the report was the social gospel movement. Popularized in the late 19th century, especially among Protestant groups, the social gospel movement helped to create a fervor for social improvement and reform that profoundly influenced the creation of social studies. Most of the founders of the field were older stock, not recent immigrants, and they had small-town pietist and Republican roots with the concomitant obligation to set the world straight. From the upper-middle-class loft from which they viewed the world, this appeared possible through the curriculum. This was behind acceptance of social efficiency doctrines, partly because of the firm faith in transformation that it inspired.

Third, at least part of the impetus for social studies reform during the era came from a desire to Americanize the masses, spurred by fear of foreign ideologies and cultures and fear of competition for limited resources. Educational leaders wanted the schools to help address modern problems of the industrial era—urbanization, industrialization, and immigration—while supporting the general status quo of liberal capitalist democracy. This would create allegiance to the state and the appearance of progress. Though aimed at social betterment, the *Report on Social Studies* was created by White, middle-class northwest European Americans who generally assumed the hegemony of their own group and ignored race as an issue (Watkins, 2001).

A fourth influence was economic necessity. CRSE was driven by social efficiency advocates and the perceived need to boost economic productivity. A curriculum emphasizing modern, progressive history and community civics would do far more to create a citizenry effective in labor and was seen as a wise investment in human capital. Certainly, this was a major aim of social efficiency advocates such as Snedden and W. W. Charters. The report might also be seen as part of a growing bureaucratization in industrial society, seeking to Americanize immigrants as part of the broader civic reform movement, which included social settlement and charity organization work (Tyack, 1974; Kliebard, 1986).

Finally, the members of the Committee on Social Studies sought to create a practical, flexible document, one that would prove useful to teachers. On its face, the report was generated by concerns of educators for social improvement and for improving the teaching of social studies subjects in schools and was aimed at providing modest help for society. Underneath the surface, in the tension between social efficiency and social meliorism, the report could be described as an attempt to reconcile competing visions (Lybarger, 1981).

SILENCE

Reactions to the committee appear mixed, at best, in the short term. In the journal *Historical Outlook*, coverage devoted to the report was substantial at first, then disappeared. The editors published a summary of the 1916 report in the journal in early 1917, then published no reference to or commentary on the report until 1920. This silence makes it appear that the social studies insurgents may have been shut out of the journal by advocates of traditional history—their enemies in the turf war, competing for status, voice, and power over the curriculum.

This gap in the debate over social studies is quite puzzling and will likely be a source of disagreement among historians of the field for some time to come. Was social studies not mentioned because of a focus on World War I, or was there a deliberate attempt to shut down the insurrection? Given the fact that other educational issues and topics did receive attention in the journal during the war, it seems highly unlikely that no manuscripts reacting to the report were received. More likely, Henry Johnson and other traditional historians who opposed social studies persuaded the journal's editor, A. E. McKinley, not to publish any articles on the report. Circumstantial evidence strongly suggests that this was a signal from the historians who provided editorial supervision for the journal that social studies was not welcome.

Later, following the end of the war, there were a number of published reactions to the curriculum proposals of the CRSE Committee on Social Studies from historians, social scientists, and other educators, much of it focused on Problems of Democracy. One reaction suggests that not all historians stood opposed to the 1916 report. The AHA Committee on History and Education for Citizenship in the Schools, also known as the Schafer

Committee, recommended a similar pattern to that suggested by the 1916 Social Studies Committee. The main outlines for Problems of Democracy were supported by the Schafer Committee. Though the report was presented to the AHA, it was not adopted or officially published as a report approved by the association (Schafer, 1921b).

The American Economic Association (AEA) made a report on the presentation of social studies in schools in 1923 and described the purposes of social studies in schools and the "distinctive contribution of each field of social study," based on contributions from historians, political scientists, geographers, sociologists, and economists. The AEA proposed a 6-3-3 social studies program somewhat similar to that proposed by the report of the Social Studies Committee of 1916 (American Economic Association [AEA], 1924). Their proposal for the junior high years recommended a fused curriculum for each grade, including ninth-grade inclusion of "principles of social organization (economic, political, social)" with a focus on asking the student "to formulate consciously the principles of social living which should guide him in later years." The report did not mention the possibility of a "problems" course in the senior high years, but did suggest that social studies "should be directed toward an understanding of the physiology rather than the pathology of social living," an apparent dig at the 1916 committee's recommendation (Proposed, 1922).

The American Political Science Association (APSA) had been concerned about the teaching of social studies for a number of years. Its 1916 report, *The Teaching of Government*, had advocated a year of social science other than history in high school, with at least one semester devoted to the study of government. A report published in 1922 by the APSA disapproved of Problems of Democracy as defined by the Social Studies Committee of CRSE. Instead, the APSA wanted civics as the 12th grade offering, and a focus on governmental organization and function. While stating that it recognized the value of the "problem method" in teaching, the Committee argued that "no effective instruction in the problems of democracy can be imparted to high school pupils unless they are given an adequate background through the study of governmental organization and functions. To provide this background, they argued, "the course must be comprehensive and systematic, not a study of isolated problems" (American Political Science Association [APSA], 1922).

At least one group outside the social studies committee of the NEA was more supportive of the *Report on Social Studies* and Problems of Democracy. A 1922 report written by the Committee on Social Studies of the National Association of Secondary School Principals (NASSP) favored economics and Problems of Democracy in grade 12. They suggested that Problems of Democracy could eventually become a full-year course. This group also suggested no history after grade 10 and claimed that there was "too much history" being taught. The NASSP's statement indicated a firm endorsement of the Problems of Democracy course, and an important one, given administrative influence over the curriculum offered in schools (Cox, 1922).

Sociologists were in general agreement with the 1916 Social Studies Committee, but did not support Problems of Democracy, and wanted a general social science course instead. They wanted no focus on problems but did state that problems could be selected and "taught . . . to facilitate the teaching of economic and sociological principles involved" (Finney, 1920).

Ross Finney, who headed the Committee on the Teaching of Sociology of the American Sociological Association, was quite critical of the proposed new social studies course Problems of Democracy. In a 1924 article he discussed the move to Community Civics and Problems of Democracy, suggested more emphasis on morals and philosophy, and recommended that the course be retitled General Social Science. He also offered the following critique:

> Emphasis on the sore spots in society has a certain morbid effect on the minds of young persons. It makes them imagine that they ought to be agitators, radicals, reformers, philanthropists, social workers or something of the sort. It tends to fill their heads with queer immature ideas, with increased danger that they may fail to function normally in the staple relations and fundamental institutions of society. And that is likely to do far more harm than good. (pp. 527–528)

Finney's remarks epitomized the feelings of many opponents of the Problems of Democracy course, suggesting that opposition was, in part, ideological. He stated that he preferred teaching scientific economics, sociology, and political science, and shifting "from social pathology to social anatomy and social physiology," arguing that this would be better and "more scientific" in terms of the practical effects on the minds of students (p. 527).

Thus, the reaction to the proposed new course Problems of Democracy was quite mixed. The leading political science and sociology organizations were opposed to the new course, and historians and economists had a muted response, with the AHA failing to adopt the Schafer Committee's endorsement of the course, and the American Economic Association supporting the social studies report only in very general terms. Only the NASSP, an organization of school administrators, gave unqualified support for the idea. Dawson's "History Inquiry" found 30 administrators favoring an extension of the course for every one who opposed it (1924). That support was to prove very important to the early establishment of the course. Unfortunately, the disapproval signaled by the majority of historians and social scientists was to foreshadow continuing disagreement over the future of social studies. The failure of several leading groups of social scientists to endorse the Problems of Democracy course reflected the powerful hold of the disciplines on curriculum formation. This proved a major obstacle to the spread of the issues-centered vision of social studies as an integrated field.

As we can see, there was quite a bit of adverse reaction to the course Problems of Democracy, recognized as the epitome of the meliorist program. Debate over the merits of Problems of Democracy was debate over social studies, over progressive education, and over competing visions of the future of the nation. The essence of this critique was summed up by Dawson as "Critics want science, proponents want problems," to which one advocate of the course replied, "Young people face problems, not sciences" (Dawson, 1927, pp. 285–286). Some critics charged that the course was too general and the subject matter not well organized. Others felt that if the course was structured via the social sciences it would be too theoretical, and if it were practical in design it would become a "hodgepodge of materials that begin nowhere and end nowhere" (Ashley, 1920, p. 502).

The main source of opposition was apparently from social scientists who believed that sociology, government, and economics should be taught as separate subjects. Modern problems could not be understood, or so the argument went, without a thorough grounding in the principles of the separate social sciences.

DEBATE ON SOCIAL STUDIES IN THE 1920S

Now that the major camps had staked out their turf, and initial reactions were in, debate over competing approaches became a dominant trend. There were several camps in the 1920s debates including those who were in favor of the new social studies proposed by the 1916 committee, those who were opposed, and those who favored a stronger place for either traditional history or one of the social sciences. By the late 1920s, arguments over the social studies curriculum were manifest in disagreement over the contents of the 12th-grade course, whether it should focus on one of the social sciences or offer a blend of several.

Disagreement seemed to center on the following key issues. First, what should be the major source of content: history, the social science disciplines, issues and societal problems, or some mix of these? Second, to what extent should content be integrated across disciplinary boundaries? Third, what should be the role of student interest versus the study of knowledge for its own sake? Fourth, what was the best form of education? Should it embody a mental discipline approach focusing primarily on memory, or should it focus on problem solving? Finally, running through the discourse on social studies during the 1920s and beyond was the question of ultimate purposes: To what extent should education aim for socialization, passing on the social traditions, or countersocialization, encouraging questioning?

While there were many critics of the new social studies, criticism was also mixed with partial agreement from most. There were also, of course, numerous advocates of the new approach, including the members of the 1916 committee, the founders of the National Council for the Social Studies, advocates of social efficiency such as Franklin Bobbitt, Charters, and Snedden, and advocates of a reconstructed social studies curriculum such as Harold Rugg and his entourage.

In addition to the reactions of organized groups of educators, we can glean insights into the turmoil over social studies by examining the continuing debate in the *Historical Outlook,* the leading journal for social studies teachers of the time. In 1920, a "Department of Social Studies" was established in the journal, edited in cooperation with the National Commission for Teaching Citizenship, an extension of the NEA Committee on Social Studies. Beginning in February 1920, the journal's board of editors included Edgar Dawson and Lucy Salmon, staunch supporters of social studies.

Also in 1920, the journal published a brief report on the reconstituted NEA Committee on Social Studies, which held a meeting on February 24, 1920, to consider "supplementing or revising" its original report. Membership on the committee included most members of the 1916 committee with the addition of several leading scholars, including Ross L. Finney and Harold Rugg. The brief report in the journal read, "At the time of its publication, the 1916 report was considered by many as a somewhat radical document, and was received in some quarters with a certain degree of skepticism. During the intervening four years, however, there has been a decided tendency to accept the essential principles of that report. The war has been very largely responsible for this, because of the shaking-up it has given to the social studies in high schools" (Editor, 1920, p. 203). The article went on to report a "high demand" for copies of the bulletin, which were being widely used as the basis for reorganization in many school districts. It also reported "increasing agreement" among committees from the various committees of the NEA, AHA, ASA, and so on, in part because of the "influence of the war period" and to a series of conferences held between representatives of various committees (p. 203). Thus it appears that in 1920, at least for the editor of *Historical Outlook,* and perhaps for many members of the NEA Committee, there was an air of optimism and cooperation on the prospects for building a broad consensus around the 1916 report.

However, in the early 1920s, articles began to appear offering reactions to the new approach to social studies described by the 1916 report. In 1921, two important critiques of the 1916 report were published. In one, Anna Stewart accused the report of "many inconsistencies" and wrote disparagingly of trends it had set in motion, among them the move to "damn history in order to boost civics," and of the complaints about the use of chronology as a "what-comes-next" principle. She argued that chronology can serve important functions in helping learners to understand closely interwoven movements, and that chronological sequence should not be put in opposition to the problem method of teaching, but viewed as compatible parts of a complete whole (pp. 53–56).

In the same year, a scathing though indirect critique of the social studies movement was written by a longtime advocate of traditional history, Henry Johnson. Johnson's critique took the form of a contribution to the report of the Schafer Committee in which he described "a vast confusion of conflicting theories" on the place assigned to history in "what we are acquiring the habit of calling the 'social studies.'" In his remarks, Johnson described three alternatives: (a) nonsystematic study of history, in which the past is used "to illuminate current events, to impress festivals, ceremonies, and holidays, to enforce moral or civic ideas, and in general to stimulate love and reverence for existing institutions without regard to any of the essential conditions imposed by history as a special branch of learning"; (b) history as a separate school subject, *"but with the promise that it shall be history controlled by present interests and problems"* (Johnson then went on to present extreme examples of the application of this principle to the sometimes capricious interests and problems identified by children); and (c) modern and scientific history, with the aim to "describe as accurately as possible, and explain as adequately as possible the past itself." For Johnson, this was the one, truly respectable approach to history, focused on understanding the past and "creating definite impressions of continuity" and conscious training in historical source method. Although he made no direct references to the NEA Committee on Social Studies, it was clear from his remarks that he had their version of social studies and history in mind in offering his criticisms of history controlled by present interests (1921, pp. 93–95).

Addressing the same dilemma, though with a more even-handed approach, Tryon, in 1922, discussed possible "adjustments" between history and the other social sciences in the course of study. The four major alternatives he described included (a) "an independent-parallel twelve-year program in history and one of equal length in social studies other than history"; (b) an "alternating of the two subjects in the elementary and high school programs"; (c) "a combined course" in history and the other social studies, in its most radical form supplanting all independent work in history and the social studies with a new course made by careful selection of material from the entire social studies field, and in a less radical version, creating two 1-year general social science courses; and (d) a combination of the independent-parallel and unified schemes. According to Tryon, each had its proponents: the independent-parallel program was recommended by an influential committee of the NASSP; an alternating plan was favored by at least three major committees of national scope; the unified plan has had many proponents over the years, though few actual applications; and the combined plan has growing influence in schools. Tryon argued in support of a combination of the two schemes (pp. 78–82).

In a volume of the journal *Historical Outlook* addressing the purposes and prospects for the newly formed National Council for the Social Studies, several authors were enlisted to provide descriptive articles, gathered under the header "Characteristic Elements of the Social Studies." The selection of articles reads like a precursor of the federationist, consensus definition later adopted by NCSS (i.e., social studies is history and the social sciences in schools). In an explanatory note that precedes the selections, and that was apparently circulated to the authors in advance to "secure their cooperation," the editor, Secretary Edgar Dawson, wrote, "There is no general agreement as yet on the matter of the organization of a course of study in man's social relations." He went on to suggest that "the time has passed for dogmatic statements about separate courses or merged ones," and that alternative proposals must be considered on the basis of a "careful analysis of what it is we wish to accomplish." Thus, what was presented in the collection of articles were statements addressing the special virtues of each of the social studies subjects, including history, government, economics, sociology, and geography along with the belief that they are "not mutually exclusive" but "supplementary," and the hope that the "Joint Commission of scholars" will present a statement to "clear the atmosphere" (Dawson, 1922, pp. 327, 337).

Continuing concern over the relative place of history and the social sciences in the curriculum was expressed throughout the decade. One writer, C. E. Martz, examined the place of history in the new social studies program and argued that history, taught well, encompasses every value claimed for social studies, and that we should not throw out traditional history when we are just beginning to see it taught well. Martz viewed social studies advocates as "casting history to the wayside." Martz presented many of the values attributed to the study of history, claiming that it is a "living subject" and that it treats every problem now confronting society, but can better help develop the habit of "weighing evidence" because of the distance it provides from matters "not now in the field of controversy." Martz also stressed the value of chronology because it gives a sense of the orderly succession of events, movements, and problems "that cannot be isolated," and argued that "societal growth must be likened to a rope with strands thoroughly intertwined, rather than as a string of beads easily separated into its parts" (1924, p. 73).

By 1926, much of the debate centered on the subject matter contents of the 12th-grade course, with the struggle continuing among proponents of the various social sciences for a home in the curriculum. Debate centered around whether the 12th-grade offering should focus on one or more of the social sciences, or whether it should be a fully integrated offering. According to Dawson, American history was the most common offering for grade 12, but was being replaced by courses in Civics, Economics, Problems of Democracy, Social Problems, and Sociology. Proponents of each of these offerings continued to make their case (1926).

By 1928, the situation apparently hadn't been clarified much. Reporting on a survey of the social studies, one writer argued that the curriculum for social studies was in a state of turmoil and in need of repair. The report presented data collected by the writer and materials assembled by other investigators providing convincing evidence of the wide variation in types of courses offered, and seemed to favor a move toward standardization and consolidation of courses (Dahl, 1928). In hindsight, the struggle over social studies between advocates of particular disciplines and curricular integration had just begun. The 1920s offered "no clear victories to any of the contending factions" or camps struggling for control of the curriculum (Krug, 1972, p. 68).

NCSS FOUNDED

At a time when social studies was "up for grabs," the National Council for the Social Studies was established in an attempt to bring some order to the field and to promote the vision of social studies created by the NEA Committee on Social Studies (Hertzberg, 1981). What they developed was a consensus definition of the field aimed at a broad, practical orientation to social studies, one that would please as many people as possible and offend few critics. Creation of a consensus definition was an understandable response to the turmoil created by social studies insurgents in the 1916 report and by the response of critics. What emerged was a lasting definition that weathered a number of storms over the curriculum, but, unfortunately, failed to adequately defend and promote a vision of social studies as a strong alternative to traditional history and the social sciences.

The effort to establish NCSS came from a group at Teachers College, Columbia University, and from Earle Rugg, who organized a "social studies roundtable" in Chicago. The first organizing meeting for the group was called by Earle Rugg in an explanatory letter that outlined plans for an organization to coordinate work in the field with the NEA. The letter cited "lack of agreement about subject matter." The first organizational meeting of the group occurred on March 3, 1921, in Atlantic City, New Jersey, during a meeting of the NEA Department of Superintendence. Most attendees were members of the continuing NEA Committee on Social Studies.

The earliest "temporary constitution" drawn up by the group in 1921 included a definition and statement of the group's object. The initial name of the organization was the National Council of Teachers of the Social Studies. The object included a statement of purpose for the organization, "to bring about the association and cooperation of teachers of the social studies (history, government, economics, sociology, etc.) . . . and others interested in obtaining the maximum results in education for citizenship from social studies" (Gambrill, 1921). The following year, the revised constitution included a new name, the National Council for the Social Studies, and the following definitional sentence: "The 'social studies' shall include history, government, economics, geography, and sociology" (Drafts, 1921). Note the difference in tone of the two name statements, from "of" to "for." Perhaps more important, this definition of social studies as a list of subjects set the organization's direction as a consensus organization.

At least two of the most prominent early leaders of the social studies movement, Dawson and Tryon, had fears about the movement's appeal and had heard the voices of critics. Far from being "directionless" (Nelson, 1995), the fledgling organization was seeking to build consensus, a stable social studies field that would be endorsed by as many interested parties as possible.

By the late 1920s NCSS was well established, with more than 1,600 members, and was growing in both membership and influence. It became a department of the NEA in 1925 and established ties with the AHA, conducting its annual meeting in conjunction with the AHA annual meeting and often holding joint sessions.

PROGRESSIVE EDUCATION AND RUGG SOCIAL STUDIES

The new approach to social studies, and the birth of NCSS, would not have occurred without progressive education. The progressive education movement emerged out of a general "culture of protest . . . against the prevailing ideology of business . . . cultural uniformity," and the "life styles" and idea of a "good life" (Krug, 1972, pp. 178–179). All three involved revulsion toward the current practice and ideology of schooling. Progressive education was also part of progressivism writ large and had grown out of the general response to problems brought by industrialization. In broad terms, it was an effort to cast the school as a fundamental lever of social and political regeneration.

The progressive education movement had its philosophic roots in Herbert Spencer and in the work of reform Darwinists such as Lester Frank Ward and Albion Small, sociologists who argued that the mind is "telic" and that evolution can be directed toward worthy social ends. Thus, education was the foremost activity and great panacea for curing social ills. John Dewey, a younger colleague of Small, wrote in 1897 that "education is the fundamental method of social progress and reform" and that the teacher was "the prophet of the true God and the usherer in of the true kingdom of God" (1899).

Progressives in education were of at least four or five strands. There was the Rousseauist, fully child-centered strand; the social reconstructionist strand, aimed at changing the social order; the social efficiency or life adjustment strand; the administrative or bureaucratic strand; and the centrist, mainstream progressive. With all these strands of thought came a great deal of misinterpretation and criticism from teachers and the public.

Perhaps the leading progressive social studies educator of the time was Harold Rugg. Harold Ordway Rugg, born in Fitchburg, Massachusetts, on January 17, 1886, attended Fitchburg public schools, which he would later describe in rather unflattering terms (Rugg, 1941b). Prior to attending Dartmouth College, he worked in a textile mill and was directly exposed to the realities of modern industry. After college, and prior to becoming an educator, Rugg studied civil engineering and worked as a railroad surveyor and as an instructor of civil engineering. He taught civil engineering for 2 years and became interested in how students learn, then attended the University of Illinois, where he earned a PhD in education under the mentorship of William C. Bagley in 1915. During World War I, service on the Army Committee on Classification of Personnel resulted in contact with intellectuals holding an aesthetic orientation, which led Rugg to read the work of frontier thinkers. Arthur Upham Pope, also working for the army, introduced him to the works of a number of contemporary social critics, including Van Wyck Brooks, Waldo Frank, and Randolph Bourne, who had written for *The Seven Arts,* a highly regarded literary journal. Another colleague on the Army's Personnel Committee, John Coss, also apparently had an influence on Rugg. Coss planned to develop an undergraduate course at Columbia University that would integrate the social sciences into a general introduction to the contemporary world. Coss seems to have started the process of Rugg's thinking of developing a similarly integrated approach in his social science pamphlets. He felt it his duty to inform youth about these ideas. Rugg was also influenced by his brother Earle Rugg, a history teacher at Oak Park, Illinois, who had urged Harold to consider devoting attention to social studies (Nelson, 1977). So, with little previous interest in social problems, Rugg became engrossed in the social and literary criticism of *The Seven Arts* and arrived at a liberal orientation to addressing social problems, fending off the skepticsm that became so prevalent in the 1920s (Carbone, 1977).

Inspired by these new horizons, Rugg was eager to develop these ideas toward reorganization of the social studies curriculum. Thus, when the opportunity came, in January 1920, he joined the faculty at Teachers College, Columbia University, and developed his interest in the history and social studies curriculum. His contacts at Teachers College with John Dewey, William H. Kilpatrick, George S. Counts, John L. Childs, Jesse Newlon, R. Bruce Raup, and others had a profound influence on his intellectual development, as did his association with the avante-garde in the New York area, including creative artists such as Alfred Stieglitz and Georgia O'Keeffe in Greenwich Village and during his later residence in the arts community of Woodstock, New York.

During his early years at Teachers College, Rugg concluded that teacher education was too difficult and didn't work. He decided to attempt to improve education through what he saw as the most influential element, the textbook. In an article published in 1921, he called for a social studies curriculum that would be entirely problem-centered, built around what he called the "American Problem" (p. 252). Rugg's vision was of a better society, which he referred to variously as "the great society," "the great technology," and "the great new epoch." The reconstructed society was to be created through a combination of large-scale social and economic planning and a new education that would cultivate "integrated" and creative personalities (Carbone, 1977, p. 4). Achieving widespread popular consent for democratic social planning could only take place if the public were made more aware of existing social problems and potential reforms; thus Rugg suggested a curricular focus on social problems and issues.

Although Rugg may have been the leading progressive thinker in social studies, his ideas regarding subject matter and curriculum planning, while innovative, were, if anything, more conservative than those of many in the progressive camp. His pamphlet and textbook series, with subject matter organized around contemporary problems and their historical antecedents, represented thoughtful planning in advance of instruction, a relatively conservative approach, more in line with Dewey than with Kilpatrick or others who tended to discount its importance.

Rugg's thoughts on "reconstructing social studies" were first published in an article that appeared in *Historical Outlook* in 1921. In that article, and in subsequent publications, Rugg argued, "All units of work shall be . . . in problem-solving form," focusing on "alternative proposals," and with historical background developed as needed for "clear thinking" about "current affairs," all sequenced through some form of "'layer' scheme" (p. 252).

Rugg would later argue that the entire social studies curriculum should be organized around problems of contemporary life (1923). Although not the only experiments in unification in social studies at the time, these ideas were clearly far ahead of their time and were later to become central guiding principles for reflective and issues-centered social studies. Nonetheless, Rugg was not without his critics. Some referred to almost any scheme for unification with the derogatory label "social stew." One early critic of Rugg's work complained that the material was too technical or difficult for the junior high school grades (Goodier, 1926). Another, Robert S. Lynd, a social scientist, suggested that Rugg focused on public issues at the expense of the skills needed in everyday social life. Lynd argued for a broader unification across the social and natural sciences (1927).

Despite criticisms, Rugg hoped to create a fully integrated social studies curriculum, abolishing the artificial divisions between history, geography, political science, economics, and sociology and grouping all the material under the general rubric of *social studies*. His first attempt at enacting this plan began with a team assembled at Lincoln School, Teachers College, which included the high school history teacher, a geography teacher, an elementary history teacher, and an elementary "room" teacher. Difficulties arose immediately. As Rugg later recalled: "My plan wasn't too clear, even to me, and to the teachers it was utterly nebulous . . . the high school history man was downright opposed to the whole idea" (1941b, p. 205).

After a year Rugg disbanded the original group and assembled a new team with his brother Earle Rugg as a key member. Earle had come to Teachers College to pursue his own doctorate and to work with Harold in developing the new materials. He decided to focus on developing materials for use in the junior high school because intelligent fifth and sixth graders had found the materials difficult and because of the confused state of social studies in the junior high. Rugg realized that a well-written series of social studies materials for the junior high years would have a good chance of being adopted across the entire country. While he saw the potential for personal gain, even more enticing, he viewed his materials as a vehicle to make a difference in the education of democratic citizens (Nelson, 1977).

The need for texts and the confused state of the curriculum for those grades made it possible that new and appealing materials could be adopted widely. Rugg contacted former students and asked them to subscribe, sight unseen, to the first pamphlet series, a prototype for the eventual textbook series. The response was overwhelming. By June 1922, he had received orders for 4,000 copies of each. Rugg and his team of associates revised the materials with the $100,000 they had made, and built a research team of doctoral students paid from the funds. The second edition of the pamphlet series resulted in about 100,000 copies of each unit being shipped to schools.

The work of the research team centered around developing "guiding principles" for developing the pamphlet series into a curriculum. The team researched current events to "scientifically" determine what the leading issues were, using four liberal journals and the literary digest and canvassing the work of "frontier thinkers." While the research team's work was being completed, insights from their work flowed into the Rugg pamphlet and textbook series only informally. The work of the research team produced what can reasonably be assessed as a highly skewed interpretation of American society. Perhaps Rugg's most grievous and fatal mistake was that he and his research team sometimes failed to include competing or dissenting ideas. Moreover, presenting a biased collection of liberal thought without competing ideas or a declaration of value was one thing, but to clothe his procedures in quasi-scientific robes was contradictory and ultimately raised many doubts.

Publication of a textbook series was planned with Ginn and Company in 1926, through Rugg's contact with a fellow Dartmouth alumni, his friend Henry H. Hilton. Originally planned to cover grades 3–12, the series first focused on the junior high school. During the ensuing years, Rugg rewrote and revised the pamphlets and added a teachers guide. The revised materials were published in textbook form, two texts per grade, beginning in August 1929. Subsequently, the texts were revised to answer critics and update material. The series became a huge financial success, and may represent the zenith of issues-centered social studies materials' entry into classrooms in the 20th century (Nelson, 1977, p. 79). We will return to the Rugg story in subsequent chapters.

LOOKING BACKWARD AND LOOKING FORWARD

In 1921–1922 the United States Bureau of Education conducted a survey of enrollments in school subjects, its first since 1915. By the early 1920s, not much had changed as a result of the 1916 report. History remained dominant (U.S. Bureau of Education, 1924). Two official studies of the "facts" about social studies, both published in 1924, were sponsored by the leading professional organizations, one sponsored by NCSS and the other by the AHA. The NCSS survey was conducted by J. Montgomery Gambrill, who described 15 cases of experimental curricula in junior high and high school, and found the new curriculum dominated by training for citizenship and the needs of contemporary society; new courses were integrated or fused; history was often focused on practical or current value; schools were still in "bondage" to the textbook and focused on treating social and political questions in a "conventional and commonplace" manner. Thus, the curriculum was very similar to what had gone before and what would come after, with a focus on routine teaching from a textbook.

Dawson's "History Inquiry" revealed a field in transition, with one third of teachers following the recommendations of the AHA Committee of Seven for a traditional history curriculum, one third following the 1916 report and its call for a new type of social studies, and one third following such a variety of curricula that no common pattern could be discerned. He wrote, "There is no doubt that ancient, medieval, and English history, as separate courses, tend to disappear from the high school curriculum," with a tendency to stress recent history (1924, p. 268).

A nationwide survey of social studies course offerings and enrollments in 1928 reported that relative enrollment in history courses had fallen and the social studies other than history showed a slight gain. The 1916 report was having some impact on enrollments, with major gains for some social science courses, and slow growth for Problems of Democracy (U.S. Office of Education [USOE], 1930). A 1930 study found the percentage of students enrolled in social studies courses increasing, with enrollments in social studies other than history showing greatest gain (Brown, 1930).

As to method, the typical teacher was frequently derided as a "routine following, unimaginative slave of tradition." Question-and-answer recitation was clearly the favorite method (Wirth, 1931). A deeper analysis found schools in the "typical community" providing civic boosterism, at least some broadening of horizons, and an intense patriotism, and reproducing and sorting students for predetermined social roles (Lynd & Lynd, 1929). Another observer wrote an article titled "Chaos in the Senior High Social Studies," suggesting that the field was an unsettled "hodge podge" with a great deal of overlapping of subject matter, and a lack of economy and standardization (Dahl, 1928).

A theme issue of *Historical Outlook*, published in 1929, provided an especially interesting look back at the early development of social studies and offered insights on the aspirations and concerns of social studies educators at the end of the decade. The articles conveyed a sense of some of the major dilemmas in the field and lament the failure of leadership to adequately address these dilemmas. Charles A. Beard provided an overview of trends in social studies and described a field in transition, from traditional history, focused on "war, diplomacy, and politics," to a field more focused on the present. Presaging many of the continuing tensions in the field, Beard wrote:

> The term is not entirely happy. The boundaries of the field are indefinite. The subject-matter is difficult to determine. Methods of teaching and testing are under debate. Intangibles are numerous. But amid all the fuss and feathers, there is substance, there is reality, in social studies. The grave public responsibilities which they are designed to meet, in some measure at least, cannot be evaded. (1929, p. 371)

Edgar Dawson lamented the opposing forces spawned by the work of the 1916 report and the founding of NCSS. He wrote that the field "missed the co-operation of some subject-matter specialists who have been unwilling to sink their particularistic interests in a single undertaking [and] have in many cases stood firm for elementary courses in their own fields" (1929, p. 372). (He was referring to separate courses in economics, government, and sociology rather than a fused offering such as Problems of Democracy). Later, he lamented the fact that "the particularistic spirit of specialists made for failure" (p. 375).

Despite such reservations and difficulties, the 1916 recommendations in the *Report on Social Studies* became the dominant curricular pattern for most of the 20th century. Looking backward from midcentury, the curricular pattern for social studies in 1950 was largely similar to the curriculum proposed in the 1916 report. The modernist and forward-looking compromise proposed in the report succeeded in part because administrators favored social studies over the traditional history program. History, the time honored core of the social studies curriculum, was still the dominant subject; offerings in American history doubled and European history was strengthened, while the earlier emphasis on ancient and medieval history was disavowed. The report was also successful because its emphasis on the broader goals of citizenship education and social efficiency fit the current trends. Its inclusion of the social gospel ethos in both Community Civics and Problems of Democracy was a good fit with American ideals, and the doctrine of appeal to student's present interests had great resonance in the modern society that was emerging. Finally, the flexibility built into the Report's proposals made it acceptable to more administrators, teachers, and members of the public.

The roots of the report's success must also be viewed as cultural, economic, and intellectual. It is important to keep in mind that the United States government sponsored the creation of the report and gave it an "official" imprimatur. The government supplied many of the key leaders of the social studies committee and paid for the publication and distribution of its reports (Saxe, 1991, pp. 117–118). The report received additional support from the NEA, the Rockefeller Foundation, and the General Education Board, all mainstream institutions with an interest in moderate and functional approaches to education that would assist the growth of American institutions within the context of liberalism and capitalism. The economic and social policy undergirding the report and the educational projections it embodied ultimately supported social control and the maintenance and continued development of mainstream liberal, democratic capitalist institutions.

On the whole the report was a compromise, a moderate and progressive approach to social education aimed at creating cooperative citizens. It was part of the moderate, piecemeal, and progressive attempt to reform society aimed at curbing the excesses of industrialism. Why did the committee create this moderate compromise instead of other possibilities, such as a child-centered or fully issues-centered plan? One reason was that the report reflected the orientations of competing interest groups over the future direction of the curriculum. At least four major camps had significant influence: historians, meliorists, advocates of social efficiency, and advocates of the various social science disciplines.

It is also imperative to keep in mind that the 1916 report was developed during a time in which the hegemony of the White, Anglo-Saxon, Protestant, middle-class male of Western European descent was largely unchallenged. The courses that made up the curriculum in 1916 were predominantly the story of the glory of Western civilization and its latest triumph, the growth of the American nation. The curriculum would establish reverence for American and Eurocentric ideals and traditions through history courses, social training for social efficiency and conformity through Community Civics, and an attitude favoring progressive social betterment through the fledgling and experimental Problems of Democracy.

The creators of the report had certain blind spots. The conception of social welfare they promoted was aimed at adjusting people to the society by addressing their deficiencies (Lybarger, 1981). Most did not see government as the solution, instead preferring piecemeal charity. Nevertheless, they did have the aim of helping, and sought to address social problems through school curricula in a sincere way.

Nonetheless, the curriculum plan they developed, when contrasted with a curriculum built on traditional history, was a move toward the modern, toward raising questions and investigating issues. It was a curricular framework that allowed the work of the reform-minded meliorists and reconstructionists such as Harold Rugg to flower, the mandarin and positivist New Social Studies to develop, and the life-adjustment version of social efficiency to come to influence. In a sense, it was an opening in the curricular architecture that allowed multiple visions to flourish and to struggle in turf battles over the future of social studies.

By the late 1920s it was clear that there were several important tensions in the field, many of which were readily apparent to at least some participants at the time. Although there were no clear victories for any of the pedagogical camps, the battle lines were more clearly drawn between advocates of traditional history and competing models of social studies. New professional organizations emerged as significant players in the battle over social studies, with NCSS and discipline organizations in an uneasy alliance and frequently at odds. The social gospel of reform emerged as a significant and continuing echo, continuing its growth in the curriculum with development of the Rugg social studies materials and the growth of the Problems of Democracy course. The grand question to emerge during the decade was, How would social studies be defined? Although an answer was not forthcoming, the alternatives were beginning to come into focus.

As we shall see in the following chapter, by the 1930s the turmoil of the national debate was much greater. Not only was social studies at stake, but the future of civilization was also. The battles over social studies took on an ideological tone of war between traditionalists and frontier thinkers, and were accompanied by serious thinking about the qualities of American institutions as compared with alternatives.

CHAPTER THREE

Social Studies in Hard Times:
Social Reconstructionism and the
Educational Frontier

DURING THE 1930s the turf struggle over the future direction of social studies hardened into a much sharper ideological battle. With its social gospel roots and social welfare orientation, social studies had always had a reconstructionist bent. Because of the sharpening distinctions and conflicts over wealth and power during the depression, that tendency grew immeasurably as George Counts, Harold Rugg, and others called for new approaches in schools that would transform an ailing social order. Although Rugg's call for a "cooperative commonwealth" and a revamped, issues-oriented social studies predated the depression years, it was during the 1930s that his influence, and that of other educational reconstructionists, reached its peak. In the 1930s, battles over the future direction of social studies became overtly ideological as the tone of educational rhetoric shifted. In social studies, this translated into increased attention to issues-centered approaches.

Social studies during the depression must be understood in the context of the era. By 1933 perhaps 15 million people—one quarter to one third of the labor force—were out of work. The American people had known depressions before and had come to expect the boom-and-bust cycle as a natural occurrence. Yet, the maelstrom of the Great Depression was different. Never before had so many Americans endured so much economic suffering. Even those who had jobs lived with the fear of unemployment, fear of seeing their life savings vanish in a bank failure, and fear of further economic collapse.

In education, the depression led to budget cuts, and teachers were often the victims. Teachers got plenty of sympathy, though little else, from the public. Educators began an open dialogue on individualism and social responsibility and the role of schooling in their development as the depression made these matters objects of public concern. As pundits attacked individualism as the cause of the depression, critics of progressive education attacked excessive individualism in education (Krug, 1972).

Progressive educators continued to promote many of the trends begun earlier, including curricular integration and the methods craze. In social studies, the turf battles between advocates of history and the newer social studies continued, along with increasing attention to the teaching of social problems, controversial issues, and Problems of Democracy. As we shall see, during this decade, and for the first time, each of the major camps in the struggle to determine the direction of social studies was fully present and accounted for.

Various forms of curricular integration were increasingly popular during the 1930s. These were known under a variety of labels but were most commonly referred to as integration, correlation, fusion or unification, and core. One teacher wrote of the correlation of current events and issues with a chronologically organized course in U. S. history (King, 1930). There were critics of the various approaches to curricular integration, some of whom viewed the trend as a left-wing assault on the curriculum. There was also a good deal of difference among educators on the meaning and application of the various forms of integration. One attempt to clarify the confusion suggested that *fusion* be used to refer to the organization of experiences and materials into learning units that "take no account of social studies boundaries as such." *Integration* meant "integrated materials of instruction from several fields," *correlation* meant "seeking and utilizing points of contact and relationships between subjects," and *core* was "practically synonymous" with *integration* (Park & Stephenson, 1940, pp. 313–316). In at least a few instances, curriculum integration became the target of criticisms from those who supported maintaining the sanctity of history and the social science disciplines (Phillips, 1933).

The turf battles between competing camps offering different definitions for social studies continued, and with new vigor, even though most historians did not take a strong stance on the matter. Amid numerous calls for rapprochement by social studies educators, many scholars and other adherents of history or one of the social sciences continued to argue for the value of study in their particular fields. In a few instances, teachers described and recommended innovative approaches such as teaching history backward, or using a "regressive" or topical method.

Social problems, controversial issues, and Problems of Democracy all received increasing attention, in keeping with the tenor of the times. If the problems approach and the Problems of Democracy course had established a beachhead in the 1920s, it was during the 1930s, particularly the second half, that meliorist and reconstructionist attention to issues and social problems took off. Aided by the obvious social problems of the Great

Depression, by the movement for educational reconstructionism, and by the growing interest in integrated approaches, an issues-centered curricula, it seemed for a time, would be the wave of the future.

The second half of the decade also saw the rise of life adjustment education, a version of the hard social efficiency championed earlier by David Snedden and other curriculum theorists. Led by Charles Prosser, a former student of Snedden's, life adjustment found root in the work of the Educational Policies Commission and the American Youth Commission.

In the main, the decade of the 1930s saw the growth of what had been called progressive education, though in hindsight, many educational historians are unsure of the label and what it meant. In the late 1930s, many progressive educators had come to question the meaning of the term and had great difficulty in agreeing on a single definition. Was it the activity curriculum? A problems approach? Was it analogous to social reconstructionism? Were some of its programs disguised social efficiency? Although it is clear that progressivism meant different things to different people, there were definite meanings to the term. The mainstream progressives stressed instruction emphasizing student activity, participation, and growth. The reconstructionist wing stressed education to foster a new social order. The administrative progressives wanted a more efficient educational system, and the Rousseauist, child-centered progressives supported the natural development of the child. These contrasting interpretations of "progressive" education sometimes confused both educators and laypersons, though they also made possible a brief consensus for change (Tyack, Hansot, & Lowe, 1985).

The Eight-Year Study of the Progressive Education Association was the single most important experimental project of the time. Preoccupied with social change, its creators "fostered an environment which encouraged continual curricular revision." The project was both an outgrowth and embodiment of the experimental trends of 1930s educational practice. It involved curricular experimentation in progressive schools and research that tracked their students through college. Although there were no clear winners in the comparisons between the experimental and control groups, the curricular experimentation under the auspices of the study involved different forms of integrated curricula, including fusion and core, and frequently centered around issues, social problems, and student's personal problems that were seen as aspects of larger issues.

One thoughtful observer described a mix of practices. Several of the trends he noted reflected approaches to course organization. First, a great many history courses were still organized chronologically, in some cases correlated with the literature of each era. There was a tendency to break away from political and military history and focus more attention on social history. And he noted a growing tendency for schools that retained a chronological framework to "bridge the gap between the past and the present," relating the history studied as quickly as possible to contemporary problems.

Looking backward, the 1930s were golden years for advocates of core and issues-centered education, and a sense of the excitement of the times remains. Those involved were young and innovative spirits. Although the teachers and students involved in the reform study experienced a heady freedom, realized a good deal of growth, and gained a strong sense of "belonging to an adventurous company," the lasting impact is much less clear (Giles, McCutchen, & Zechiel, 1942).

LARGER BATTLES

The attacks on progressivism in the 1930s were largely a continuation of the 1920s debates casting progressives against anti-progressives. Press critics of the progressives portrayed domination of schools by a small group of educationists at Teachers College, especially Dewey, Kilpatrick, Russell, and Counts, in association with Beard. Of course, there were enemies both within and outside the gates of education. Within progressive education there were some friendly critics who pointed out the impracticality of many progressive ideas. Others espoused "traditional education," "that vague entity of disrepute," which amounted to a declaration of treason (Krug, 1972, p. 285). Essentialists were the treasonist group, led by W. C. Bagley. Other articulate critics included William S. Learned of the Carnegie Foundation; Abraham Flexner; John L. Tildsley, associate superintendent of schools in New York City; and Robert Maynard Hutchins, the new, youthful president of the University of Chicago.

Criticisms were of at least two types. There was the stereotyped and approved pattern of criticism. Without risking one's professional reputation it was permissible to charge that progressivism was "anti-traditional and anti-academic" with the object of making a case for change, or that it was nearly a "religious crusade." Then there was the criticism that progressive education was leading to "lower standards, coddling, the decline of work . . . fads and frills, trivialities . . . vocationalism," and too much focus on "practical subjects." Much of the criticism amounted to "sustained muttering" against modern education, frequently employing stereotyped images of progressivism. The article "Lollipops vs. Learning" is a good example (Krug, 1972, pp. 286–287).

The most well known critique came in a form that became known as essentialism. The essentialist platform, created in 1938, had various facets.

W. C. Bagley was the most visible essentialist. As an advocate of social efficiency, he had been denouncing progressivism since the early 1920s. He attacked the softness of progressivism and saw numerous defects, including
the emphasis on "pupil-initiative vs. teacher-initiative" . . . "personal experience v. race experience," and "immediate needs vs. remote goals"
(1938, p. 244).

There were many other critics as well. Henry Johnson continued to be
one of the main critics of progressive social studies and remained an advocate of traditional history to the end. Most notable among the many critics
both within and outside of education by the late 1930s, none other than
John Dewey himself had become a critic of progressive education as it had
been put into practice. In *Education and Experience,* Dewey criticized educators for allowing too much freedom in the name of progressivism and for
straying too far from the use of the organized subject matter (1938).

EDUCATION FOR SOCIAL RECONSTRUCTIONISM

In 1932, at a meeting of the Progressive Education Association (PEA),
George S. Counts delivered an address titled "Dare Progressive Education
Be Progressive?" It has been described as an "electrifying" speech, with a
"yeasty" response. The audience was so moved by the speech that they sat
in silence, contemplating the prospects and the vision that lay before them
(Krug, 1972, pp. 235–236).

"Dare the Schools Build a New Social Order?" the pamphlet created
from the 1932 speech, became the main source of reconstructionist thought
in education as Counts's challenge "burst upon the profession." The aim
was not simply to save the PEA, but to cast the school as a lever in transforming the society. Arguing against the child-centered tradition, he challenged educators, "to face squarely and courageously every social issue,
come to grips with life in all of its stark reality . . . develop a realistic and
comprehensive theory of social welfare, fashion a compelling and challenging vision of human destiny, and become less frightened . . . at the bogies
of *imposition* and *indoctrination*" (1932, pp. 9, 12). Arguing that schools cannot be neutral, Counts wrote, "All education contains a large element of
imposition . . . the real question is not whether imposition will take place,
but rather from what source will it come." He did not support the notion
that teachers should "promote particular reforms through the educational
system." Instead, he hoped they would endeavor to provide a "vision of the
possibilities which lie ahead" and "enlist (students) loyalties and enthusi-
asms in the realization of the vision." Teachers and students would "critically" examine "our social institutions and practices in the light of such a

vision" (pp. 12, 27, 87). Thus, Counts's vision held special implications for social studies education, supporting issues-centered study in the vein of Harold Rugg's work.

In education during the 1930s, the idea of social change was already in vogue. The reconstructionists added the notion that change was something people could direct. These theories implied a "revitalized" social studies. Reconstructionists called on schools and teachers to lead in creation of social change, and social studies teachers were to be the vanguard. The idea of using schools to change the social order was far from new but was recapitulated by Counts and other reconstructionists in such a way and at such an opportune time that it gained currency.

The social reconstructionist crusade was centered at Teachers College, Columbia University. Counts was the lead reconstructionist, but the ranks included William H. Kilpatrick, Rugg, Jesse Newlon, John Childs, and R. Bruce Raup, and the group had links to Dewey. It was a modern expression of a long "messianic tradition," a new language to express traditional faith in utopian reform through schooling (Bowers, 1969).

In 1934, educators sympathetic with reconstructionism launched a new journal, *The Social Frontier*, with Counts as editor, to help advance their cause. Over the years of its existence the journal served as a lively forum for debate on social reconstructionism and on the role of schooling in creating a new society. "To exercise educational leadership can only mean to define the issues of contemporary life and to initiate persistently and consistently clear-cut movements, in the school and out, calculated to achieve the goals of a good life," the journal's editors declared. While the most persistent theme of the journal was the evil nature of laissez-faire capitalism and rugged individualism, differences emerged on the efficacy of the class struggle as a means to bring social change. A major focus of the journal was the debate over whether teachers had the right to indoctrinate students with perspectives critical of mainstream institutions.

Reconstructionists were critiqued from both the left and the right. The left viewed reconstructionists as naive and unrealistic in their hopes that schools could change the capitalist social order. These critics charged that reconstructionists failed to recognize the deep hold of class structure and capitalist ideology (Tyack, Hansot, & Lowe, 1985). Another critic, David Snedden, called reconstructionism "romantic nonsense," labeled its advocates "utopians, subversive of 'civic decency,'" and charged that its supporters played into the hands of communists. School administrators were largely alienated from reconstructionism because of "its lack of prospects for success." As one argued, "Schools and schoolmasters are not . . . permitted to take the lead in changing the social order." Reconstructionism was a visionary romanticism that "wouldn't work" (Krug, 1972, pp. 238–239).

One superintendent reportedly said that the Teachers College oligarchy "should be put in rear seats and muzzled" (p. 251). Another mused, "The stream of words and books about a new social order which has poured over teachers in the last few years seems very much like the proverbial water on a duck's back" (Moseley, 1936).

Hearst newspapers and other sources, in cartoons and editorials, reacted to Beard and the AHA Commission on Social Studies by seeing them as a "red menace." State legislatures reacted by passing loyalty oath laws and by requiring patriotic instruction and rituals. Patriotic and business groups reacted as well. The Daughters of the American Revolution listed the NEA as an organization in "sympathy with communist ideals," and the American Legion led a drive promoting loyalty oaths for teachers. By 1936, 21 states had enacted special oaths of allegiance. The National Association of Manufacturers used advertising to improve the image of capitalism and commissioned a textbook survey that led to attacks on the Rugg texts and others. Anticommunists vilified many progressive and reconstructionist educational leaders as communists or sympathizers. Counts, Rugg, and Dewey even came under Federal Bureau of Investigation (FBI) surveillance (Dilling, 1934; Nelson & Singleton, 1978; Tyack et al., 1985, pp. 63–64).

Despite all the criticism, during the 1930s many publications for teachers reflected a reconstructionist emphasis, though the degree to which social reconstructionism trickled down to the classroom is more difficult to assess. Reconstructionists succeeded in creating a lively debate on the purposes of education and contributed to increasing attention to the Problems of Democracy course and an emerging focus on social problems as the high point of the curriculum. Despite this growing attention, course texts for Problems of Democracy continued to embody a somewhat disjointed, piecemeal, meliorist approach rather than looking at the whole pattern of inequality and power relationships that educational reconstructionism called forth. However, on the whole, it appears, the impact of reconstructionism on the educational mainstream was somewhat limited. In part, this was because many teachers feared community reaction. One survey found that only 5.6 % of superintendents and 11.6% of teachers believed that students should be led to enter discussions on reform and social issues, and 82% of teachers agreed that "educators should avoid partisanship" (Tyack et al., 1985, p. 67). Given these attitudes on the part of the vast majority of teachers, the prospects for success were slim.

THE COMMISSION ON SOCIAL STUDIES OF THE AHA

Social reconstructionism did have a profound impact on the ideas of social studies educators in several camps and on the practices of at least some educators. Perhaps the most notable impact on the social studies dialogue of the period came with the work of the AHA Commission on Social Studies. The commission represented a huge contribution of talent, scholarship, and funds. Begun in 1929, the commission was an outgrowth of previous AHA committees on school history.

In the past, most national committees examining the curriculum had operated under sponsorship of one parent organization, resulting in a restricted view with specialists from only one subject area. This commission was instead created as an academically diverse group largely to avoid this problem. Its members included four historians, three professors of education, two economists, two political scientists, one professor of the teaching of history, one geographer, one sociologist, one college president, and one superintendent of schools. The chair, A. C. Krey, was deeply committed to a broad approach to social studies. His 1926 book on the education of youth for social efficiency sounded like the work of an education professor; Jesse Newlon, a longtime progressive educator, served as NEA president and was a proponent of curriculum integration; Henry Johnson was long a staunch supporter of traditional history; Leon C. Marshall was chair of the AEA Committee on Schools and favored an interdisciplinary, issues-centered approach to the social sciences.

Charles A. Beard, the most prominent and influential member, is difficult to classify but was known primarily as a historian and as a progressive reformer. George S. Counts was to become the leading spokesperson for social reconstruction in education. The commission had a total of 16 members. Its diversity was its strength, and perhaps its downfall. One can imagine that this group had some interesting discussions. Many other notable scholars were also involved through subcommittees or consultation, among them Harold Rugg, Boyd Bode, and Franklin Bobbitt.

The findings and recommendations of the commission were diverse, voluminous, and somewhat unclear. The first publication of the commission, *A Charter for the Social Sciences in the Schools,* written by Beard, appeared in 1932. This introductory volume laid out several of the key beliefs of the commissioners and had a strong reconstructionist bent. The report began with the sentence "Such is the unity of all things that the first sentence on instruction in social studies in the schools strikes into a seamless web too large for any human eye." Thus, Beard would postulate the need for the disciplines as a powerful conditioning force in the creation of social studies in schools. Then, he wrote, the commission would "assume in the beginning" that the "spirit and letter of scholarship" would "seem to set a certain inevitable framework" for instruction. Thus, the opening passages seemed to suggest a discipline-based orientation (pp. 1–3).

Later, and at some length, Beard discussed his misgivings about a curriculum devoted to social issues or current events. Admitting "grave problems" are "all about us in society," and suggesting that such questions cannot be ignored, he cautioned against "the hasty opinion that the public schools can solve the problems of democracy," or the contention that "the chief purpose of the social studies is to assure a presentation and discussion of current issues." He then went on to provide a detailed argument against the problems of democracy as a guiding framework for the curriculum: problems are temporary; lists of problems are "partial, one-sided . . . trivial"; they cannot be solved by "classroom consideration"; discussion of some issues may jeopardize a teacher's position; and schools are "merely one agency" of information (pp. 42–47).

He suggested, instead, an emphasis on "wide knowledge of facts and a discipline in thinking," and went on to write:

> To be sure, many facts presented should be immediately germane to problems, and the mind may be whetted on live issues as well as dead issues, but there is something to be said for giving pupils a thorough grounding in the historical records of human experience before they attack the more elusive questions of the living present. (p. 47)

Later, Beard described the tentative nature of knowledge, and expressed a preference for inquiry, not indoctrination, in the education of citizens, stating that "no fixed set of dogmas" would be appropriate (p. 95). Then he outlined the knowledge, skills, attitudes, and values that needed to be acquired to allow the fullest possible development of each individual. In addressing the purposes of social studies, the commission developed a "ten-point platform" to shape instruction, including "national planning in industry . . . expansion of insurance systems . . . universal education," and so forth (pp. 79–81). The volume also described creation of "rich, many sided personalities, equipped with practical knowledge and inspired by ideals" as the purpose of civic instruction. By this statement Beard and the commission meant that students should possess information and attitudes that would lead to sufficient development of independence in judgment to make "fateful decisions" and preserve freedom (pp. 96–113).

The commission rejected a general social science and a curriculum detached from the disciplines, and found a curriculum based on problems of democracy to be insufficient. Beyond this declaration, which may have been aimed at Rugg and others who supported an issues-centered curriculum, the report did little to clarify the relationship between history and the social sciences, or what was to be included. History was described as the "crown" of social subjects and the synthesizing and integrating force, but what this meant was left unclear.

Alongside the *Charter*, in 1932 the commission also outlined a list of vol-

umes it planned to sponsor, several of which have become works of enduring value. The commission published the majority of these works prior to
the appearance of its *Conclusions and Recommendations* in 1934. Several of the
volumes had a reconstructionist orientation. This was especially true for a
volume authored by George S. Counts, who believed that instruction in social studies should be "organized within a frame of reference provided by
the ideal of democratic collectivism." Less forthright, but also reconstructionist in orientation, were volumes by Beard, Newlon, and Merle Curti.

Drafted by Beard and Counts, the *Conclusions and Recommendations* of
the commission expressed a "democratic American radicalism" that could
only have appeared in 1934, at the height of the depression. Under way since
1932, creation of the volume was controversial among the members of the
commission and led to several rewritings. It presented a subtle, reconstructionist view. The volume covered many matters, frame of reference, philosophy and purpose, materials of instruction, method of teaching, tests and
testing, the teacher, public relations, and administration, thus creating
many opportunities for controversy and attack. Much of the outside attention centered on its statement of philosophy and purpose and its "frame of
reference," especially its comments on the nature of society and the social
order. It stated that "the age of individualism and laissez faire in economy
and government is closing and that a new age of collectivism is emerging"
(p. 16). It argued that we would see the emergence of a consciously integrated society, in which "individual economic actions and individual property rights would be altered and abridged." The commission was against
regimentation, but for personal, cultural, and individual freedom.

The volume gave a good deal of attention to the curriculum, discussing
the disciplines and other nations, as well as contemporary American life
and theories and philosophies designed to deal with the problems of industrial society. It put forward the theory that learning must be related to
the life interests of the pupil and that "almost any topic is appropriate if related." The themes and subjects discussed included regional geography,
comparative economics, government, cultural sociology, major movements
of thought and action in the modern world, and recent international developments. The commission neither suggested a scope and sequence, nor did
it exclude integrated or interdisciplinary study, leaving readers with a
somewhat nebulous impression. The commission did clearly "embrace the
traditional disciplines . . . including history, economics, politics, sociology,
geography, anthropology and psychology," and repudiated "the notion that
any general or comprehensive social science has been created which tran-
scends the disciplines themselves" (Commission, 1934, pp. 6–7).

Thus, the commission clearly championed the distinct disciplines
as the source of content for social studies. But, they also wrote, "the social

sciences as bodies of empirical data contain no inner logic which determines clearly and positively either the scope, the content, or the structure of social science materials to be taught or the social activities to be encouraged" (pp. 6–10). It is likely that this position represented a compromise. Although portrayed as a relativist and a progressive historian, Beard believed that to make sense of any social phenomenon a historian, and by implication a student, had to develop a broad conceptual framework depicting the overall order, meaning, and direction of history. Beard's "act of faith" was that history was moving "forward" toward "a collectivist democracy." He conceived of social science scholarship as including everything that humankind had ever done, and he saw the necessity of separate disciplines for study of such a broad field. Thus, he thought of social studies more as a mosaic made up of separate disciplines than as a single unified field or a seamless web (Whelan, 1997b). Apparently, the membership of the commission could not agree on the implications of their allegiance to the social sciences for the curriculum, perhaps reflecting the diverse makeup of the commission and the fact that curricular integration, fusion, and core were still gaining in popularity in the schools.

In the *Charter*, Beard had written that social studies instruction was conditioned by "the spirit and letter of scholarship, by the realities and ideas of the society in which it is carried on, and by the nature and limitations of the teaching and learning process." He suggested that these conditions "seem to set a certain inevitable framework" for determining "the content and applications of civic instruction" (p. 2). Despite numerous meetings and several years of work considering these questions, the commission, it appears, did not reach a firm conclusion.

Thus, in the realm of the continuing definitional battles over social studies the commission took something of a middling ground, though their joint reports clearly supported a discipline-based orientation and support for history as the synthesizing discipline. The work, findings, and recommendations of the commission expressed the meliorist version of social efficiency, within a social reconstructionist framework. The commission's failure to specify a scope and sequence may have resulted from ideological differences over the frame of reference and differing understandings of what a "problems approach" might mean in practice. In any event, the commission's deep divisions were a reflection of its diverse makeup and the differences in perspective brought to bear on their project.

Given the reconstructionist orientation of Counts, Beard, and others on the commission, the deliberations of the group did produce dissent and debate among the commissioners. Charles Merriam and others considered Counts too radical, opposed use of the term *collectivism*, and saw the *Conclusions* as calling for "indoctrination." Four members, Frank W. Ballou, Charles E. Merriam, Ernest Horn, and Edmund E. Day, refused to sign. The geographer Isaiah Bowman signed with reservations. Two of the four dissenters later expressed their reasons for not signing the final report. Ballou's statement focused on educational issues, and Horn's published dissent expressed his disappointment with the commission over its handling of the chapter on testing (Ballou, 1934; Boozer, 1960). Neither Day nor Merriam published his reasons for refusing to sign the report. Merriam considered Counts too radical in his position that schools could take a lead role in social reconstruction, and was wary of his influence on Beard (Boozer, 1960; Karl, 1974). Both Merriam and Day held more moderate views on the relationship of schooling to social change (Boozer, 1960). The dissention on the commission may partially explain their failure to take a stronger position on the problems-versus-disciplines controversy brewing in the schools, and the failure to issue a specific framework for social studies scope and sequence.

Reactions

The reaction to the commission was an immediate storm in the general press, then a continuing and long-term controversy in pedagogical publications and books. The *New York Times* published a story on May 10, 1934, describing the upcoming release of the commission's report under the headline "Social Study Row Stirred by Report, Four of 16 Educators Dissent on 'Radical' Conclusions in 5-Year School Survey. 'Political' Foes Hinted." The story went on to note rumors that the report had been "'suppressed' supposedly because of its alleged radical nature" and to discuss the possible opposition to the report from "powerful financial interests feared by foundations and universities" or "from political enemies of the present national administration." Later in the article George S. Counts was cited as saying "that he did not know of any such pressure brought to bear by financial or other outside interests against the report, and said it had merely been delayed by differences of opinion."

Apparently the rumors of suppression surfaced the previous fall when word leaked out that the commission had prepared a "very sweeping and progressive document." It was also rumored that pressure had been put on the commission by "the great financial interests which endow Foundations and that the majority of the Commission had been frightened into modifying the report . . . in the direction of conservatism." As it turned out the report was published in nearly its original form, with a minority on the commission protesting that it was too radical. Writing in a column titled "The Liberal Viewpoint," Harry Elmer Barnes suggested that the content of the report "indicates well enough why those who habitually play ball with the great Foundations" might hesitate (1934, n.p.).

Subsequently, following release of the *Conclusions*, the *Times* described the report's contents under the headline "Collectivist Era Seen in Survey, Transition from Individualist Age Under Way . . . Asks School Adjustment." The *New York Herald Tribune* carried a similar story, as did many other newspapers. One editorial appearing in the *New York Sun* on May 23 was titled "Propaganda in Education" and cited a liberal critic of the commission who argued that it was "not the schools' mission to predetermine the economic and social status of society and to shape the minds of pupils." The critic preferred "to educate for the open mind." The following year, the *Philadelphia Evening Bulletin* carried a story titled "Breeding Communism," in which a department head in a South Philadelphia high school protested the infiltration of radical economics and cited the Commission on Social Studies (1935). And so the public controversy surrounding the report continued.

Among educators there was a mixed reaction. Beard's statement from the commission's discussions was praised by Rugg for favoring social reconstruction through educational reconstruction (Krug, 1972). However, the reaction from the profession on the whole was more critical. Franklin Bobbitt called the report an "astounding" and "rather startling social document" and charged that it displayed the "tone" of the "revolutionary hysteria that grips all the collectivizing nations" (1934, pp. 201, 208). Charles H. Judd observed that the *Conclusions* commented on topics beyond its purview. Judd left it for the reader to decide what to do about social studies in schools. Haggerty compared the report to a movement for evangelical religion in the 1890s, with feelings as a substitute for facts and little to help the teacher (Krug, 1972).

A number of reactions were also published in *The Social Studies*. Boyd H. Bode viewed the conclusions as a threat against free choice with its desire to have a frame of reference inculcated in schools, and saw its basic defect as the attempt to "combine an authoritarian 'frame of reference' with the cultivation of effective and independent thinking" (1935, p. 346).

R. O. Hughes criticized the failure of the commission to provide a clear position on its view of a proper "scheme of organization" for the curriculum and lamented, "We are just where we were when we started" (1934, p. 287). Kenneth Gell, a high school teacher in Rochester, New York, critiqued the commission for failing to seek "proper and sufficient advice of the group to be served" and suggested that this diminished the report's effectiveness. Gell also criticized the commission's "failure to understand teaching conditions as they do exist," as well as the report's preponderance of "generalities rather than specific recommendations" (1934, pp. 289, 291).

For the most part, teachers and practitioners who commented had an adverse reaction. The report had no scope and sequence and was full of "glittering generalities." The central tendencies among the criticisms of the commission appeared to center around its "frame of reference," the word *collectivism*, its comments on tests, and the lack of a specific and definite program for schools (Wesley, 1936, p. 448).

For their part, the commissioners stated that they did not believe in "one body of material, one way of organization, or one method of teaching." They added, "It had not been instructed to provide a detailed syllabus and texts to be imposed on school systems." In its *Conclusions,* the commission had made a gallant but unrealistic appeal for bold actions that teachers were generally not permitted. The commission took a strong position on social theory and in the struggle between history and issues-centered education, favoring the continuation of chronological history. They did not comment in much depth on other trends in education. The cooperative involvement of educators and academics was a plus, but the commissioners assumed, mistakenly, that an academic focus would affect schools. In hindsight, the commission's failure provide a scope and sequence may have proved its most serious flaw. It appears, as detailed above, that several commissioners were at odds. Furthermore, some may have had a disinclination to agree with specific curricular recommendations given the controversies that followed many previous commission reports. Also, the "find your own way" approach fit well with social reconstructionism and the commission's stated objection to lockstep authoritarianism.

On the whole, the influence of the commission may have been quite diffuse, for while the group created a large body of work on social studies, it took a timid stance on scope and sequence and seemed generally uncomfortable with the realities of schools. Its total body of work may rightly have been viewed at the time as "probably the most important contribution in the whole literature of the social studies in the secondary schools" (Read, 1938, p. 729).

Despite its voluminous publications and the controversies, reactions, and extended discussions it inspired, the commission's influence was undoubtedly weakened by its decision not to specify a scope and sequence. The commission failed to bridge the gap between the departmentalized and discipline-based orientation of academic historians and social scientists and the emerging focus of teachers and curriculum specialists on curriculum integration, problems, and issues, trends that were rising to new heights in schools.

RUGG AND PROBLEM-CENTERED SOCIAL STUDIES

Another major area in which the rhetoric of social reconstructionism had an impact was in the continuing development of the Rugg social studies program. Harold Rugg's continuing pursuit of changing social studies and

further developing his textbook series built around an issues-centered vision was the most important development in the history of issues-centered
social studies during the 1930s.

Rugg was a long-term advocate of problem-centered instruction and,
as early as 1921, had advocated a social studies curriculum built around
"the American problem." As we have seen, during the 1920s Rugg and his
associates at Teachers College, through a strenuous effort, had created a
successful pilot for an integrated social studies program at Lincoln School.
Mimeographed materials were transformed into a pamphlet series mar-
keted, sight unseen, to former students and associates across the nation.
And publication of the pamphlets as a textbook series focused on the junior high school years began in 1929. The first text was published in August
1929 and another volume in the series every 6 months thereafter.

During the decade of the 1930s, sales of Rugg's textbook series sky-
rocketed. Each volume of the series averaged more than 20,000 copies per
year until 1938. During the 10-year period to 1939, the series sold 1,317,960
copies at approximately $2.00 each, and more than 2,687,000 workbooks
were sold. According to a sales agent for Ginn and Company, the books
were the easiest to sell of any that he handled. Rugg and his associates had
created a unified social studies program and his books attracted world-
wide attention and imitation. He had clearly become the leading social
studies educator in the United States (Winters, 1967).

The content organization of the Rugg textbooks was supposedly centered around guiding principles distilled from the frontier thinkers, including the growth of modern cultures, development of loyalties and attitudes for decision making, and the synthesis of knowledge through social
studies. The methodology for introducing this content included the dramatic episode, planned recurrence of key concepts, practice in skills of gen-
eralizing, and learning by doing. The six volumes of the junior high school
program were "designed to provide a comprehensive introduction to
modes of living and insistent problems of the modern world," with the purpose of "introducing young people to the chief conditions and problems
which will confront them as citizens of the world" through a unified course
in social studies. Rugg defended his development of a "unified" course by
alluding to students' need to "utilize facts, meanings, generalizations, and
historical movement" in understanding modern institutions. He cited the
need to tie various factors "closely together in their natural relationships"
to help students understand the modern world. He wrote:

> Whenever history is needed to understand the present, history is presented. If
> geographic relationships are needed to throw light upon contemporary prob-
> lems, those geographic relationships are incorporated. The same thing has been
> done with economic and social facts and principles. (Rugg, 1931, pp. vi, vii)

Although the books contained a great deal of historical narrative, not unlike many other texts, the overarching aim was to make the study of history and the social sciences relevant, interesting, and meaningful to students with the goal of social melioration. Material from history and the social sciences was framed with issues and problems of present concern. In addition, the writing was engaging and down to earth. For example, the narrative for one text began with an imaginary meeting of the Social Science Club of "George Washington Junior High School of Anystate, U.S.A.," in which members of the club discussed the problems and issues to be taken up in group study (pp. 3–10). The description is lively and engaging and undoubtedly helped to interest many students in the remainder of the text.

Over the course of its development, and Rugg's self-described "struggle with a blank sheet of paper," the organizational scheme for the pamphlet series and the textbooks remained relatively constant (Winters, 1968). The textbook series was titled *Man and His Changing Society*. Titles included *An Introduction to American Civilization, Changing Civilizations in the Modern World, A History of American Civilization,* and *An Introduction to the Problems of American Culture*. The final volume of the first edition was published in January 1932. Revised editions appeared from 1936 to 1940, partially in response to adverse criticism and in an effort to keep the books up to date (Nelson, 1977).

During the 1930s Rugg's growth as a scholar and thinker continued. He had already established his credentials as a leading scholar in education. The social studies program, the publication of a number of highly regarded books and articles, and his activities during the hard times of the Great Depression greatly enhanced his reputation. He remained energetic on the faculty at Teachers College and was an active member of the PEA. Also, during the early part of the decade, he came to be known, along with his colleague, George S. Counts, as one of the leading social reconstructionists in the nation and was a respected participant in the debates over educational and social policy in the *Social Frontier* and other venues.

Rugg had been a long-term advocate of social reconstructionism through the schools, but in the 1930s his rhetoric became more strident. During the 1920s Rugg's social thought was influenced in two main directions. He read social criticism and was feeling the thrust of arguments for social engineering and, at the same time, was investigating the views of those who held that artists and writers should lead the way to social improvement. These strands matured in his thinking in the 1930s and stood behind his work on the textbook series and his books and articles calling for reform. In *The Great Technology,* published in 1933, Rugg called for social engineering in the form of technological experts who would design and operate the economy in the public interest. For Rugg, the economic problem "is to design and operate a system of production and distribution which will produce the maximum amount of goods needed by the people and will distribute them in such a way that each person will be given at least the highest minimum standard of living possible." An additional share of our abundance would be permitted to those who made excellent contributions through "greater creative ability and initiative" but this would be restricted to only "a low multiple of the minimum" (p. 106). Rugg's central concern continued to focus on his hope that social education could be used to help in the "scientifically designed reconstruction of society" for the general benefit of all. He called for "a mammoth and creative program of educational reconstruction" (pp. 18, 233). He frequently described his vision as a "thousand year march" of democracy toward a "cooperative commonwealth" (Price, 1983). Despite such rhetoric, his social vision was not as radical as his critics portrayed, but placed him somewhere between New Deal liberalism and democratic socialism. Above all, it was a democratic vision.

Early criticisms of the Rugg social studies materials foreshadowed what would transpire during the late 1930s and early 1940s. One of the earliest attacks occurred during the 1924–1925 period. The second edition of the social science pamphlets was being used in Bayonne, New Jersey, known as a "Standard Oil town." One of the pamphlets contained an illustration of a man working for Standard Oil and included the caption "Working on a job of this kind reduces your life 20 years." Fearing a reaction, Preston H. Smith, the schools superintendent, threw the series out. Then, in April 1927, the first concerted attack took place, when Otis Caldwell, director of the Lincoln School, received a large packet in the mail from a major corporation describing the pamphlets as "subversive and un-American." Rugg and associates prepared a defense, and after a 3-hour luncheon with company officials the controversy was resolved (Winters, 1968, pp. 136–137).

Rugg's writings underwent a shift in the early 1930s with a more pointed advocacy of social reconstructionism and the goal of moving toward some form of "collectivism." It was primarily these writings and subsequent media coverage of speaking engagements that attracted the attention of self-appointed censors to Rugg's work. His success, combined with his affiliation with unpopular causes, made him a target for criticism. Shortly after publication of *The Red Network*, in which Rugg was listed, the first attack on the Rugg textbook series occurred in 1935, when the Federation of Citizens Associations of the District of Columbia requested that the local school board remove the books. After an investigation, the request was denied.

During 1935 Rugg spoke out against American Legion attempts to censor a classroom magazine. For the balance of the decade, in a series of major speeches, Rugg attacked patriotic societies, including the Advertising Federation of America, the National Association of Manufacturers, and the United States Chamber of Commerce—and the New Deal itself. His comments and outspoken views critical of the legion and other groups had the effect of making him a chief target of attacks.

By 1939, controversies over the Rugg textbooks flared anew, and the American public was treated to a spectacle that received continuing national media coverage. The attacks centered in the New York metropolitan area and were orchestrated by a relatively small number of people, with many of the specific criticisms being used over and over again. According to an analysis of the attacks by Rugg and associates, of 240 incidents more than 160 were from New York or New Jersey. Only eight other states were represented. Thus, it appears that there was no real popular uprising against the Rugg textbooks, but instead an intense campaign orchestrated by relatively few people. The bulk of the attacks came from a group of business writers and publicists, retired military of the American Legion, professional journalists, and a few loose cannons. The flames were fanned by extensive coverage in the Hearst newspaper syndicate. Although the campaign was apparently not very well organized, it was marked by informal cooperation among the attackers, who liberally quoted, cited, and reprinted each other's work. Attacks on the Rugg materials were part of a blanket attack on American writers and texts, with Rugg gradually becoming the main target.

Among the most well publicized attacks was one by Bertie C. Forbes, who in his own magazine raged against the books in an article titled "Treacherous Teachings," in which he charged Rugg with being against private enterprise and urged boards of education to "cast out" the Rugg books (1939). The Advertising Federation of America, led by Alfred T. Falk, attacked the books for carrying "anti-advertising propaganda." Merwin K. Hart, president of the New York State Economic Council, which he had organized, entered the battle, addressed a number of conventions and meetings, and charged Rugg with "making a subtle sugar-coated effort to convert youth to Communism" and accused him of suggesting that capitalism "has been a failure and socialism should be substituted in its place" (quoted in Myers, 1940, p. 18).

Controversies over the books in a number of cities and towns eventually led to school board decisions to either censor the books or, conversely, to declare that they contained "nothing subversive." The typical pattern was a complaint, followed by appointment of a committee to investigate, then debate and, frequently, public hearings. In a number of well-publicized cases, Rugg appeared in person to defend the textbook series. In several communities concerned citizens and school board members responded to the attackers and pressured for the continued presence of the books.

The outcome of the controversy varied from place to place. In Englewood, New Jersey, despite the best efforts of Forbes, who was a school board member, the effort to remove the books ultimately failed. Similar decisions to uphold either student use of the books in social studies classes or the mere presence of the books in the school library were made in Philadelphia and in Atlanta. In at least a few cases, notably Binghamton, New York, and Bradner, Ohio, the books were removed. In Bradner, where he was already under attack, the superintendent ordered the books taken down to the furnace room and burned. Although the localized attacks on the Rugg textbooks had attracted a great deal of attention, the accusers were relatively unsuccessful in removing the books from schools.

Given the number of attacks and the concerns of so many citizens over their contents, the question is raised of whether the Rugg textbooks were problematic. The books were definitely left leaning, though they were not the communistic propaganda Rugg's critics claimed them to be. Previous reviewers of the Rugg materials have disagreed over the degree to which the textbooks reflected Rugg's social vision. For example, one writer called the text series "quite moderate" and suggests that they did not reflect his "more radical views" (Stanley, 1982). Another author concluded that "there can be little doubt that the books clearly echo his own socioeconomic orientation" (Carbone & Wilson, 1995). My own look at a few of the Rugg texts suggests that they were progressive in orientation and relatively moderate in outlook, given the rhetoric of the times. They also contained a great deal of narrative history and dramatic stories well told, as well as stimulating photos and cartoons. They were, decidedly, oriented toward raising serious questions in the minds of students about the social and economic institutions of the nation. Yet they were typical of many progressive texts of the era.

The research program of Rugg and his associates that lay behind the Rugg social studies program also had an ideological orientation, despite being clothed in "scientific" language. Rugg believed that he had developed a "scientific method" for selecting content, partially on the basis of examining key writings recommended by "frontier thinkers" in the social sciences. From these sources, Rugg and his associates distilled approximately 300 current problems to be used as the focus of their curriculum. As early as 1921, this plan for curriculum making was challenged by a scholar from the traditional history camp, Joseph Schafer, who questioned the process that Rugg recommended, seeing it as "merely 'opinion' camouflaged by the cant of a professed 'scientific' investigation" (1921a). The process was also challenged by another scholar, J. T. Phinney, in 1934, who questioned the representativeness of the books and articles that had been selected as the source of "problems and issues" and concluded that Rugg's work was not really very "scientific." Phinney went on to argue that "the question of how the curriculum should be organized must remain largely a philosophical question." Of course, a glance at Rugg's list of writers and advisors reveals a definite liberal strain. The process was not scientific at all but was an attempt at thoughtful curriculum construction with the aim of raising questions about social, economic, and cultural institutions posed by what Rugg had called the American problem (Phinney, 1934a, 1934b).

In conclusion, Rugg's influence on social studies in the schools was quite extensive, despite the attacks, which would eventually lead to the discontinuation of his textbook series. Workbooks for the series continued to sell well after the attacks, an indication that the books were still being used for some time in many schools well into the 1940s (Winters, 1967). Despite, and perhaps partly because of, the lasting fame generated by public uproar over his textbook series, Rugg's achievement remains to this day the high point of progressive reform in social studies.

Paralleling the development of Rugg's social studies materials, the decade saw the rapid growth of issues-oriented approaches. These developments included attention to the Problems of Democracy course, increased curricular attention to controversial issues and social problems, plans for the infusion of current topics and issues in discipline-based curricula, and integrated or core curricula that centered around problem topics or issues. The pages of social studies journals witnessed a steady growth in articles devoted to various aspects of teaching social problems. Articles related a variety of successful plans, procedures, and approaches to teaching the modern problems course. Several gave attention to the rationale behind the study of problems and the problem method of organization. Others indicated serious consideration of many difficulties and unresolved issues relating to the course. A few were critical and called for instruction in the social science disciplines in order to avoid superficiality, or a grab-bag approach. The vast majority of articles were supportive, however, and sought to win converts or simply to improve practice. By the late 1930s, the number of articles devoted to instruction that was centered on social problems had grown to the point that it was one of the dominant ongoing themes of the journal now known as *Social Education*.

Academic Freedom Concerns

All this attention to social issues and the idea of social reconstruction through education that lay behind it generated a good deal of opposition from conservative groups who wanted schools to continue to teach in the old ways, to teach "My country right or wrong." Although the Rugg case was most prominent, he was by no means alone. Opponents emerged to condemn virtually anything critical of American society. By the mid-1930s

a broad array of academic freedom issues and cases emerged as a consequence of these trends. If the pages of *The Social Studies* were any indication,
academic freedom concerns reached a high point by the mid-1930s. The
section of the journal titled "Recent Happenings in the Social Studies" suddenly filled with reports of academic freedom resolutions, conferences on
academic freedom, infiltration of PTAs by ultrapatriotic groups, loyalty
oaths, and intellectual lynchings. One of the more famous cases was that of
Victor Jewett, a junior high social studies teacher who was singled out for
censure in Eureka, California. Jewett was said to have "criticized the government while extolling the Russian government, belittled great men of
American history, received money from Russia for spreading propaganda
in the local schools, engaged actively in the lumber strike and made inflammatory addresses at union meetings, and was seen in the company of
pickets of the lumber workers union." Despite having taught social studies for 5 years, Jewett was transferred to teach mathematics and later sus-
pended from teaching altogether. A sober-minded observer in California
noted: "Californians interested in education, justice, and civil liberties . . .
are witnessing with increasing alarm the growing tide of terror, repression,
and violence which is sweeping even the respectable guardians of our most
sacred institutions" (Staff, 1935, pp. 482–483).

Hearst newspapers were responsible for many of the academic-
freedom battles of the times, or at least for fanning the flames. Newspapers
of the Hearst syndicate generally reported charges against the schools in
the most inflammatory language and in a prominent place in their papers.
In 1935, several leaders in American education called on a government
committee, the McCormick-Dickstein Committee, to investigate "a campaign of terrorism against teachers in American Colleges, universities,
schools, and even private schools." The leaders, including Beard, Counts,
Kilpatrick, Bagley, and others based their accusation in part on a ploy by
two Hearst reporters who posed as prospective university students at Syra-
cuse and Teachers College in an attempt to secure information regarding
"radical" professors (Kappan, 1935, pp. 106–107). The "red scare" campaign was launched partly in response to the report of the AHA Commission on Social Studies, and the news of the publication of the *Social Frontier,*
a journal believed to be aimed at bringing the social reconstructionist recommendations of the commission into the school curriculum of the nation.

RHETORIC VERSUS REALITY

At decade's end, the rhetoric of change was reflected in a superb volume
titled *The Future of the Social Studies*, edited by James A. Michener (1939).
The volume was intended to be what Michener called "the first step in what

may become a sustained effort to bring some order into a confused field." It offered a glimpse of several scholars' visions of the field's future, and contained chapters by Harold Rugg and several other advocates of a social problems orientation. Proposed history courses tended to be broad and fused with a strong emphasis on "problems" and on social and economic aspects. The 12th-grade offering was almost invariably some form of Problems of Democracy, and in several of the chapters, that course was fused with American history in a 2-year sequence. If this volume were the only indication of the status of social studies instruction, a reader would think that advocates of problem-centered instruction had made huge inroads into the curriculum. Of course, the volume was not intended as a description of actual practice, but instead encapsulated many of the hottest trends in the rhetoric of the field. Apparently, not everyone was thrilled with the visions of social studies presented. Following its initial publication, Howard Wilson of Harvard said that he would like to see a follow-up in which a group of experts would be asked to write "a reasoned, mature reaction" (Minutes, 1939).

If the rhetoric of social studies was reflected in the Michener volume, what about actual practice? American history continued to enroll the highest total numbers, followed by world history. Ancient, medieval, and English history had all declined in enrollment. Among the other social sciences, community government had the largest share, followed by economics, sociology, and Problems of Democracy, which was declared to be "one of the fastest growing subjects in the high-school curriculum" (Jessen & Herlihy, 1938). The Rugg social science course and other similarly unified approaches were having some influence on the junior high years.

Another survey found a general social studies trend "in the direction of fusion or integration." Among the general trends were a gain in social studies other than history, condensation of world history into a shorter course, new courses such as Community Civics, movement toward integration, and increased emphasis on recent history (Editor, 1934).

As to teaching methods, one thoughtful observer found that schools "stress conformity" and "only flirt with or entirely ignore the glaring and not infrequently unpleasant realities"; they stressed "the superiority of our civilization," supported imperialism, and selected episodes of history that illustrate steady progress. Despite the trend toward integration, content varied little in final form from that in traditional subject courses. History tended to be a thin survey of the past in which students understand little of the "significance of history." Question-and-answer recitation remained the most typical procedure (Wilson, 1938, pp. xii, 272).

Many of the recommendations of the 1916 report of the Committee on Social Studies were gaining ground, largely at the expense of traditional history, which was viewed by many as hopelessly out of date. Enrollments in the four blocks were sharply in decline. It appears that the reconstructionist approach to teaching lay in a field where most teachers were not allowed freedom to venture. Teachers were, for the most part, still going about their work in routine ways. In many if not most communities, teachers were restrained by community opposition to reconstructionist ideas. At the same time, traditional approaches to education were under assault as never before, and the wave of questioning represented by educational reconstructionism undoubtedly had some influence on both the tone of discussion and the topics to be considered. The Rugg social studies program and both the Problems of Democracy course and teaching organized around social problems had found an enlarged niche in the curriculum. On the whole, however, it appears that the rhetoric of educational change in social studies had outdistanced educational practice. Social studies suffered from what one writer described as "impotence," from bad teaching, and from the imperviousness of long-established routine to new ideas and approaches.

By the end of the decade, social studies trends had resulted in only a little substantive change in classrooms. Still, the period was a high point in social studies history, especially for Rugg and advocates of a social problems approach. By the end of the 1930s, each of the major social studies sects had developed a presence in the rhetoric over reform and held at least a toehold in the curriculum. During the decade, the struggle over the social studies curriculum had also become more overtly ideological, reflecting the turmoil of the times. Curriculum trends included greater experimentation than before, within the broad stream of classroom constancy. Social reconstructionism hit full stride, boosted by hard times, and affected the success of one of the major projects of 1930s, the Rugg texts. The AHA Commission on Social Studies reached conclusions much different from those of the AHA Committee of Seven of only a few decades before, and did not call for a return to traditional history. This was significant because it showed that moderates, progressives, and reconstructionists had meaningful influence among historians at the time and that compromise was possible.

Many of the key issues in the field were being addressed, sometimes more clearly than ever before. At one conference session held in Portland, Oregon, on June 29, 1936, and led by the then president of NCSS, R. O. Hughes, a roundtable discussion was held on the following key questions confronting the field:

1. Shall the social studies accept conventional social-science school subjects as fundamental categories, or shall they arrange and present experiences directly related to the performance of functions in society?

2. Shall the social studies present merely organized knowledge, or shall they also assume responsibility for attitudes and ideals?
3. Shall the social studies be primarily an activity program, or shall they be handled through an organized social-science program with activities for enrichment?
4. Shall the social studies seek to enable pupils to adjust themselves to current or developing social ideals, or shall they seek the reconstruction of society? (Editor, 1936, p. 349)

The questions touched on purpose, content, and method, raising many of the concerns that would continue to inspire multiple positions and struggles among educators, social science scholars, and the concerned public. The fact that at least a few educators were discussing them so forthrightly was an indication of hopefulness for the future (Staff, 1936). However, by the close of the decade, it seemed to at least one prominent NCSS leader, Edgar Dawson, that the struggle over social studies might best be characterized as "National Council for the Social Studies vs. 'United States' of America or the civilized world . . . which I am more interested in, than in any other movement I know of" (Dawson, 1940).

In closing, the decade of the 1930s saw some gains for social studies instruction on the whole. There was a general shift to the left and toward increasing innovation in curriculum planning, toward approaches centered on social problems, and toward curricular integration. These shifts were inspired by the depression and by a growing questioning of societal institutions by George Counts, the movement toward social reconstructionism, and Rugg's social studies program. But the "new" questioning of the social order was short lived, as substantive critiques and challenges from patriotic groups began in earnest by mid-decade. As we shall see in the following chapter, the winds of war being felt in the 1930s eventually had significant implications for social studies. The field would emerge in the 1940s with many similar trends continuing, the fires of criticism flaming, and advocates of the traditional history camp beginning to reassert their views.

CHAPTER FOUR

War and the War on Social Studies

ONE COMMON VIEW of the 1940–1945 time period is that in education and American culture generally, the climate changed, from one of questioning American political, social, and economic institutions and focusing on the problems of American society, to one of emphasizing what's right about our institutions. In light of the rise of dictatorships in Europe, the shift in attention seemed warranted. For many progressives at the time, the shift toward defending American democracy was prudent. Even the frontier thinkers supported the idea of armed conflict if it became necessary. And so, a focus on preparing students to give their lives for democracy became a very real purpose for many educators.

The impact of World War II on social studies education during this period was both immediate and long lasting. In the short term, the war led to creation of wartime educational ventures, including the education of defense workers; increased attention to geography and war-related topics; air education; postwar concerns for building a lasting peace; and intercultural education, a forerunner of multiculturalism. The war also had an immediate impact on progressive educational trends, casting a pall over experimentation and, in the long term, leading to the death of progressive education as an organized force, at least in the form of the PEA. Curiously, even as the looming conflict cast an ideological shadow over reconstructionist and issues-oriented approaches, the war began to engulf American attention and involvement just as several progressive ventures were bearing fruit. In spite of the war, progressives continued to experiment and develop curricula, and some trends that had begun earlier continued to grow.

The progressive belief in the perfectability or improvement of society was dealt a heavy blow of realism by the war (Krug, 1972). Ideologically, the war had an impact on curriculum and courses, on beliefs about education and its goals, on teaching about past wars, and on ideological purposes. Schools generally communicated the belief that it was honorable to give one's life, if necessary, for democratic ideals.

In recent years World War II has been characterized in a number of popular works as a "peoples' war," or "the good war," fought by "the greatest generation" of Americans. Was the war an effort to preserve democracy and to resist totalitarianism, as its advocates claimed, or was it something else? It was a war against "an enemy of unspeakable evil" (Zinn, 1980, p. 398), and the overwhelming majority of Americans considered the fight a necessity. However, significant numbers of people viewed the war as a struggle for imperialist control. At least 43,000 American civilians refused to be drafted. Of these, 6,000 went to prison. One noted historian, Gabriel Kolko, after a careful study of American policy, concluded that the central economic war aim of the United States was to save capitalism (Kolko, 1968). As Howard Zinn points out, a good deal of corroborating evidence supports this conclusion. These questions must be considered, for the answer has implications for the role played by social studies education during the war. If the war was a struggle for imperialist control, much of educational policy then becomes a form of either propaganda for the war and the inculcation of "democracy," or a deceitful effort at social control.

WAR AND EDUCATION

The war was to have an early impact on education in the United States, even prior to U.S. entry. Educators became preoccupied with a massive national defense effort that brought with it changes in the social and pedagogical climate. One national initiative was the formation of the National Defense Advisory Commission in 1940, through which educators, and Commissioner of Education John Studebaker, assumed responsibility for preparing defense workers. The program was created in early July, after Hitler's invasion of the Low Countries, to provide 10-week courses to 150,000 youth and the unemployed. Also, 55 educational organizations formed the National Coordinating Commission on Education. By November 1940, more than one million defense workers were generated by crash programs, providing a "massive" morale booster for school leaders. In addition, the war lifted vocational training to unprecedented levels (Krug, 1972).

    During 1942 and 1943, following U.S. entry, several wartime commissions and panels made specific recommendations regarding the social studies curriculum. The group most directly responsible for social studies teaching during the war was the Commission on Wartime Policy of NCSS. Their report, *The Social Studies Mobilize for Victory*, was widely distributed and cited as an important document with useful recommendations. The report suggested "new emphases, readjustments, and acceleration" in social studies programs. It described the need to prepare citizens who would "face the dangers of combat—willingly." The report went on:

Total war requires an informed and thoughtful population, aware of the task to be done, determined to preserve a democracy which it understands, and convinced of the responsibility of each citizen in the drive for lasting victory. The stamina of a fighting democracy depends upon widespread understanding of the issues at stake, of the stark necessities of total war on a global scale, and of the complex tasks of achieving a peace. An informed and aroused citizenry is the foundation of victory in both war and peace. (1943, pp. 3–10).

The Social Studies Mobilize for Victory was the major statement of the social studies profession during the war and included discussion of virtually all aspects of the social studies program. The general thrust of the commission's recommendations was toward an efficient citizen education program that would assist in the war effort. Social criticism and social problems were generally deemphasized in favor of efficiency-oriented citizenship education with emphasis on strengthening the peoples' faith in democracy. The commission recommended that schools and agencies "utilize dramatic incidents and impressive ceremonials for the purpose of building the emotional drives of loyalty to democracy." During the latter 1930s educators had held an open and often acrimonious debate over indoctrination. During the war, it seemed, there was no debate. Indoctrination was deemed necessary.

Despite the general drift toward inculcating democracy as a faith, there were still some doubters and, apparently, significant disagreement. I. L. Kerrison, a high school teacher in Detroit, wrote in 1944 that teachers should abandon "the pedantic aim of objectivity" and hit hard, in class and out, for the interpretations and programs in which they believe; his argument was countered by a former president of the National Council for the Social Studies, R. O. Hughes, who suggested that teachers have a prior obligation to present facts, to maintain balance and perspective, and to protect "freedom of thought and action" (Kerrison & Hughes, 1944, p. 79). His view was undoubtedly shared by many others with a progressive orientation.

PROGRESSIVISM CONTINUED

Progressive education continued to draw supporters and critics, and a good deal of the discourse made it into magazines outside education. In September 1941, the *Rotarian* ran a debate under the title "Shall We Have More 'Progressive Education'?" Carleton Washburne, superintendent of the Winnetka, Illinois, schools, a longtime leader in progressive education, and then president of the PEA, answered in the affirmative. Washburne briefly explained the origins of progressive education, contrasting it with the traditional method, which was often disjointed from the life of the child and autocratic in spirit and method. Progressivism, he asserted, had two basic tenets, education of the whole child and education for the democratic way of life. He argued that subject matter and skills needed to be learned in connection with their use and related to life experience. Students also needed, he suggested, "a participative understanding of democracy—patriotism, citizenship, and character are all combined in a genuine civic consciousness, in an identification of one's own well-being with that of one's fellows." He posited a conception of the teacher as a "guide, counsellor, and friend," and of the curriculum as broadened and flexible with "no sharp boundaries" between school subjects (pp. 26–28).

A response to Washburne was written by Mortimer J. Adler of the University of Chicago. Adler argued that many progressive educators had expanded the school into a grandiose institute, regulating "everything" and solving the social problems of the community. The trouble with this vision, he wrote, was that the school would become "a sort of totalitarian colossus, benevolent, it is true, but nonetheless totalitarian, presiding over every moment in the life of the individual, from cradle to grave." Adler argued instead for schooling to focus on intellectual development first, and moral virtue second. Although he seemed to have some affinity for moderate progressives, he was most critical of the child-centered camp, whose members he characterized as "extremists who would abolish all authority on the part of the teacher." Moderates, he wrote, applied the "principle of interest to method . . . . to make what should be learned interesting and attractive," an approach that he described as sound (1941, pp. 29–30, 56, 57).

In some ways it seemed as if these two combatants were talking past one another. Washburne made a strong case that progressive education was infinitely preferable to the old traditional schooling. Adler seemed to respect moderate progressivism, but had little use for social efficiency–oriented bureaucracy or teachers and institutions seeking to propagandize democracy.

Developments in Social Studies

In social studies there were a number of interesting developments. Progressive social studies educators were still working on the project of orienting social studies teaching around the problems of American society, especially in the Problems of Democracy course. Interest in the course remained strong and appeared to continue growing through the war years, though the wave of articles devoted to social problems and problem-centered teaching declined, displaced by war concerns. Nonetheless, Americans on the whole seemed emotionally caught up in the war effort as a campaign for democracy and viewed the Problems of Democracy course as one way to further the cause.

Concern for improving teaching within the "modern problems movement" was strong during the late 1930s and early parts of the war. Many aspects of the curriculum were focused on problems and issues, and American history and contemporary problems were often combined into a 1- or 2-year course (Hunt, 1941d). Thus, NCSS took the unusual step of preparing materials for teachers that would serve to help them in the effort to make Problems of Democracy and other problem-centered offerings more teachable. The pamphlet series Problems in American Life was a 28-part set of materials focused on problems and issues in American society, many of which received treatment in the Problems of Democracy course or in fused American history and problems offerings. The series was a joint venture with the National Association of Secondary School Principals aimed at providing useful, up-to-date materials for teachers in the form of resource units and teaching ideas. A resource unit, as encapsulated in the series, included, first, an in-depth analysis of the problem/topic by a leading scholar, and second, teaching aids, materials, and suggested student-centered activities. The result was a series of pamphlets with thoughtful, thorough, and current analysis, combined with state-of-the-art teaching suggestions and resources (Quillen, 1942). Although the pamphlet series apparently enjoyed a wide distribution, its publication was discontinued sometime during the war years. It remains an unheralded, little-known contribution.

An important development in the theory of reflective teaching, and a refinement of the Deweyan tradition in social studies, appeared during the war, with the completion of Alan Griffin's doctoral dissertation, "A Philosophical Approach to the Subject Matter Preparation of Teachers of History." This proved to be a seminal work primarily because of its quality and because of its subsequent influence on theories of reflective teaching developed later by Griffin's protégés. Griffin's main contribution was to elaborate, in both practical and theoretical terms, the meaning and implications of Deweyan reflective theory for the teaching of history (1942).

As we shall see below, turf battles over the social studies curriculum would continue with attacks on social studies both from outside the field and from within the academy. The times, and the public, seemed to be calling for more traditional teaching and the indoctrination of democracy. In the final analysis, you don't prepare young people to give their lives for their country by raising troublesome questions about its institutions. If it was a capitalist war, raising troubling questions about the vagaries of the capitalist system certainly would not aid in military recruitment or compliance.

THE GATHERING STORM

Attacks on the Rugg social studies program continued to increase during the late 1930s and early 1940s, becoming national in scope. The following round of controversy was generated by two articles that appeared in nationally circulated magazines. The first of these was by Augustin G. Rudd and was published in the April 1940 issue of *Nation's Business* under the title "Our 'Reconstructed' Educational System." Rudd posited that the growth of radical youth organizations, such as the American Youth Congress and the Young Communist League, was inspired by an "entire educational system" that had been "reconstructed" with textbooks and courses teaching "that our economic and political institutions are decadent." He blamed the widespread teaching of "'Social science,' an omnibus course practically supplanting specific study of history, geography and U. S. Government." Rudd cited the Rugg textbooks as the major culprit and argued that Rugg "subtly but surely" implied a need for a state-planned economy and socialism. Rugg, he argued, used "dramatic episodes" to emphasize the worst aspects of our institutions. "Time after time," Rudd wrote, "he uses half-truths, partisan references, and an amazing liberty with historical facts, the net effect of which is to undermine the faith of children in the American way of life. The constantly recurring theme is an effort to sell the child the collectivist theory of society" (p. 94).

The second article, by Orlen K. Armstrong, was titled "Treason in the Textbooks" and appeared in the *American Legion Magazine* for September 1940. This was the official journal of the legion and was distributed to one million homes. The article contained a bitter denounciation of the writers and teachers of the "new history" and quoted extensively from Rugg's text *A History of American Government and Culture* and from its teacher's guide. He used these and other books by the "frontier thinkers" to document the books' subversive goals:

  a. To present a new interpretation of history in order to "debunk" our heroes and cast doubt upon their motives, their patriotism, and their service to mankind.
  b. To cast aspersions upon our Constitution and our form of government, and shape opinions favorable to replacing them with socialistic control.
  c. To condemn the American system of private ownership and enterprise, and form opinions favorable to collectivism.

    d. To mould opinion against traditional religious faiths and ideas of morality,
       as being part of an outgrown system. (Armstrong, 1940, pp. 51, 70)

Armstrong also attacked fused courses that consolidated "history, geography, civics and social science" and stated flatly that "these courses form
a complete pattern of propaganda for a change in our political, economic,
and social order" (pp. 51, 70). The author went a step further and published
a list of "subversive" books and magazines, which was reprinted elsewhere. Once again, Rugg's textbook series was the central target.

    The legion article created an immediate storm of controversy. Authors,
educators, and even some legionnaires attacked it, and a number of the
blacklisted publications received an immediate retraction from the legion.
The associate secretary of the NEA wrote that the attack had "no adequate
basis in fact." He argued, "It is not 'treason' to teach that American ideals
require a fair chance for everyone in terms of economic, social, and educational opportunity" and that it was not treason "to teach that these ideals
are not yet fully achieved" and to inspire youth to attain them (Carr, 1940).
Armstrong admitted, in the wake of the controversy, that he had not inves-
tigated a number of the publications he listed. Yet, as is so often the case,
the damage was done. Rugg, who had once boasted that "the only way to
get somewhere in education was to attack someone big," had apparently
met his match (Winters, 1968).

    In his presidential address to the NCSS membership in November,
Howard R. Anderson countered the charges against social studies and suggested that Armstrong had made "sensational charges without great concern for buttressing them with facts" (1941). Rugg read Anderson's speech
"with great interest and agreement" and offered his own analysis of the
sources of the attack, made by "eight hitherto unknown persons of almost
no prestige or influence," who were "artificially keeping it alive." The persons and groups included Hart, Forbes, Rudd, E. H. West, Fries, Dilling,
George Sokolsky, and Armstrong. They were, he charged, gaining success
via access to national agencies, chiefly the Hearst papers, patriotic groups,
and business organizations. Rugg went on to suggest that the critics were
limiting education by characterizing certain "bad words" as subversive or
un-American, essentially labeling them as naming taboo topics. Rugg
wrote that the "Bad Words," which point out deficiencies in American life,
"simply cannot be introduced into the school, in any form, without arous-
ing the bitter opposition of certain special-interest groups—persons
like . . . the Forbes-Hart-Rudd-West combination" (Rugg, 1941a, p. 178).

    Meanwhile the entire controversy had gathered increasing national at-
tention. According to an article in *Time* magazine, by the end of the spring
term in 1940, the Rugg textbooks had been banned from a half-dozen school

systems. Critics objected to the Rugg texts, the article reported, "for picturing the U.S. as a land of unequal opportunity, and giving a class conscious account of the framing of the U.S. Constitution." The books were increasingly under attack "in the small town American Legion belt," the article reported, citing two fresh book "burnings" in the towns of Mountain Lakes and Wayne Township, N. J. ("Book Burnings," 1940, pp. 64–65).

The Storm Builds

The following major development in the Rugg story raised the stakes considerably, as it involved the activities of the National Association of Manufacturers (NAM), an organization with considerable resources. NCSS and the NAM had a relationship that went back at least to May 1940, when H. W. Prentis, president of the NAM, wrote to NCSS offering to provide conference speakers to address "Fundamentals of the American Way." These fundamentals included "Opportunity, Freedom of Religion and Speech, Representative Democracy, and Private Enterprise." Furthermore, he wrote, "Behind these watchwords is a story—a dramatic and inspiring message which, in the best interests of our country, cannot be told and retold too often." Evidently, the NAM believed that social studies teachers needed a strong reminder (Prentis, 1940).

On December 11, 1940, the *New York Times* reported that the NAM announced that it would initiate a survey of textbooks then in use in the schools to see if it could find evidence of subversive teaching. In addition, the activities of the NAM received extensive coverage from George Sokolsky in the Hearst papers and were featured prominently in the *New York Times*. Ralph Robey, an assistant professor of banking at Columbia University and a columnist for *Newsweek*, was hired by the NAM to prepare a series of abstracts of some 800 currently used social studies textbooks to show the author's attitudes toward government and business. The *Times* reported that the congress of NAM annually consolidated the opinions of 8,000 members, employing some 2 million workers, and that it spent $1,600,000 a year on staff work and public information. Robey's study was undertaken so that the NAM members might move against any works that were found prejudicial to the U.S. form of government, society, or system of free enterprise. As a well-known critic of the "socialism of the New Deal," Robey was far from an unbiased reporter. Nonetheless, the association pointed out that he was hired merely to develop abstracts, and that the reader could then judge the merits of the books (*New York Times*, December 11, 1940, p. 29).

Announcement of the NAM study was met by a good deal of concern and controversy and drew reactions from a number of social studies educators. Tyler Kepner, a teacher in Brookline, Massachusetts, and a member of the Commission on History a few years earlier, wrote to the Academic Freedom Committee of NCSS and suggested that the NAM study was "quite a different thing from the attack recently emanating from a well-organized minority group." Assuming that "more of this business is yet to come," he asked whether the council had in mind any "specific action" to offset the attacks. "How long," he wrote, "do leaders in social education propose to let Mr. Rugg carry the burden practically alone?" (1940). Howard Wilson responded that he agreed with Kepner's assessment of the NAM project, calling it "both ridiculous and dangerous." He was "a little disturbed" by Kepner's question about Rugg, and wrote, "Generally speaking, Rugg has enjoyed carrying his burden alone, I think. He has said and done a good many things that I, for example, could not support him on. However, on this one issue of freedom of speech and writing I agree wholeheartedly that we must support him." How to do so, "without at the same time supporting some of his educational positions which are not acceptable, is a difficult matter to decide." Wilson also mentioned that faculty at Harvard had recently appointed a committee to consider ways and means to defend "educational interests," and that NCSS would do something to help (1940).

The Harvard committee, on January 2, 1941, issued a statement warning of the dangers in the process of abstracting textbooks and urging that the NAM join with other groups in support of a broad study of education. "The first and most obvious danger," they wrote, "is that the abstracting of the textbooks may be done with bias. . . . The second is the grave possibility of misuse of the abstracts which are produced" (Harvard, 1941, p. 1). Their statement received a reassuring reply from the NAM, who claimed to be in complete accord with the group of Harvard professors in their view of education. The NAM went on to say that it had received many requests for information regarding the "growing volume of criticism" of what is being taught in our schools, and undertook the study with the intent of providing information to their members. Their intent, the statement read, was "merely to determine the facts—to determine whether there is any basis . . . for the growing apprehension about school textbooks." The response indicated that the NAM and Professor Robey would "refrain from interpretation," but would let readers make up their own minds (National Association of Manufacturers, 1941, pp. 2–3).

Despite such reassurances, not everyone was satisfied that the NAM acted with such a benign intent. In his editor's column, Erling M. Hunt wrote that there was still "cause for concern" because of other disturbing factors in the situation. Moreover, he wrote, H. W. Prentis, Jr., president of the NAM, had made vigorous and repeated declarations repudiating the development of political and social democracy during the past 150 years. Hunt described the repeated "investigation of textbooks" by various groups over the past quarter century as "unfortunate and ineffectual." Specifically, he charged, "The implication that teachers, administrators, textbook authors, and publishers are delinquent in their patriotic duty . . . is unjust and misleading," and that "focusing of attention on individual statements" rather than the school program as a whole obscures the main issues rather than helping the situation (1941b, pp. 88–89).

The Storm Unleashed

On Saturday, February 22, 1941, a headline at the top of the front page of the *New York Times* read:

UN-AMERICAN TONE
SEEN IN TEXTBOOKS
ON SOCIAL SCIENCES

Survey of 600 Used in Schools
Finds a Distorted Emphasis
on Defects of Democracy

ONLY A FEW CALLED RED

Tendency Chiefly is to "Tear
Down," Dr. Robey Holds—
Propaganda Study Decried

The article reported:

A "substantial portion" of the social science textbooks now used in the high schools of this country tend to criticize our form of government and hold in derision or contempt the system of private enterprise, Dr. Ralph Robey, assistant professor of banking at Columbia University, said yesterday in summarizing his personal conclusions from abstracting the textbooks for the National Association of Manufacturers. . . . There is a notable tendency, he said, for books to play down what has been accomplished in this country and to stress the defects of our democracy. Only a few of the textbooks are actually subversive in content and follow the Communist party line, according to the study. On the whole, the books do not bow to any "line" as such, but tend to create discontent and unrest by their approach and treatment of government and business questions, the educator found.

The article went on to describe the sponsorship of the study, and pointed out the NAM's statement that "no position would be taken" by the organization, that it would be purely an objective study designed to give members a firsthand view of the books. Then the article reported:

During the last year or so a controversy over subversive textbooks has disturbed the educational world. The social science textbooks by Dr. Harold Rugg of Teachers College have come in for a particularly severe attack. Several school systems have banned his books from the classroom, charging them with being too critical of our existing form of government. In one or two communities they were publicly burned. (Fine, 1941, p. 1)

All this, including the reference to Rugg, appeared on the front page. Excerpts from the abstracts, printed on page 6, were included from texts labeled *economics, government, history, social problems,* and *social studies.* Of the seven abstracts published in the *Times,* two were from Rugg books; one was from a book by Leon C. Marshall, an advocate of a social process approach; and another was a problems text titled "Society and Its Problems." The abstracts provided selected and provocative quotations from the texts, segments in which textbook authors critically described or raised questions about the functioning of government, the distribution of wealth and incidence of poverty, or the interplay of power and wealth. The quotations were provided without any sense of the remainder of each text, much of which would be found utterly innocuous. Yet the selected evidence cited did suggest, quite strongly, that many textbooks were raising difficult questions about the real functioning of American institutions.

"Protests, corrections, and replies" to Dr. Robey's findings came quickly. The *Times'* earlier editions on February 22 had cast Dr. Robey's statements as part of his report, while later editions, as cited above, identified his remarks as "his personal conclusions." Robey later confirmed that the remarks were his personal opinion, and that the NAM had not authorized his statements or the release of excerpts from the "abstracts." Nonetheless, the story led to a flurry of communications, clarifications, and statements of concern and other developments (Hunt, 1941a).

On the day of the story, Wilbur Murra, executive secretary of NCSS, wired a telegram to Walter D. Fuller, new president of the NAM, stating that the board of directors "instructs me to express its deep concern about generalized statement on textbooks made by Ralph Robey in New York Times for Saturday, February 22. Please wire collect whether National Association of Manufacturers repudiates or endorses statement" (Murra, 1941b). On February 24, Mr. Fuller replied, "Dr. Robey's opinion entirely personal. The National Association of Manufacturers neither endorses nor repudiates it because such endorsement or repudiation would infer that our organization has an opinion of its own." The wire went on to restate the NAM's official position that it did not have an opinion but merely wished to "epitomize the attitude expressed" in the textbooks under study (Fuller, 1941).

On the same day, the NAM issued a press release that included a letter sent to all NAM members declaring that Dr. Robey's criticisms represented his "personal opinion only" and insisting that the abstracts themselves were "completely unprejudiced." The letter also included several "considerations" printed at the beginning of each abstract, suggesting that textbooks should not be condemned for explaining unpopular political or economic philosophies "provided they are not advocated." And that they should treat "favorable aspects" of our institutions but "should not be required to ignore unfavorable aspects or important dissents" (Hunt, 1941a).

Meanwhile, statements condemning the "recent attacks upon textbooks" were issued by a number of organizations. NCSS charged that the attacks were "unjust and misleading" and that they brought discredit upon the entire school system. Press accounts of a meeting of the PEA, which happened to coincide with the *Times* story, included quotes from Rugg and from the authors of one of the other textbooks, vigorously defending their texts, attacking the critics, charging that the excerpts selected were unfair, and defending their books against the charge of un-Americanism. In addition, a committee of ten social scientists was appointed by the American Committee for Democracy and Intellectual Freedom to examine the textbooks charged with being subversive. The School Book Publishers National Association also issued a strong statement, published on February 24, objecting to Dr. Robey's criticisms: "It is the consensus of this group that the charges made by those representing the National Association of Manufacturers cannot be substantiated by truth, that we believe there are very few if any of the texts used in the schools deliberately or otherwise written to break down the American plan of life" (Hunt, 1941a, pp. 289–290).

Editorials appeared in many newspapers and took positions on both sides in the controversy, though many were critical of the NAM and Robey. The *New York Herald-Tribune* gave some support to the criticism and suggested that "conflicting theories" were unsuitable for schools, given the possibility of bias and oversimplification and the immaturity of youth. The *New York Post* was critical of both the NAM and Robey and suggested that the NAM's attempt to "disassociate itself" from Robey's comments would be a "hard trick" and calling the response from educators and publishers, along with the NAM backtracking, "a fine show of democracy" countering a threat to free speech. The *Des Moines Register* characterized the NAM study as a "witch-hunt"; the *St. Louis Post-Dispatch* argued that there was "more real hope" in the criticisms contained in the texts "than in all the platitudinous whitewash in the world"; and the *St. Louis Star-Times* defended "intellectual freedom and the spirit of inquiry" as the "essence of education in a democracy." For his part, Erling M. Hunt, editor of *Social Education,* expressed a skeptical attitude toward the manufacturers' failure to "disavow" Robey's comments. Hunt concluded that the entire enterprise created "confusion, suspicion, and embarrassment for teachers and administrators . . . who stand in devotion to American government and the bases of our economic system" (1941a, pp. 291–292).

On April 3, the NAM released a belated statement attempting to further distance itself from the entire controversy and offering to "cooperate with teachers at any time" to assure proper use of the abstracts. The NAM also sent a long letter to 38,000 social science teachers and 10,000 school officials in which Mr. Fuller asserted the NAM's confidence in American teachers and expressed regret that "distorted" impressions of the project had been given such wide currency. He also asserted that from the beginning, the NAM "believed that the issue of subversiveness in textbooks was being immensely exaggerated" (Hunt, 1941c). Later, in September 1941, the NAM explored the idea of an exhibit at the annual meeting of the NCSS, but confessed a "hesitation . . . born of a very strong feeling that it might be misinterpreted. We do not wish to create the impression that we are seeking to promote, advertise or urge the use of NAM literature" (Abbott, 1941). Wilbur Murra, executive secretary, replied, "You are right in anticipating that teachers might misunderstand your motives" (1941a).

The Aftermath

The defense against the attacks on the Rugg textbooks was mounted on several fronts. The Academic Freedom Committee of NCSS issued a statement supporting academic freedom and later prepared "a packet of reading matter on freedom of teaching in the social studies area," which included a 66-page booklet on fending off attacks on textbooks (Curti, 1941). The Council of the American Historical Association asked Professor A. M. Schlesinger to draft a statement regarding controversial issues in textbooks. The statement, which was approved by the council, gave strong support for the inclusion of controversial questions in "the historical account" and for encouraging a "spirit of inquiry" in young people. However, the statement also read that the textbook writer has "an obligation to give both sides" and made no mention of current issues (American Historical Association, 1941). Many textbook writers, including Rugg, had failed to follow fully the edict to "give both sides," and many historians were less than fond of the focus on social problems and social issues in schools. So the statement of support from the AHA was not as strongly worded as it might have been.

Rugg himself was undoubtedly the chief advocate for the defense of social studies, and the Rugg textbooks, against the attackers. And, almost from the start of the attacks on the Rugg books, numerous friends and colleagues rushed to his defense. One of the most active groups was the Committee on Intellectual Freedom and Democracy, organized by his colleagues at Columbia and chaired by Franz Boaz. Another group that furnished support was the Association of Textbook Publishers and also supportive were Rugg's associates on the journal *Frontiers of Democracy*, who were very active in his defense (Winters, 1968).

Rugg gave an able defense of his work and attempted to meet every attack directly, appearing in person "whenever and wherever possible." It seemed that Rugg enjoyed face-to-face confrontations with his attackers, and it was said by people who knew him that Rugg "lived for an argument," often playing the role of devil's advocate to stir up controversy, provoking opponents into making rash statements, which he would tear apart with cold and sarcastic responses (p. 183).

Rugg's confrontations with his accusers followed a familiar pattern. First, he would be accused of being a communist, then criticized over his plan for a socialistic society in *The Great Technology*. Then the accusers would turn to the textbooks themselves. Confronting a similar situation again and again, the critique and Rugg's responses became routine. When pressed, critic after critic would admit that they had not read the books. Under siege on every side, Rugg wrote an autobiographical work to tell his side of the story. *That Men May Understand* was published in April 1941 and received generally favorable reviews. The *New York Times Book Review* scoffed at the idea of Rugg being a communist and described his generation of educational reformers as having "imbibed the antique liquor of utopianism which was always turning New England heads." *The Nation* compared Rugg to Saint Paul carrying the gospel, and Teachers College to the early Church. *Publishers Weekly* endorsed the book and joined Rugg in attacking his critics, accusing Dilling, Forbes, and Hart of working on "the prejudices of the American people" and calling Rugg's book "a vigorous and adequate reply to his critics" (Winters, 1968, pp. 187–189).

After a little more time had passed, heated discourse on the controversy largely subsided, yet discussion of the general pattern of attacks continued in the professional literature. One article, written by a school superintendent, argued that many of the attacks were part of a deliberate effort to undermine "public confidence in the schools so that school appropriations may be reduced" (Dannelly, 1941). Another author provided a larger historical context for the attacks and suggested that they were part of a larger "war on social studies." "The real animus of the critics," he wrote, "is against the whole modern conception of the social studies as a realistic approach to life." In opposition to the critics, he argued that young people have "the right to know what the world is all about and to learn what can be done about it" (Gould, 1941, pp. 90–91). Later still, one social studies professor wrote that "controversial issues ought to be taught," but he cautioned that treatment of issues must be "intelligible" to students; that it must be "rational," appealing primarily to reason rather than emotions; that it should be used in conjunction with the "historical method," a critical examination of sources; that it must be "fair to both sides and all viewpoints"; and that presentation must be clear and complete (Haefner, 1942, pp. 267–268). There is little doubt that this more "balanced" approach was the new order of the day.

As it turned out, February 22, 1941, the date of the Robey story, was a watershed in the war on social studies. Up to that point tension built while the movement for integrated social studies and a focus on issues and problems with a meliorist or reconstructionist purpose gathered steam. After the Robey article, the tide had turned. The struggle over the Rugg textbooks continued in many communities. In a few cases the attempt to censor the texts was successful. In others, they were retained for some time, then quietly dropped when it came time for the adoption of new books. By the middle of the decade, the Rugg textbook series and program had virtually disappeared. Social studies in general, it seemed, was on the defensive. The possibility of a critical, reflective social studies was seriously in doubt, and attacks on progressive educators continued to mount throughout the decade.

Progressives would have both proponents and defenders, but criticism of progressive education seemed a rising tide that no seawall could restrain. The attacks on the Rugg textbooks, and the war against social studies of which it was a part, were pieces of a much larger pattern, one that would continue for some time to come.

THE CONTROVERSY OVER AMERICAN HISTORY

A second important controversy occurred in the 1940s and centered on charges from a respected historian, Allan Nevins, in an article published by the *New York Times*, that U.S. history was no longer sufficiently taught in the nation's schools. Once again, the bogey was social studies. Hugh Russell Fraser, who joined what came to be referred to as the *New York Times* crusade against social studies, blamed "extremists from NCSS and its twin brother, Teachers College," for the decline in the teaching of history. Social studies educators, including Edgar B. Wesley, Wilbur Murra, and Edgar B. Hunt, responded vigorously and provided evidence that U.S. history was a "universal requirement" in the nation's schools. The net result of the stalemate was that social studies was once again portrayed as faddish, implying that attempts at innovation by "educationists" led to a dilution of the study of political history and of American heroes. The controversy over American history combined with the turmoil over the Rugg textbooks to serve as a major turning point, transforming a turf battle between competing camps into a war on progressive social studies.

The wartime controversy over the teaching of American history began with a short article by Pulitzer Prize–winning historian Allan Nevins, professor of American history, Columbia University, which appeared in the *New York Times Magazine* for May 3, 1942. The article was titled "American History for Americans." With inflammatory language, Nevins charged that "young people are all too ignorant of American history," and that schools and colleges were to blame. "Our educational requirements in American history and government," he wrote, "have been and are deplorably haphazard, chaotic and ineffective." To support his charges, Nevins cited the fact that laws requiring American history existed in only 26 states and that 22 states had no legal requirement. The requirements were often "vague and unexacting" and resulted in "the greatest unevenness." The problem was, he went on, that in many schools "a little American history is interjected into a course of 'social studies,' confusedly and halfheartedly. In still others it is taught as a hasty pendant to world history. In others it is simply ignored. Probably the majority of American children never receive the equivalent of a full year's careful work in our national history." Nevins also charged that very few colleges and universities required American history.

The consequence of this neglect was that it undermined the "patriotism and unity of the country. No nation," he wrote, "can be patriotic in the best sense, so people can feel a proud comradeship, without a knowledge of the past." And it was needed in a time of war. In fact, he went on, the "Army camps are hastily organizing classes in historical instruction." Neglect of American history left young men "without a very deep faith in the democratic way of life." Such instruction would provide the people with "its richest source of cultural interest," to "quicken the pulse and feed the mind." Nevins argued that national identity and ideals are rooted in history, and that, "We cannot understand what we are fighting for unless we know how our principles developed."

"It is time for us to catch the true spirit of America, yes, the spirit of its past and its destiny." This could best be accomplished, he argued, by passing similar state laws with mandatory requirements for thorough courses on American history, "divorced from social studies, cosmic history and like fetters." "In these grim times," he suggested, "we must re-examine the sources of our moral and spiritual strength. A thorough, accurate, and intelligent knowledge of our national past—in so many ways the brightest national record in all world history—is the best ground for faith in the present and hope for the future" (Nevins, 1942a, pp. 6, 28). It was a rallying call for action, for tapping "this fountain of inspiration" in the national interest.

The Survey

The Nevins article led to a *New York Times* survey of college level teaching conducted by *Times* education writer Benjamin Fine, published on June 21, 1942. The survey found that "schools throughout the nation were giving instruction in United States history to relatively few students." The *Times* sent questionnaires to virtually every liberal arts college, professional school, and teachers college in the nation, a total of 1,225 institutions. The survey revealed that 82% of the institutions of higher learning in the United States do not require the study of U.S. history. It also found that 72% of the colleges and universities do not require U.S. history for admission. As a result, the author of the survey claimed, "many students go through high school, college, and then to a professional or graduate institution without having explored courses in the history of their own country."

One observer, reporting on the findings of the survey, wrote that while the results were probably "astounding to many parents," they only confirmed what many historians had suspected for years. That "history was on the way out," and that more "utilitarian" courses were being created, dealing with contemporary problems and attempting to "'fuse' all phases of knowledge—sociology, government, economics, history, literature, geography, and even religion and philosophy." Thus, for many, the *Times* survey only confirmed the suspicion that courses in United States history were "none too popular with either students or educators" (Jordan, 1942).

With the Nevins article as inspiration, the *Times* survey had apparently proved the charge that American history was in trouble and that social studies was to blame. The survey, which was assumed to be accurate and reliable, resulted in an outpouring of editorial opinion generally condemning the failure of the schools and colleges. The tenor of commentary was captured by editorials in the summer of 1942 titled "Education's Blind Spot," "We Must Teach U.S. History," "Neglecting History," and "Selling U.S. Short."

A few weeks later, the *Times* carried a response to the charges from Erling M. Hunt, professor of history, Teachers College, under the headline "History Charges Called Untrue: Professor E. M. Hunt Says Subject Is Being Taught in All Schools." Hunt responded to the charges that American history had been "pushed out by something new, called 'social studies.'"

Those charges were, he argued, "uninformed and irresponsible." He explained that from primary grades through high school, attention to "American history, American life and American institutions has steadily increased." Furthermore, he went on, "in public high schools American history is a universal offering and a universal requirement." Although legislative requirements exist in about half the states, the laws are "unnecessary" as every school board and faculty enforces the requirement. Hunt also explained the maligned term *social studies*, stating that "the expression social studies was introduced in 1916 as a group name for history, geography, civics, economics, sociology, and current events" (1942b, October 25).

Hunt included many of the same comments in his column for October in *Social Education*, though he added stronger rhetoric and a good deal more evidence to buttress his case, and he focused his comments on Nevins. In his column, Hunt called Nevins's demand for more American history "nationalistic and not very well-informed." He chided Nevins for confusing statutory requirements with actual practice, and countered, "Every high school in the country offers American history. . . . Few indeed are the graduates of public high schools who have not studied American history in at least one year of the high school." He argued that there was "simply no foundation" for Nevins's assertion that "a little American history is interjected into a course in 'social studies,' confusedly and half-heartedly." And he called the charge "uninformed and irresponsible" and asserted, "every statement is untrue" (1942c, pp. 250–252).

In part, Nevins and others were mistaking labels for reality. The fact that some courses were now labeled *social studies* did not mean that they were so different from what had gone before. Experimentation in some schools had made few inroads into the near universal requirement for a high school course in American history. The few "exceptions" were those cases in which American history and Problems of Democracy were fused in a 2-year offering.

For its part, NCSS took up the defense by passing resolutions at its annual convention in November 1942. The resolutions read, in part, that the council "recognizes the preeminent importance of the study of American history" and "commends the present policy of giving attention at all school levels" to the study. The resolutions also directly challenged the *New York Times* survey, calling it "misleading," because of its neglect of related fields of American study. Another resolution stated that the council "condemns further State legislation prescription regarding the social studies curriculum as educationally unsound" (NCSS Resolutions, 1942).

The battle between Nevins and the *New York Times* on one side, and Hunt and NCSS on the other, continued for some time. Correspondence between the two makes for interesting reading. Nevins wrote to Hunt, on October 13, 1942, following Hunt's critique: "Of course I must answer your article. You are only 99 and 44/100 percent wrong. . . . I am loaded for bear" (Nevins, 1942b). Hunt replied, "Perhaps it will be possible to judge how wrong I am somewhat better after you have moved from the realm of impressions and prejudices into the realm of facts and realities" (Hunt, 1942d).

Nevins wrote a six-page response to Hunt's critique, citing support for his argument on the need for "statutory requirements," and reiterated his claim that "probably a majority of children never receive the equivalent of a full year's careful work in our national history." He argued in support of this claim that "nearly everyone knows some child of his immediate circle who leaves the schools without a year's such education, or anything like it. (One of my daughters has just gained a secondary-school diploma, after six years at Horace Mann School and the remainder at St. Agatha's School, without any American history whatever.)"

It appears that Nevins's own experience with his daughter's schooling may have angered him and motivated his attack on the schools. Moreover, he wrote, "I am convinced . . . that a considerable number of teachers are using fusion courses or social-studies to slight, or evade, or mangle the study of American history." He went on to charge that schools of education "sometimes encourage this effort to slight, evade, and mangle" (1942b, pp. 1–2).

Nevins then quoted, at some length, Mr. Hugh Russell Fraser, whose paper "How to Avoid Teaching American History" presented three examples: one drawn from Milne, the 6-year secondary laboratory school of the New York State College for Teachers in Albany, another drawn from the lab school at the University of Wisconsin, Madison, and a third from the Eugene, Oregon, public schools. In each case, Fraser described unit titles reported in brief overviews contained in a bulletin on teaching published by NCSS. From the unit titles he drew the conclusion that the courses have the tendency to "ignore major phases of United States political history and to substitute for them economic, social and industrial history." Nevins stated that based on Fraser's summary, he could understand why "Dr. Matthew Page Andrews believes that 'fusion' courses are widely used to kill American history rather than give it vitality" and why such courses are sometimes referred to by students as "social slush" (pp. 3–6).

While conceding that the charges against social studies "could be simply a well-intentioned, if mistaken, wartime enthusiasm," Hunt then suggested that the quotations from Dr. Andrews and Mr. Fraser, together with Professor Nevins's arguments,

> recall a familiar pattern of attacks on social studies teaching: data carefully selected and organized to support a thesis, appeals to patriotism and nationalism, identification of the program under attack with communism or radical-

ism, disparagement of teachers colleges, efforts to bar consideration of current affairs and contemporary problems from the schools. . . . They are aiding, whether consciously or not, groups that fear consideration in the schools of the realities and vital issues of the present day. . . . Who demand that the schools concern themselves not with the troubled present but with the glorious past. (1942a, pp. 351–352)

The next development in the continuing controversy was the appearance of an article written by Edgar B. Wesley, published in one of the prime journals for historians of American history, the *Mississippi Valley Historical Review*. Wesley addressed the controversy and attacked historians for their general lack of involvement in the schools. At the start of his article, Wesley discussed the difficulty of interpreting educational statistics and lay much of the blame for the controversy at its doorstep. He pointed out, as had Hunt, that many courses labeled *social studies* were actually courses in American history. This was especially common in the junior high school. Wesley drew the conclusion that history "as such" had declined in frequency, but characterized the decline as "largely in nomenclature rather than in basic elements, a shift in form rather than a loss in content." Wesley went on to charge that history had "declined" because historians "refuse to participate in school problems . . . [and] have scorned teaching and bemoaned high school teachers of history." He suggested that increased statutory requirements were not the answer, and argued that "the wisest policy is to do nothing" (1943b).

At the meeting of the Mississippi Valley Historical Association the month following publication of Wesley's article, the association responded by setting up a committee to look into the controversy and to prepare a report to be presented the following October.

The Test

As the committee was beginning its work, another major development occurred, adding fuel to the flames of the controversy. On Sunday, April 4, 1943, the *New York Times* published the results of a test on American history given to 7,000 college freshmen in 36 institutions. The headline that accompanied the report read:

Ignorance of U.S. History
Shown by College Freshmen

Survey of 7,000 Students in 36 Institutions
Discloses Vast Fund of Misinformation
On Many Basic Facts

The report began: "College freshmen throughout the nation reveal a striking ignorance of even the most elementary aspects of United States history, and know almost nothing about many important phases of this country's growth and development. . . ." "For the most part," the report went on, "these students had taken courses in American history, social studies or government in high school. . . . Few of the students were studying American history in college." One of the conclusions drawn was that "students are in need of United States history on the college or university level even though they have taken courses in this field in high school" (Fine, 1943, p. 1).

The report indicated, according to the author, not only an ignorance of elementary aspects of American history but also a large amount of misinformation. The questionnaire had been developed by Hugh Russell Fraser and Allan Nevins. The resulting report as published in the *Times* contained not only a statistical summary of student performance, but also a lengthy collection of sad but somewhat humorous anecdotes detailing the misconceptions and misinformation that students possessed. An editorial in the *Times* called the survey "highly discouraging" and stated that "since most of these college students had only recently completed high school courses in American history, the conclusion is inescapable that our high schools need better teaching in that subject" ("American History Survey," 1943, p. 10E). So it appeared that Nevins and Fraser had turned their guns on the quality rather than the quantity of American history teaching that went on in schools and had intensified their campaign for more history at the college level.

The test was followed in the *Times* with comments from Hugh Russell Fraser, blaming NCSS and Teachers College for the sorry state of affairs. Fraser was quoted as saying:

> The vicious system of teaching whereby the social study extremists have a contempt for the facts of American history must be corrected. If money is needed [to improve history instruction], it is to combat the practices of the National Council for the Social Studies and its twin brother, Teachers College, Columbia. ("Fraser Quits Post," 1943, p. 30)

Wilbur F. Murra responded to the *Times*, in a letter published on its editorial page, that Fraser's statement and others published by the *Times* tended to give laymen an "unfortunately erroneous notion as to the accepted pedagogical use of the term 'social studies' and an incorrect picture of the National Council for the Social Studies." Murra then proceeded to define social studies, providing a Wesleyan definition, and suggested that it was "absurd" to speak of social studies as being "opposed to history." He went on to explain that social studies and NCSS were aimed at improving practice in teaching American history and other social studies subjects and that "improvement of instruction in American history" had been one of the most persistent goals of NCSS "since it was founded twenty-two years ago." He also explained that American history was the "predominant" subject in the field (Murra, 1943, p. 24). On the same day, the *Times* published an editorial, stating that it did not "endorse" Mr. Fraser's statement and that it agreed with Murra and did not have the slightest doubt about the "value of the so-called social studies" ("History and 'Social Studies,'" 1943, p. 24).

The *Times* test led to yet another flurry of editorials and comment in newspapers across the nation. Many, if not all, Hearst newspapers ran an editorial titled "Our American History" (1943). The editorial asked:

> What has happened to the American schools, that they have fallen so far short of their fundamental responsibility to the American people? How do subversive textbooks, of the type so properly and patriotically but BELATEDLY purged from San Francisco's schools, find their way into American schools? . . . the American people . . . . have left supervision of the schools to radicals and theorists who have no respect for American history and no faith in American tradition. But the actual perversion has been accomplished by Socialistic and Communistic pseudo-educators who have conspired to disparage American history and to give American children a distorted conception of the principles which inspired the founders of their country.

The editorial went on to imply that social studies was a "menacing conspiracy." Another editorial contained a similar tone, parroting the *Times* survey, but going beyond, charging that American schools were failing "to teach any sort of history." This particular editorial also lambasted Murra's attempt to define social studies and charged that until social studies was clearly defined, the field would be "under the suspicion that Social Studies means something that Social Studies teachers are not willing for the general public . . . to know . . . . It is a dark suspicion indeed" ("Missed," 1943). The continuing controversy also led to a U.S. Senate resolution calling for study of the ways "the Federal Government may most effectively promote a more thorough study of the history of the United States" (1943, p. 2).

Hunt, of course, commented on the "test" in an article in *Social Education* and lambasted Nevins, Fraser, the quality of the test, and the *New York Times*. Moreover, he blamed the publisher. Apparently at Nevins's suggestion, Fraser approached Mrs. Sulzberger, who was the daughter of the late Adolph Ochs, the publisher of the *Times*, and the wife of the present publisher, to ask for her support in a campaign to improve the teaching of American history. Hunt blamed the *Times* for supporting and printing the views of Fraser and Nevins and their campaign to persuade the American public that American history is neglected and that social studies was to blame. "Why," Hunt asked, "does the *New York Times* take the educational views of Fraser, alias the Committee on American history, seriously?" (1943, p. 200).

Antidote

The final and concluding phase of the controversy came with publication of the report of the Wesley Committee, *American History in the Schools and Colleges*, in January 1944. The report, which echoed many of Wesley's earlier conclusions, was prepared in a few months, after the committee had administered its own test on American history to a representative sample of high school and college students and selected groups of adults. It found that American history was taught in both the schools and colleges, that enrollment in elementary and junior high school "approaches 100 percent." The committee also found that "enrollment in American history courses in senior high school is so high that the Committee sees no need to urge any change in programs at this level." The committee presented direct evidence in tables, charts, and narrative supporting its conclusion that "the evidence is overwhelming" that American history is taught in the schools in three cycles, and that "nearly all senior high school students study American history." The committee did support Nevins and Fraser in one area, finding that "the percentage of college students who study American history is small." The committee also found that Americans did not know their history as well as they might, especially if "by knowing history one means the ability to recall dates, names, and specific events." But it found that "Americans in general do know a reasonable amount of American history," if one means "understanding" and "appreciation" (Wesley, 1944, p. 1).

As to the charge that social studies was undermining American history, the report did not address this question directly, but did make an effort to clarify misunderstandings and misuse of the term *social studies*. In its conclusion, the committee steadfastly endorsed the continued prominence of American history in the social studies curriculum and reiterated that, based on a thorough review of evidence, "American history is now taught with sufficient frequency." It recommended that "improvement in quality" of teaching should be the major focus of educators and the public and found no need for more laws to require the teaching of American history or other social studies subjects. The committee recommended, "State legislatures should not write the social studies curriculum," but argued that it should be created by teachers, educational experts, and social scientists (pp. 119–121).

The report made no direct mention of the charges made by the Nevins-Fraser campaign. It referred directly to the "controversy concerning the teaching of American history" only in reporting its charge. It did refer to some of the criticisms obliquely, however, with statements in the preface, such as "The war has caused a reexamination of the purposes, extent, and quality of instruction in American history" and "Educational policy should be based upon evidence." This may have been a calculated attempt to quell the controversy. An early outline for the report was titled "American History for Americans," reprising the title of Nevins's original article, and another draft outline included a "preamble" with a comment implying that the committee "sees no war" between social studies and the social science subjects and stating that "this Committee eschews derogatory comparisons among subjects" (Wesley, 1943a).

The findings of the Wesley report poured cold water on the flames of controversy and brought it to a close, at least temporarily. Its findings suggested that the controversy was a tempest in a teapot over the impression that "social studies extremists" had taken over, rather than a genuine crisis in the "neglect" of American history.

The controversy over the teaching of American history continued several of the themes of the controversy over the Rugg textbooks. Wartime concerns relating to the inculcation of patriotism appeared to be at the root of both episodes. Behind the continuing war on social studies that these controversies represented were charges of subversion, a perception that a cabal of radical pedagogues at Teachers College and elsewhere was attempting to foist its views on innocent American schoolchildren. These episodes could be viewed as purification rituals, attempts to rid the culture of topics and activities deemed taboo.

Conflicts over the social studies curriculum seem to play out again and again, with many of the same arguments reappearing. In the final analysis, the controversy over the teaching of American history was built on a number of unfair and inaccurate charges not supported by the weight of evidence. Nonetheless, many of the charges probably stuck. The dramatic headlines were gained by the most sensational claims, not by the responses that followed. The controversy also claimed a great deal of the time and energy of all concerned. As one thoughtful observer on the NCSS Academic Freedom Committee wrote, "Major activity of past two or three years has been related to the attack of the *New York Times* group on American history teachers. That issue is temporarily closed with the publication of the Wesley Committee on American history. However, I anticipate that other attacks may be made in the near future" (Quillen, 1944).

CONCLUSION

Despite the battles over the social studies curriculum, evidence on the status of social studies in secondary schools suggests only relatively minor changes during the war years. One study revealed general stability in course offerings and a good deal of flexibility and tinkering with unit topics in specific courses, largely as a result of wartime needs and interests. U.S. history was the most frequent offering in both 7th and 8th grades (more commonly the 8th), with geography the second most frequent offering in those grades. Civics was the dominant offering in 9th grade, world history in 10th, and American history in 11th. In 12th grade, Problems of Democracy or some variation was the most common offering, with economics, sociology, government, or U.S. history a distant second. In most cases social studies courses were required at each level, with the exception of world history, which was usually an elective. Although there were many new course offerings, these were most often electives available in the upper grades and consisting of courses with names such as Global Geography, Contemporary History, Air-Age Geography, Latin American History, Postwar Problems, and International Relations.

Ancient, medieval, and modern history were dropped in many schools, in line with the increase in world history. Civics was also dropped in a few cases. Geography was the most commonly introduced new topic, often finding its way into the 10th-grade world history or geography course. Latin America was close behind, frequently receiving attention in U.S. history courses. Twelfth-grade Problems of Democracy was the course most likely to emphasize international affairs, social and economic planning, and international relations.

In summary, it appears from the evidence reviewed in this chapter that the war accelerated some trends, contributed to the end of others, and created a new set of demands on the curriculum. During this period there was an absence of general calls for reform or of development of new scope and sequence statements. Yet sudden changes and modifications in social studies programs were at least recommended, if not imposed, on the basis of the wartime emergency.

In the rhetorical drama that accompanied developments in social studies, the war seemed to bring something of a restoration of traditional values. Social studies was increasingly depicted as communistic or un-American, at worst, or leading to the neglect of American ideals, at best. In fact, during the middle and later 1930s, many educators with a social reconstructionist orientation had challenged the wisdom of the American social structure. Their challenge would be largely answered during the war. The period saw social studies buffeted by two nearly all-consuming controversies. First, the controversy over the Rugg textbooks and, second, the controversy over the teaching of American history. Both were directly linked to wartime concerns over patriotism, and both challenged social studies to clarify, and to purify, its aims. The challenge to the Rugg materials resulted in their eventual disappearance from schools. The impact of the controversy over American history was perhaps less direct. As we shall see, these controversies were only the beginning in a long period of national concern over the direction of social studies curriculum in schools.

CHAPTER FIVE

The Cold War and the Return to Academic Study

IF WORLD WAR II signaled the death of progressive social studies, the cold war completed the act. During the second half of the 1940s and throughout the 1950s, social studies was one of the bogeys for attacks on progressive education in general. The tone of the earlier attack on social studies by historian Allan Nevins, along with many of his specific charges, were repeated vociferously. The postwar era was a time of conformity and of economic prosperity and expansion, and a time during which American power around the globe was rivaled only by that of the Soviet Union. That rivalry, and the ideological struggle between the two industrial giants, between communism and capitalism, set a tone for the entire era. It was a tone of confrontation, secrecy, and self-righteousness, which established a pattern of attacks on academic freedom and freedom of speech and thought that affected schools and society as nothing had before. Only the red scares of the 1920s and 1930s had a similar effect, though they did not exert so much influence over the direction of the curriculum. In the postwar era, a chill settled over the discussion of controversial issues, and by the late 1950s, the pendulum in education had swung so far to the right that government set a course to ensure an academic curriculum centered in the traditional disciplines. In social studies, this led to a move away from the study of social issues, and toward a greater focus on the disciplines.

This was a critical time for social studies and gave historians and social scientists an advantage in years hence. The dominant theme of the era, both in schools and out, was the struggle over communism. Throughout the postwar era, communism, when it was given attention in schools, was portrayed as a threat to democracy. This focus represented an attempted ideological purification of the American citizenry through the influence of schools. Indeed, as one prominent educational historian has argued, one cannot understand the 1950s and 1960s in American education without the basic understanding that the cold war and the battle against communism was its central theme (Karier, 1986). As a focal point in citizenship education through social studies courses, anticommunism became a topical vehicle for the enactment of education for social efficiency and for the direct inculcation of mainstream American values via the discrediting of ideas that were seen as un-American.

Direct anticommunism took up residence in a number of educational locales during the postwar era: in school textbooks and supplemental materials, in the professional literature of the time, and among educational leaders. Moreover, anticommunist sentiment was one of the driving forces in the major curricular trend of the times. The 1950s brought a renewal of emphasis on traditional disciplines and a focus on both traditional and newer academically oriented approaches to education, which resulted in federally funded curriculum projects in numerous areas, including the new math, the new science, and the new social studies.

I do not mean to assume that the anticommunist viewpoint was, on the whole, "bad." It simply was a fact. A number of the leading progressive educators had an anticommunist perspective. However, in its excesses, anticommunism created an unhealthy atmosphere for the airing of dissent, thus profoundly influencing schools and society. Much of the anticommunist crusade in schools illustrated the subtle dangers of citizenship transmission and the potential limits it may place on free expression and free thought, creating a one-dimensional curriculum that could, potentially, repel all alternatives.

ATTACKS ON PROGRESSIVE EDUCATION

During the late 1940s and early 1950s a growing crescendo of attacks on progressive education emerged. The deluge of articles and books attacking progressive education began in 1949 and peaked in 1953. The first strand of attack was from intellectuals, best symbolized by Arthur Bestor, a historian and leading critic of education. The second strand of criticism, red-baiting attacks, grew from the ideological conflict of the era, from those who viewed progressive education as a communist plot. A third strand attacked the public funding of mass education. Each of these was conditioned and voiced against the urgent backdrop of cold war crisis. In social studies, and in education generally, the impact of these attacks was to impose a chill, an atmosphere of restraint, censorship. The attacks precipitated a tilt toward conformity in the curriculum, toward discipline-based subjects, toward a denatured form of inquiry, and away from modern problems and anything in the curriculum that took a questioning attitude toward society.

The intellectual critique of progressivism came largely from university professors and journalists. These critics charged that the curriculum in schools was soft, anti-intellectual, and weak when compared to schools in Europe and the USSR. The first major book capturing the essence of the intellectual critique was *And Madly Teach*, published by Mortimer Smith in 1949. Smith charged that the progressive philosophy of education was undemocratic and anti-intellectual because it failed to "adhere to any standards of knowledge" and abandoned the notion of educating every child with the world's wisdom by embracing "utilitarian how-to courses." In 1953 at least four important books were published critiquing progressive education. These included Robert Hutchins's *The Conflict in Education in a Democratic Society*, Albert Lynd's *Quackery in the Public Schools*, Arthur Bestor's *Educational Wastelands*, and Paul Woodring's *Let's Talk Sense About Our Schools*. Among these, Bestor's critique was by far the most widely read.

Bestor, a respected historian at the University of Illinois, who became the leading intellectual critic of education, charged that modern education had become anti-intellectual, a position in general agreement with Lynd and much of the accumulated criticism. In *Educational Wastelands*, Bestor favored an old-style progressive education with respect for the disciplines and the primacy of intellectual values. He charged that a conspiracy existed among "professional educationists," through an "interlocking directorate" of progressive leaders.

Bestor charged that educators had "undermined public confidence in the schools" by focusing on trivial purposes and by "deliberately divorcing the schools from the disciplines of science and scholarship." Bestor posited that schools existed to teach "the power to think" and argued for the restoration of "liberal education" (1953, pp. 9–10). Bestor argued that the decline of liberal education threatened the national welfare and the security of our democratic institutions. He argued for "the disciplined mind" and made a case for the academic disciplines as the core of the curriculum, and for history as the core of social studies (p. 59).

Bestor had few kind words for social studies; he urged the elimination of the term and a return to history and the "logical organization of knowledge" and derided the study of contemporary problems as "an easy door" (p. 22). He was hypercritical of social studies and called it "social stew" (p. 46).

Bestor's work did find critics. William Clark Trow responded that Bestor had drawn a "badly distorted" picture of American education, that Bestor's program for developing the disciplined mind would limit the relevance of education, and that "no one would be ready to solve a problem until he is at least through college." He characterized Bestor's ideas as "dubious," and suggested, "We don't march backward" (1954, pp. 25–26).

Bestor's critique of social studies was apparently treated as one of the many attacks, but did receive a somewhat belated response, published in 1958 in *Social Education*. Describing Bestor as the most "embattled opponent" of the term *social studies*, Leo J. Alilunas charged that Bestor had lumped together life adjustment and social studies and had little appreciation for the attempts at defining the field. Alilunas charged that Bestor made no effort to understand the development of the social studies movement and ignored the attempts to adjust the demands of history and the other social sciences. Simply put, Bestor hadn't done his homework.

Educational Wastelands was widely read, and it made Arthur Bestor the leading spokesperson of his time on education. A good deal of his activity over the ensuing years was based on the book and the fame that it bestowed. The Council for Basic Education was formed by Bestor and others to advance the intellectual and moral development of youth and to champion a reform agenda calling for a restoration of traditional academic approaches to schooling. A new consensus emerged, based on the primacy and integrity of the academic disciplines, the value of inquiry or discovery learning, the appropriateness of academic study for the high school, support for gifted education, production of change materials, development of curriculum reform projects, and appropriate inservice teacher training.

Red-Baiting Attacks

Many of the 1950s attacks on progressive social studies were ideologically based. These attacks had origins much earlier, in the red scare, in the work of Sidney Hook, and in the hearings conducted by the House Un-American Activities Committee and similar government panels in the 1930s and 1940s. By the early 1950s, the fear of having one's career destroyed by the House Committee was very real. This was the "silent generation" of the McCarthy era. Also, during the same period, the Central Intelligence Agency (CIA) developed books and reports, labeled *manpower studies*, which held education as part of the solution to a cold war personnel shortage projected by Harvard president James B. Conant, Vice Admiral Hyman G. Rickover, and many other military, educational, and political leaders (Karier, 1986).

Behind rising fears of communism were the realities of living in the atomic age. Simply put, people became less optimistic about the human prospect. In the years immediately following the first use of atomic weaponry, the nation was seized by atom bomb hysteria. Numerous articles appeared in the popular press that captured the fears and hopes of many Americans. Among the titles: "The Challenge of the Atomic Bomb," "Sovereignty in the Atomic Age," and "I'm a Frightened Man" (Atomic, 1946).

Long before the development of cold war fears and atomic bomb hysteria, critics of progressive education had frequently asserted that it was subversive and had made numerous efforts to save the schools by routing progressive educators and "left-wing" textbooks, notably in the 1920s and during the Rugg controversy. In the late 1940s and early 1950s, criticism reached new heights. The thesis of the political criticism of progressive social studies in the postwar era was stated clearly in an article by John T. Flynn that appeared in the *Reader's Digest* in 1951. Flynn charged that a group of progressive educators "set out to introduce into the social science courses of our high schools a seductive form of propaganda for collectivism—chiefly of that type we call socialism." Flynn wrote that the "propaganda" put forth in schools, largely by the Rugg textbook series, taught that the "American system of free enterprise is a failure," that our "republic of limited powers is a mistake," and that "our way of life must give way to a collectivist society" (p. 24). He cited a string of quotes from the early writings of Counts and Rugg to support his thesis. However, Flynn failed to note that the Rugg textbook series had been discontinued and fallen into disuse.

Other red-baiting critics included Kitty Jones and Robert Olivier in *Progressive Education Is REDucation,* and Mary Allen in *Education or Indoctrination,* both published in 1956. These books mirrored many of Flynn's charges but went even further. Jones and Olivier charged that progressive educators were at work "making little socialists" and criticized the plan of the "frontier thinkers" "to indoctrinate this and future generations with their view" and to have the entire nation "participate in solving problems." The book also critiqued the "scrambling" of history, geography, and government into the "social studies," and the "anti-intellectualism" of educationists (pp. 40, 45, 98–99, 130). Allen reviewed much of the literature critiquing progressive education. She criticized Dewey's pragmatism, traced linkages between progressive educators and socialist organizations, critiqued the social reconstructionist agenda of the frontier thinkers, and charged that communism had attached itself to progressive education with the subsequent threat of "communist infiltration in our schools." In sum, she warned, "there is overwhelming evidence to indicate that there is a well-organized, well-financed plan to impose a new social order on the people of America whether they like it or not" (p. 52).

A number of right-wing groups contributed to the general ferment against the communists and socialists who were supposedly subverting American education. The best known of these was Allen Zoll's National Council for American Education, which supplied speakers and pamphlets to community groups, published a periodical, and disseminated critiques of "un-American" textbooks and lists of Communist-front affiliations of professors at leading universities (Anderson, 1952b). The attacks on progressivism and social studies were reinforced by support from politically potent groups such as the American Legion, the Sons and Daughters of the American Revolution, and the Minute Women. Attackers sought out the schools not because they were rife with subversion but because they were accessible. Weeding out controversial books and teachers was an attempt to do something about the communist menace; it was a "crusade to purify American education of its political and ideological errors" (Ravitch, 1983, p. 121). While instances of ousted teachers were rare, manipulation of the communist issue put teachers, textbooks, and the curriculum at the mercy of right-wing pressure groups and imposed serious limits on academic freedom.

What was behind the attacks? As in the Rugg controversy and earlier, attacks on education often seemed to have local origins among concerned citizens, but were in fact being orchestrated and supported by national pressure groups joining informal "coalitions" with "interlocking directorates." All of this was taking place within the context of a national crisis over communism, a critical fact to bear in mind. Loyalty programs and fear of subversion were on the rise, accompanied by sensational spy trials and congressional hearings. Two national committees, the Senate Internal Security Subcommittee and the House Committee on Un-American Activities, were investigating educators on a national stage. Mandates for loyalty oaths and legislation providing for the ouster of disloyal teachers were passed in an increasing number of states. In this context, right-wing extremists found a ready audience for their allegations.

In sum, the atmosphere in the schools was heavily influenced by the anticommunist crusade. While university professors split on the question of whether Communists should be allowed to teach, 90% of the public believed that Communists should be fired. Yet charges of subversion were difficult to refute and tended to damage, and sometimes destroy, careers. At the very least, they spread an atmosphere of fear and distrust and led to the closing of many minds (Ravitch, 1983). The notion that progressive educators, especially in social studies, were subversive, socialist, or linked to communism, gained increasing currency and undoubtedly damaged the cause of progressive-, meliorist-, and reconstructionist-oriented social studies.

The Response

Educators responded to the attacks, as they often do, primarily by writing books and articles examining, explaining, and countering the attacks. The journals *Progressive Education* ("Attacks on Education," 1952) and *Phi Delta Kappan* ("Attacks on Education," 1953) ran special issues devoted to analysis of critics and aimed at helping teachers, administrators, and professors counter attacks from local groups. At least one book provided an anthology of literature on "the great debate" on education, as it was often called. In *Public Education Under Criticism*, C. Winfield Scott and Clyde M. Hill presented excerpts from critics and included sections on general and philosophical matters, progressive education, the fundamentals, religion, social studies, and teacher education. The book also included sections defending education, providing analysis and evaluation of the criticisms, and a final segment titled "How to Handle Criticisms" (1954). The fact that social studies was the only specific subject field given its own section is a significant indication that social studies was one of the prime targets.

Most of the articles written in response to the wave of criticism admitted that schools could be doing a better job, but also offered counterarguments and evidence on the issues. Archibald W. Anderson, a professor of education at the University of Illinois, undertook a painstaking review of evidence related to most of the critiques. Regarding the charge that schools were neglecting the fundamentals, he found substantial research evidence to contradict the charge and argued that the basic skills were often included in newer subjects and activities. In response to the charge that modern methods were an inefficient waste of time, he found considerable research evidence pointing to "one inevitable conclusion: Schools using modern and progressive methods of teaching and a modern curriculum are doing a good job, and in most instances a better job of teaching the fundamentals as traditional schools." Moreover, he argued that attention to "social problems" was a necessity in a democratic society and in keeping with the American tradition (1952a, pp. 98, 104).

Most of the responses to the attacks on education were not as thorough as Anderson's, nor were they published in journals and magazines that would reach the general public. Once again, attacks and sensational charges received more attention from the public than did the reasoned and often thoughtful responses of educators. In the realm of social studies, the response seemed particularly anemic and deferred. It seemed that the critics of progressive education had the upper hand and the nation's ear.

Perhaps many of the attacks were not taken seriously. Similar criticisms had been voiced earlier and were seemingly repeated again and again. Despite mounting criticism, it seemed that most progressive educators continued business as usual, and that schools were largely operating much as they had for years, in traditional ways. Near the peak of the controversy, in 1955, the PEA folded up its tent and went out of business. Two years later, the magazine *Progressive Education* ceased publication. Progressive education had gone from a high point in the 1930s during which it seemed that a growing number of educators claimed the mantle of progressivism, to a new time during which progressives took the blame for all the ills of education. In hindsight, their response was muted. Given the suspicious tenor of the times, this was understandable.

NCSS Responds

There were several critical responses from social studies educators to the attacks on education, including a number of articles, books, and special issues of journals. Yet despite a good deal of discussion of and resistance to criticisms of social studies during the postwar era, by the late 1950s it appears that the NCSS had largely caved in to critics and followed their recommendations for a different approach to social studies, one built around the disciplines.

Many progressive leaders failed to respond adequately to the attacks on progressive education "in large part because they were retired or about to retire from Teachers College" (Karier, 1986, p. 296). To its credit, from 1953 to 1955, in conjunction with other groups of educators, NCSS sold kits titled "Attacks on Education," which were aimed at helping teachers and school administrators fend off attacks. In the main, however, social studies educators cowered under the weight of the attacks, and even elected a critic of the field, with views similar to Bestor, to the office of president of the NCSS. In his presidential address to the organization in 1957, William H. Cartwright decried a "drift from scholars and scholarship" in social studies and called for new spirit of cooperation among educators and "their natural allies, the academic scholars" (pp. 5, 6).

Three volumes published by NCSS in the late 1950s and early 1960s illustrate the extent of the cave-in. First, in 1958, NCSS published a yearbook edited by Roy A. Price, titled *New Viewpoints in the Social Sciences.* In the volume the academic disciplines were represented in essays by scholars from a variety of social science fields. Notably, the volume ignored educators and schools. Also, in 1961, NCSS published a book by Cartwright and Watson titled *Interpreting and Teaching American History.* The volume included era-by-era essays reviewing the latest scholarship on American history, including an essay by Arthur Bestor, and some work on educational practice. Another project, begun in 1958 as a collaboration between NCSS and the American Council of Learned Societies, resulted in publication of *The Social Sciences and the Social Studies* (Berelson, 1963). Each of these volumes emphasized an academic- and disciplines-oriented approach in keeping with the nature of the criticism. Perhaps the trend toward more disciplines-oriented work was simply a reflection of the times. In any event, the criticisms of social studies in the early postwar era had apparently borne fruit.

If the winners were the disciplines, the losers were advocates of reflective or issues-centered social studies. The crusade against communism sent a chill through social studies and could not have been healthy. One factor that undoubtedly had an impact was the change in key leadership positions within NCSS. Merrill Hartshorn had replaced Wilbur Murra as executive secretary during the World War II years, and Lewis Paul Todd had replaced Erling M. Hunt as editor of *Social Education* during the postwar era. Murra and Hunt were among the great progressive leaders who had helped with the birth of social studies and frequently came to its defense. Many other progressive educators had retired or were nearing retirement age. It appears that the younger generation of progressive educators was not up to the challenge brought by criticisms. Perhaps they simply had no choice but to lie low and let the national crisis pass. In any event, the decline of progressive social studies was part of the larger decline of progressive education in schools and was a lasting consequence of the war on social studies.

CURRICULUM TRENDS

The golden age of curriculum development had occurred in the 1930s. In many cases, trends begun in the 1920s or 1930s continued into the postwar period, or morphed into a new variation or hybrid. During the postwar era, several distinct yet overlapping curriculum trends emerged. Among these were general education, life adjustment, and core. General education was a trend that began in the 1930s, but came to full fruition with publication of the Harvard "Redbook" on education published in 1945. This report was the work of the Committee on the Objectives of a General Education in a Free Society, led by Harvard president James B. Conant. For secondary schools the report recommended both a "general" and "special" focus with attention to three areas: natural sciences, social sciences, and the humanities—both the bodies of knowledge and the distinctive methods of each. It postulated that the major aims of general education were to develop students who thought effectively, communicated efficiently, and were skilled and thoughtful at making judgments and discriminating among values. The aim was to develop "the good man, the good citizen, and the useful man" with integrated personality (Harvard Committee, 1945, p. 51). It supported both history and the problems course, but seemed to recommend postponing the formal study of the social sciences other than history until college.

Another still emerging trend that was to exert its greatest influence during the postwar era was life adjustment education. Begun in the 1930s, its official birth can be marked by Prosser's 1939 Inglis lecture and his call to focus on student "needs." Life adjustment represented a new reformulation of an old trend, and a prominent one. This was the "new social efficiency," and Prosser was the Snedden of his time. The life adjustment movement led to proposals for significant though small changes in the social studies curriculum, including an emphasis on personal problems, as in the Senior Problems course, and a deemphasis on global and national issues, which was ironic given the new stature of the United States in the world.

During the postwar era, Life Adjustment Education became an official program of the U.S. Office of Education. In 1947, Commissioner John W. Studebaker appointed the National Commission on Life Adjustment Education for Youth. It was decided that life adjustment would focus not only on those who were neglected, but would be aimed more broadly, at all American youth. Life adjustment programs focused on utility and at the same time lowered the bar. Business arithmetic was substituted for geometry, physical fitness for foreign language. Moreover, math and foreign language were to be dropped as required studies (McGrath, 1951a, 1951b).

Time magazine, which heralded the arrival of the program with a brief article titled "Get Adjusted," compared the notion to Aldous Huxley's description in *Brave New World* of human hatching and conditioning centers in which everyone was taught his or her place. From the Alphas at the top, to the Epsilons, or sewer workers, the whole process aimed at "making people like their unescapable social destiny" (1947, p. 64). Life adjustment in practice meant a stress on "functional" objectives, including vocation, health, and leisure, and was a partial rejection of academic studies, at least as a steady diet for all students. It led to many instances of curricula focused on trivialities, such as "What is expected on a blind date?" and "Development of an Effective Personality." The clear objective was adjusting the student to group norms and societal expectations.

On the question of the impact of life adjustment education on actual school programs there is little certainty. *Social Education* contained references to life adjustment but it was never a strong presence. However, there were a number of complaints voiced about the "overcrowding" of social studies with new demands. There were also a number of new textbooks that had life adjustment titles: *Getting Adjusted to Life, Social Living, Teen-Agers, Building Your Life, Marriage and Family Living,* and *Facing Life's Problems.* Perhaps the greatest impact on the social studies curriculum came in Senior Problems courses, which were a variation on Contemporary Problems and Problems of Democracy with a focus on life adjustment and personal problems. In many schools, problems courses were transformed into a vehicle for life adjustment (Franklin, 1987). On the whole, however, given the mixed reception in the literature from scholars and teachers, it is likely that most teachers ignored the program (Broder, 1976).

The body of criticism hurled against the life adjustment program during the 1950s was a major reason for its demise. As we have seen, life adjustment was pronounced anti-intellectual by multiple critics, and numerous flaws were raised in that critique (Hofstadter, 1963). Although much of the critique was caricature, many of the supposed flaws were accurate. Life adjustment was not a movement that would lead to higher academic achievement. Although well intended, it was built on inequitable and undemocratic assumptions regarding the life prospects of the majority of students, denying many students their right to a full and equal chance at success in the American system.

Other significant trends were at work as well. Business and industry cooperation had been anathema to many social studies educators in the 1930s, but it was back in the postwar era, with corporations openly courting social studies educators and producing "free" materials for classroom use. NCSS moved cautiously into this arena, partly because of the opposition of organized labor. Social studies educators were understandably skeptical of the intentions of business groups, given the continuing propaganda flowing from the NAM and others (Minutes, 1951).

One of the most persistent issues in the curriculum was the continuing trend toward various forms of curriculum integration under the labels *integration, correlation, fusion,* and *core,* though by the postwar period, *core* had become the most common terminology. Core courses were also known sometimes as *general education, unified studies,* and *basic living.* By 1949, according to a survey conducted by the U.S. Office of Education, 20% of junior high schools with more than 500 students had developed a core curriculum, as had 11.3% of high schools of similar size. English and social studies were "invariably part of the core," making up 72.7% of all core courses (Wright, 1950, p. 13).

Interest in various forms of integrated curriculum continued in *Social Education* through most of the postwar period, at least until the mid-1950s. Core was often portrayed, especially by critics, as a choice between "subject versus core." In reality core was simply a different way of getting at the subjects, rather than a reaction to subject areas or disciplines. The early postwar years marked a revival of core experimentation in its purest form, centering study around a social issue, perhaps in local manifestation, for interdisciplinary study, undergirded by a faculty-planned framework of subject matter. Social studies was by far the largest source of problems for study, and core represented a reorganization of social studies under the perennial goal of education for citizenship. The subject matter of both core and traditional plans of organization was largely the same. However, core simply seemed, to many, to furnish a better vehicle for doing the same job. There were, of course, some misapplications by extreme utilitarians (Harvill, 1954).

THE CONTINUING STRUGGLE TO DEFINE SOCIAL STUDIES

During the postwar era, there were many competing groups struggling over the direction of the curriculum. This situation caused one social studies teacher to describe the field as "chaotic," and to lament "sprawling pedagogical confusion" and "incompetence" in the schools which he described as an "embarrassing manifestation of rapid growth of an American institution" (Robinson, 1959, p. 322). Conditions within social studies were quite unsettled, it seemed, with renewed attacks on the field and the continuing growth of competing traditions. A number of scholars viewed the overcrowding of the social studies curriculum with some alarm, or called for new attempts at clearer definition. One observer, recently returned from military service, wrote, "The social studies are in a mess" (Taylor, 1946). Another, a young social scientist, called for the "immediate abandonment of the term" *social studies,* and recommended replacing it with "social science" (Kidd, 1953). Lewis Paul Todd, in his editor's column, described the dilemmas of the field as a result of "the cult of specialism," with curricula in secondary schools and colleges organized by specialists, knowledge "fragmentized and compartmentalized," and students expected to become specialists (1949).

Largely in response to criticism of the field, the NCSS board of directors adopted a resolution attempting to clarify the situation and to quiet critics. The board resolved that it was "deeply concerned by indications that the term 'social studies' is misunderstood or misused." It then provided a standard umbrella definition, with a pointed addendum:

> The expression "social studies" as introduced in 1916 is the overall name for a group of subjects that includes history, geography, civics, economics, humanities, and the natural sciences. It is comparable to such terms as mathematics, humanities, and the natural sciences. This is the usage, and the only implication of the term as used. . . . The term "social studies" carries no implications of a particular organization of subjects or of any political or social or economic point of view. (1953, p. 1)

Ever the thoughtful and balanced analyst, Dorothy McClure Fraser, NCSS president during 1954, asserted that the battle over "content vs. method" was fraught with misunderstanding and confusion. She argued that the issue was not, "Shall we have content or method?" but rather, "WHAT content is needed, ON WHAT BASES shall it be chosen, and HOW SHALL IT BE ORGANIZED." She went on to suggest that the arguments among different camps were, in essence, over "the criteria to be used in selecting the content, the purposes for which it is to be studied, and whether or not a given set of facts is essential" (NCSS Board of Directors, 1955, p. 104). Later, she worried whether social studies educators were preparing frameworks that would be a "kind of hash that is not going to be much good to anybody." Similarly, another observer from within the fold wondered whether some approaches to social studies "would simply permit people to roam all over the lot and they would not focus on something specific" (Fraser, 1957; Hartshorn, 1965).

A perceptive social scientist noted that too often the term *social studies* had become "a mark of derision, denoting a 'watering down' of subject-matter," leading to "innane and often meandering discussions." He urged the value of the social sciences as a means to keep "a steady middle-of-the-road" approach and called for teachers to become familiar with the techniques and materials of the social sciences and to integrate them into their teaching (Watson, 1957, pp. 25–26).

Lewis Paul Todd discussed the confusion over the term *social studies* in his editorial column. Borrowing a metaphor from Bestor, he lamented the complications, for definition and for teaching, that came from adding "ingredient after ingredient to the social studies brew until it now includes everything from driver education to personal grooming—and we're still tossing ingredients into the boiling kettle at an alarming rate." He compared the situation of the social studies teacher to the circus juggling act, with the juggler throwing plate after plate, and facing the impossibility of keeping all the plates in the air (1957, pp. 245–246). These thoughts reflect a time of contradiction and turmoil, during which the definition and approach to social studies was once again up for grabs, contested among multiple factions.

Citizenship Education

One approach popular at the time was centered around the perennial guiding light for the field. Several projects and programs were aimed directly at citizenship education. The Detroit Citizenship Education Study was a research project, of 1945–1953, prompted by the wartime Detroit race riot. The project was directed by Stanley E. Diamond and attempted to take a problem-solving approach to teaching problems of citizenship education. The project focused on several areas of development in eight Detroit schools, including understanding children, the meaning and practice of democracy, solution of social problems, the improvement of human relations, and school-community relations. Another project aimed primarily at producing stimulating materials for teachers was the Civic Education Center at Tufts University. Participants at the center produced the Living Democracy Series, a series of pamphlets for student use focused on social issues and civic education. The 32nd Yearbook of the Superintendent's Association was titled *Education for American Citizenship*. The volume combined citizenship inculcation with problem-solving skills, as did most of the projects in this genre. At the time, it seems, there was no apparent contradiction between these two goals.

By far the largest and most influential of the projects was the Citizenship Education Project (CEP) based at Teachers College, Columbia University. The CEP disseminated extensive and suggestive materials for teachers, including the book *Premises of American Liberty* (1952) and its revision, *When Men Are Free: Premises of American Liberty* (1955). The materials produced were used in school systems across the country, and in the army, navy and air force. Perhaps most important, the CEP launched a new style of curriculum development project and set a pattern for many of the projects that came later. It had a professional university staff that conducted studies and produced programs and materials for national use over a period of years. It also sought to train teachers and to diffuse the entire package. Unfortunately, the project relied on one teacher in each school to spread the program, an approach that proved to be too thin.

Some of the materials were quite standard as they aimed at inculcation of democratic principles through the schools and other agencies. The project's scholars developed boxes of annotated reference cards with brief readings on issues and bibliographic references to sources from a variety of ideological viewpoints. The program centered on the *Premises of American Liberty* text and on the dissemination of "laboratory practices," reality-based activities in which students worked with the machinery of politics, including elections, government agencies, courts, boards, and commissions. The text was a compilation of the basic core principles and beliefs of American democratic society, focused on inculcation of the American creed, and contained little that could be deemed objectionable.

Like the Rugg materials during an earlier period, the portion of the CEP materials that were focused on issues came under attack. Frank Hughes, an editorial writer and reporter for the *Chicago Tribune* visited the CEP headquarters in July 1951 and wrote a series of five articles that appeared on the front page of the *Tribune* in August 1951, charging the Columbia Citizen course with feeding leftist views and "New Deal Propaganda" to high school students.

Subsequent articles covered familiar ground, charging that the project was pouring propaganda for socialism and the welfare state into the public schools, virtually unchallenged. William Fletcher Russell, president of Teachers College, and William S. Vincent, the project director, prepared a 10-page, point-by-point rebuttal to the articles, which was distributed to newspaper people, educators, politicians, and others to allay any fears about the project. Like many other curriculum reform efforts before and since, the CEP had some influence. But the project failed to reach its stated objective of changing citizenship education programs in all the schools of the United States. Project directors failed to appreciate both the enormity of the task and the general resistance to and difficulty of change in the public schools, foreshadowing much of what would come later (Streb, 1979).

Issues-Centered Developments

Ironically, during a time of educational conservatism and retrenchment, the issues-centered camp made major gains in theory. There was a great deal of attention in the literature to the social problems approach, problem solving, and the Problems of Democracy course. One of the earliest works to appear was an article by Shirley Engle, "Factors in the Teaching of Our Persistent Modern Problems," published in 1947. Engle's article advocated a "values"-centered problems approach. Samuel P. McCutchen, a major advocate of the problems approach at the time, attempted to allay the fears of teachers and encouraged use of the problems approach. He stressed the process of problem solving as "education for democratic living" in which students trained in problem solving would become citizens proficient in dealing with the problems of society (1947).

Attention to the problems approach during the 1950s included an entry in the NCSS Curriculum Series, *The Problems Approach in the Social Studies*, first published in 1955 and reissued in a revised edition in 1960. These volumes contained theoretical work and some direct application, with an emphasis on problem-solving skills rather than societal issues or social transformation. Most significant, the approach as outlined in this period was detached from an explicit vision of societal reform, such as the goal of a "collectivist commonwealth" cited by Rugg. It was described as pedagogical method and was conceived in less political terms (Fersh, 1955; Gross, Muessig, & Fersh, 1960).

One major work published early in the postwar era was *Education for Social Competence*, by I. James Quillen and Lavonne Hanna, which appeared in 1948. Overlooked by many, this methods textbook supported a balanced issues-oriented approach to social studies education, and it was the first methods text to be built around a large-scale research project. It provided substance built on scholarship and a philosophical base. Two chapters on the problems approach reported research comparisons of chronological, topical, and problems approaches via experimental research in the "Stanford Social Education Investigation." The book also outlined criteria for selection of a problem, including its commonality, significance, relevance, and suitability.

Another important work was the methods textbook published in 1955 by Maurice P. Hunt and Lawrence E. Metcalf, *Teaching High School Social Studies: Problems in Reflective Thinking and Social Understanding*. A landmark work, this book had a major, lasting impact on social studies theory. Hunt and Metcalf expanded on the foundation provided by Alan Griffin, one of their mentors, and held that reflective inquiry could be brought to bear on the teaching of the disciplines via an emphasis on controversial issues. The first part of the book presented theoretical background. The field theory of learning was espoused as most consistent with democratic values and higher thought processes. The method of reflective thinking was examined and illuminated by contrast with nonreflective thought and behavior. Subsequent chapters were devoted to the relationship of values to reflective thought, practical applications of the method of reflecting thinking, specific teaching techniques, classroom climate, discussion, and their suggested focus on eight "closed areas" of culture in which teachers were to lead students into the "reflective testing" of beliefs.

Another seminal item was an article by Donald Oliver that appeared in the *Harvard Education Review* in 1957, titled "The Selection of Content in the Social Sciences." The article formed the basis for the Harvard Project of the 1960s. In the article, Oliver critiqued the approach to content selection as proposed by the American Historical Association's Commission on the Social Studies and the NCSS Committee on Concepts and Values. He suggested that both had "failed to consider adequately the school's right to mold personal values of the student," had confused the term *knowledge* and the relationship between "knowledge and values." He went on to argue that both failed to take into account the "ferment and conflict over competing ideas and values" which is allowed under a creed of mutual tolerance, and to "consider the difficulty of adequately describing American society." In its stead, Oliver wrote:

> We propose that the relationship between personal values, the general canons of tolerance of our society, and the determination of public policy for the regulation of human affairs be made the center of the social studies curriculum in the public school. The basic core of content would consist of the study of existing and predicted conflicts caused by differing definitions and interpretations of the meaning of liberty, security, and public welfare. (pp. 291–292)

This would be accomplished by teaching students to recognize and define areas of human conflict, to define alternative means of regulating human affairs on specific political and social issues, and to make thoughtful predictions about the consequences of various alternatives. The central objective of the approach was "to introduce young people to the fire and controversy that rages within a free society over ways of regulating human affairs." The hope was to provide students with a way of approaching conflicts and controversies that is more "'rational' than blind adherence to some ideology . . . learned during early socialization." The approach meant a dramatic shift in content implied by inquiring into major areas of conflict. It meant a strong emphasis on sociological, political, and economic disciplines and less reliance on traditional historical literature, though episodes from history and related data would be relevant in predicting consequences. As with the Rugg program, disciplinary boundaries would, of necessity, be broken down. The approach combined valuing and social science with an emphasis on ethical considerations. It was, Oliver asserted, a "tough-minded scientific approach" (p. 293). Both Hunt and Metcalf and Oliver and his associates called for a dramatic rethinking of the content of social studies instruction, or at least a rethinking of the purposes and ways of organizing materials in established courses.

Despite these gains, by the end of the 1950s, it appeared that the problems approach was in disarray. Enrollments were declining and Problems of Democracy was being replaced by a diverse set of alternatives such as Senior Problems, Basic Citizenship, Senior Social Studies, Critical Analysis, Foreign Policy, World Problems, and Contemporary Government. One dissertation study on teacher attention to social problems found that teachers in Ohio devoted little class time to discussion of controversial issues (Hall, 1953). It also appeared that the social problems approach had, in many iterations, been largely gutted of anything controversial. There was an increasing focus on the process of problem solving, the trivialization represented by many Senior Problems courses, and the declining attention to critical perspectives on American society. It also appeared that critiques of social studies, from both intellectuals and red baiters, were having an impact.

Stirrings in Other Camps

The social science and history camps were a growing presence during the postwar era. The year 1959 saw the publication of an important book in social science, *The Sociological Imagination*, by C. Wright Mills. The book expressed the intellectual goals of social education very clearly, as permitting the scholar to understand the meaning of history and the biographies of individuals and to grasp the relation between the two.

Despite such broad and relevant thought, many social scientists continued to lobby for their area of specialization. Some were calling it the age of specialization. Over the course of the postwar period a greater emphasis on both the social sciences and a social science approach to social studies emerged. By the end of the 1950s, emphasis on social science was the central trend in social studies rhetoric, partly as a result of the critiques of social studies and partly as a result of the growing emphasis on science in most any curricular form.

The teaching of traditional history continued to have many adherents as well and was the favorite reference point for many critics of social studies. One central question during this period of turmoil in the rhetoric over social studies instruction was, What kind of history would be taught? Some asserted that while history had scientific elements, the field properly belonged to the humanities. Others noted the popularity of metahistory and the examination of factors leading to the rise and fall of civilizations (Albrecht-Carrie, 1952). Several writers cited progressive historians or developed progressive, meliorist approaches to the teaching of history such as beginning with current problems, or teaching history upside down but not backward (Frymier, 1955; Gross & Allen, 1958). Still others asserted the primacy of historians' questions for the curriculum and challenged the historical profession to be more involved in the schools, much as Edgar B. Wesley had in the 1940s, though one writer cautioned that historians would "encounter hostility, idiocy, suspicion, implacable opposition" (Lillibridge, 1958, p. 115).

Thus, as we have seen, each of the camps involved in the struggle for social studies in schools was represented in the postwar era. Traditional history had a presence in the schools, in critiques of social studies, and in the social studies literature. The mandarin or social science camp had a growing presence and appeared to be the wave of the future. Education for social efficiency found its most pernicious and trivial form in life adjustment and as part of "citizenship education." The consensus approach, as embodied in the Wesleyan definition, also appeared to have staying power. And the progressive, reflective, Deweyan approach had a strong and growing following among purists. Though the reconstructionist camp was a minor presence in the literature, it continued to wield influence via the persistence of the social problems approach and the Problems of Democracy course. On the whole, however, in the struggle among history, the social sciences, and a unified, problem-oriented social studies, by the end of the 1950s it appeared that social studies was losing ground.

THE ANTICOMMUNIST CRUSADE

In trying to understand the NCSS cave-in to attacks on social studies, the near disappearance of social reconstructionism, and the decline of the social problems approach and Problems of Democracy course, it is important to remember the context of the cold war. The development of an anticommunist perspective and emphasis on the academic disciplines were both parts of a long-term trend toward educational retrenchment. The major ideological focus of the cold war era centered around the threat of communism.

In the main, communism was perceived as a threat to democracy. It was seen as a form of totalitarian fascism that was monolithic in nature, and teaching about communism was deemed necessary in order to defeat it. Evidence on the impact of anticommunism on the social studies profession may be found in the journal *Social Education,* the official publication of the NCSS. Articles related to the threat of communism began to appear throughout the cold war period (Greenawald, 1995).

Evidence of staunch anticommunist thinking may be found among certain influential social studies leaders. Merrill Hartshorn, longtime executive director of the NCSS (1943–1974), was a fervent anticommunist, with links to the power elite in Washington, DC and membership or board service on several strongly anticommunist organizations. As late as 1969, Hartshorn was concerned about the threat of Communist infiltration of American organizations and institutions (Hartshorn, 1947–1972). Several sources of evidence on Hartshorn and NCSS strongly suggest that Hartshorn's leanings influenced the leadership and direction of NCSS. Hartshorn's attitude toward communism was captured in an interview during his retirement years. Somewhat ironically, Hartshorn shared a story illustrating his strong commitment to academic freedom as he "recalled being the target of harsh criticism from those who thought he was preaching subversion when he advocated that schools teach about Communism." According to Hartshorn, "Some people interpreted that as teaching Communism. But I was just saying that we should teach *about* communism. We can't deal with something we don't understand" (Stone, 1985, p. 656). For Hartshorn, to "deal with" communism meant to defeat it.

Several important issues related to communism were being decided during the period: Should Communists be permitted to teach in public schools? Should controversial material including communism be taught in the schools? Are loyalty oaths appropriate for teachers? (DiBona, 1982). One of the most famous debates over whether Communists should be allowed to teach found a forum in a pair of *New York Times Magazine* articles under the title "Should Communists be Allowed to Teach?" (Hook, 1949). In the lead article, Sidney Hook argued no. Hook argued that Communist party members are not free to search for the truth because "according to the Communist party itself politics is bound up, through the class struggle, with every field of knowledge. . . . A party line is laid down for every area of thought from art to zoology. No person who is known to hold a view incompatible with the party line is accepted as a member" (p. 26). He wrote, further, that "once he joins [the Communist party] and remains a member, he is not a free mind" (p. 28). Hook argued that a college professor's academic freedom included the duty to maintain an open mind, as well as the usual rights.

In a response to Hook, Alexander Meiklejohn, in an article that appeared one month later, argued that Communists should be allowed to teach and that their ideas should be evaluated along with others. He suggested that democracy would win the "competition of ideas" and decried the "probationary" status deriving from academic freedom cases in which tenured professors could be dismissed. Meiklejohn described the cases of several "dismissed" professors and argued that their dismissal illustrated an administration "misled by the hatreds and fears of the cold war" and reflected an overly zealous interpretation of the "control" of Communist Party members by Moscow. He argued that such scholars joined the Communist Party because "they accept Communist beliefs," and are of like mind, as could be said for members of any political party (1949, p. 65).

NCSS joined the national debate as well. Direct ideological attacks set a tone, one that saw communism as taboo and one that was in favor of the traditional disciplines as the heart of social studies. In 1955, at its annual meeting, the board of directors of NCSS passed a resolution stating that "teachers should be free to deal with controversial issues and to present all sides of such issues" (NCSS Board of Directors, 1955). In fact, NCSS has a long history of resolutions on academic freedom throughout the postwar era, beginning in 1948 with a resolution against bans on newspapers and magazines such as *The Nation* and *Building America*. In 1953, the NCSS board of directors passed a major resolution called Freedom to Learn and Freedom to Teach that was developed by the Academic Freedom Committee of NCSS and that made a strong statement in favor of classroom freedom "to study and discuss significant moral, scientific, social, economic, and political issues," and to have access to a variety of materials "expressing different points-of-view" (Hartshorn, 1953). Virtually every year, NCSS adopted one or more resolutions supporting academic freedom. Despite such efforts, an atmosphere of repression gripped the nation and limited the freedom of teachers.

SPUTNIK AND THE NATIONAL DEFENSE EDUCATION ACT

The ideological backdrop for the National Defense Education Act developed over many years of red baiting and criticism of progressive social studies from academic critics. The stage was set, and the launching of Sputnik, the Soviet satellite, on October 4, 1957, affirmed the criticism and unleashed funds for educational reform. Sputnik served as a clarion call for American education in science and math and in studies that would strengthen U.S. brainpower in the cold war. That call was answered by the National Defense Education Act, passed in 1958, which provided unprecedented categorical aid in the hundreds of millions of dollars for the improvement of mathematics, science, and foreign-language instruction. The NDEA was supported by two main arguments: that national security required the "fullest development of the mental resources and technical skills" of American youth, and that the national interest required federal "assistance to education for programs which are important to our national defense" (Gutek, 1986).

Social studies educators were aware of the trend. Just prior to the launch of Sputnik, a committee appointed by the board of directors of NCSS made its report on "ways and means of strengthening the social studies." A resolution addressing our national "preoccupation with science and math" read, in part: "Science and math themselves, important as they are, cannot provide solutions to many of the grave problems that we face today. The most serious issues of our time lie within the field of human affairs. For the solutions to these problems, we must look to the social sciences and the humanities" (Minutes, 1958). Notwithstanding the efforts of social studies educators, the first two versions of the National Defense Education Act, in 1958 and 1961, did not include funds for social studies (Greenawald, 1995).

Following Sputnik, national magazines stoked the fires of a renewed "crisis" in education. Critics such as Vice Admiral Hyman G. Rickover, known as the originator of the nuclear submarine, blamed the schools for the nation's falling behind the Russians in science, math, and engineering, endangering the national security, and called for a renewed emphasis on those subjects. Rickover planted some of the seeds for this interpretation of the Soviet success in a series of speeches he gave, beginning around 1956, which were later published in a book titled *Education and Freedom* (1959). In this book, in his criticisms of American education he called attention to Soviet advances and described the superiority of the Soviet and the European educational systems. He criticized life adjustment and asserted that John Dewey and a mistaken, misapplied notion of equality had led to the decline of American schools and neglect of the nation's most talented students. He argued, with force and impact, that development of intellect was the key to winning the cold war.

One of the more vociferous critics of social studies, E. Merrill Root, authored a critique of textbooks that exemplified the anticommunist tenor of the times and contributed to the crisis mentality. In *Brainwashing in the High Schools*, published in 1958, Root sought to show that "the United States is losing the cold war" because of what is said or left unsaid in senior high school American history textbooks. Root charged that "one third of all the American soldiers made prisoner in Korea succumbed to brainwashing," becoming Communist sympathizers or collaborators. According to Root, these young men yielded because of the failings of their education, because they had never been taught to understand "American politics, American economics, American history, and American ideals" (pp. 3, 11).

Using incomplete quotes taken out of context, reasoning from false premises, and employing other dubious tricks, Root supported his thesis with evidence from the 11 textbooks he cited. He described the books as critical of free enterprise, belittling authentic patriotism, and preaching class war.

Shortly after Sputnik, another book appeared that seemed to sum up many of the criticisms of education spawned by cold war competition. *Second Rate Brains* contained a compendium of thought on Soviet schools and scientists, describing the achievements and long-range goals of the Soviet "educational machine" and offering critiques of "mediocrity" in American schools, including articles from Rickover and Bestor. The volume concluded with an assessment of the education crisis and suggestions on how to meet it, with the goal of developing "First Rate Brains" (Lansner, 1958). The cumulative effect of these persistent and strident attacks on education led to a shift in direction toward a renewed emphasis on academic study. The attacks led social studies away from its progressive roots and toward the social science disciplines.

CLASSROOM REALITIES

Although the rhetoric of education underwent profound changes during the postwar era, teaching practice in schools was probably less changed. Studies reported a substantial increase in United States history enrollments, with smaller gains for world history, civics, geography, and modern history, though some of the change may reflect changing labels for courses. The greatest decline was in ancient and medieval history (Anderson, 1950). Problems of Democracy reached its peak of 5.24% of all high school students, a major increase. Economics and Sociology remained relatively steady and Community Civics was no longer reported. In terms of absolute enrollments, the social studies curriculum continued to focus on history and government (Latimer, 1958).

While progressive schemes for course offerings had some influence, the vast majority of schools provided courses that were fairly conventional in their organizational pattern, despite the claims of some critics. United States history, government, world history, and a problems course were the "Big

Four" among social studies requirements. Moreover, fears that United States history was not being taught were shown to be groundless (Jones, 1954).

As to teaching methods, one thoughtful observer noticed the "lag between theory and practice." The major weakness was the teachers' "own inadequacy, impotency, and basic ignorance." Many teachers reported that they had difficulty teaching a unit, were unable to integrate other subjects, and had difficulty in setting up and organizing a problem. Teachers knew the buzzwords of education but couldn't put the words into practice (McAulay, 1960).

Further evidence that social studies faced a divide between theory and practice may be found in three articles that appeared in the mid-1950s. One perceptive observer, in an article titled "The Split Within Our Ranks," addressed the split between teachers and theorists. Teachers, he wrote, believe professors "to be dwelling in an ivory tower . . . divorced from reality" and tend to "underestimate" the impact of a heavy student load. Many teachers "do not have the time nor the energy to do many of the things she would like to do. It is a case of teachers not teaching as well as they know how" (Fink, 1955, p. 9).

The following year, Lewis Paul Todd received an "unusually interesting" letter from a teacher, which he quoted on the Editor's Page in *Social Education:*

> After I had summed up my reading on the subject of methods, the leitmotif, it seemed to me, was the student-centered and problem-centered approach. Very well, that's what it was going to be. We listed problems on the blackboard, formed committees, and away we went, nowhere! Committee sessions in the classroom were nothing but social gabfests. Individuals released from the classroom to gather information in the library simply goofed off. After a month, I abandoned the idea, and attempted a return to the traditional daily assignment, lecture and question method. I say "attempted" because these classes, after those heady weeks of freedom, never fully recovered.
>
> Well, editor, the burden of my song is this: Students as well as teachers need preparation in the newer methods. It should be the duty of any writer, or any advocate of the problem approach or any other approach, to point out the pitfalls. All of the literature on the subject, as far as I can determine, is of the boy-who-made-good variety, the "success story" kind of thing. . . . [The] professional literature [is] laden with articles which, lacking a better term, I'll call the Horatio Alger type. It's not hard to see why. Who's going to write an article entitled, "How I Fell Flat on My Face?" (1956)

The following year in an article titled "The Problem in Problem Solving," another teacher provided a response. He agreed with the letter writer on the difficulty involved in using the problems method, and asserted that it required adequate teacher preparation, a "fiery zeal to go beyond the routine type of teaching," a "probing mind which excites or stimulates deep thought, even healthy controversy." In short, he wrote, "the use of the problems method . . . requires a teacher's teacher." In closing, he cautioned, the problems approach "should not be used until control of a class is clearly established" (Avery, 1957, p. 166).

Although long forgotten, and perhaps not even recognized at the time, the authors of these comments on weaknesses in the social studies program and on the gulf between theory and practice were closer to the pulse of the profession than were many of the most prolific writers and researchers. Social studies had a problem, and it was a problem that was shared with many other subject areas in the schools. The literature had created a vision of the potential for innovative and engaging teaching for social understanding, but the majority of practitioners were unable to pull it off.

CONCLUSION

Schools, the curriculum, and social studies in particular have frequently served as an ideological battleground and as a site for the attempted purification of American ideology. The era of anticommunism in schools provides strong examples of the ideological nature of schooling and the potential impact of educators' ideological biases and fears of subversion on schooling and on educational organizations. It offers a warning of the problems that may result from blind patriotism in defense of our ideals and of the need for continuous effort to preserve free thought, free inquiry, freedom to teach, and freedom to learn.

One of the most important changes in the national conversation over social studies during the 1950s was the beginning of a shift away from a social problems approach and toward a reemphasis on academic disciplines. Perhaps the most interesting question to ask is, Why did this shift in direction occur? There was a rising cultural aversion toward controversial topics in schools and society, and this came at a critical juncture for the social studies curriculum. Unfortunately, just as issues-oriented approaches to social studies reached a peak, they were relegated to alternative status. Before World War II it appeared that an issues-and-problem-solving orientation was headed for the lead. Then, near the start of the war, the Rugg texts and other problem-oriented textbooks were subjected to attack. In the 1950s a slew of related attacks emerged, critical of social studies and any forms of education that were not traditional. By the time of Sputnik, the disciplines had the full advantage. Also, there were other factors in education that contributed to the decline of progressive social studies. Two cultures existed, that of theorists and that of practitioners, with strikingly different visions of the field. Advocates of reflective or problem-oriented teaching often assumed that teachers could apply their ideas. From the perspective of the practicing teacher, many progressive ideas proved difficult to implement. The reality was that institutional obstacles and traditional ways of thinking were often difficult to surmount.

During the postwar period, rhetoric in education passed from that of the progressive life adjustment curriculum planner of the late 1940s to the rhetoric of the cold war manpower planner of the late 1950s. The cold war and related fears dominated educational discourse, influenced practice in social studies classrooms, and weakened the potential influence of the problems approach at a crucial time. Cold war fears combined with the critique of progressive social studies ensured that a new reform, the New Social Studies movement, would take an academic, discipline-based approach to social studies.

Why did progressive social studies decline? Diane Ravitch writes in *The Troubled Crusade* that progressive education died of "old age," unable to respond adequately to attacks, and was ossified in textbooks in schools of education (1983). Although it is true that the progressive response to attacks was relatively weak, it is important to remember that many of the great progressives had retired or passed on. To assert that it died of old age or simply went out of fashion ignores the accumulated impact of years and years of derisive attacks from scholars and extremist crackpots. It matters little that many of the critics got the facts wrong. Their attacks often made front-page-headline news, through which media magnates and conservative critics manipulated a naive public. Too frequently the responses of educators, who had their fingers on the evidence, were buried in the back pages when they appeared at all. It is also difficult to comprehend the cumulative power of red-baiting attacks, which reached their peak in the 1950s and undoubtedly played a major role in the decline of progressive social studies, the focus of many of the most extreme and inaccurate charges.

Moreover, many of the attacks did contain substance, an element of truth that innumerable educators refused to hear until the launch of Sputnik more or less ended the debate. Life adjustment education, while addressing several of the very real needs of youth, was misplaced in the schools, and it deserved ferocious attack and the labels *anti-intellectual* and *undemocratic*. The academic disciplines have ready advocates, prepared to take on any perceived slight to their survival in the schools. It is also true that the disciplines have provided powerful lenses for interpreting the world, and that many "progressive" approaches appeared relatively weak. However, mainstream progressive education, the reflective, Deweyan variety promoted by Dewey, Bode, Hullfish, Hunt, Metcalf, and others, hardly deserved such criticism. As Larry Metcalf observed after presiding over a wake for the PEA, an idea can't fail if "it was never tried." Progressive education did not die in the 1950s, though its leaders fell from prominence and its influence was confined to fewer teachers. Progressive social studies, in the form of reflective and interactive teaching that addressed social issues, would continue to live in schools of education and would have hope of greater influence again during another time.

CHAPTER SIX

The Era of the New Social Studies

AS WE SAW in the previous chapter, the impetus for the new social studies grew out of cold war personnel studies conducted by the CIA and the critique of schools from Bestor, Rickover, and others (Karier, 1986). It emerged from the bitter debate on schooling, with critiques as catalyst for change, and cold war fears and Sputnik as the wellspring for funds. The general thrust of the criticism was that a return to the basics was in order, along with a new focus on disciplined knowledge.

The furor and flurry of interest in education that followed Sputnik provided an invaluable assist to those who wanted schools to raise academic standards and give more attention to gifted students. At the National Science Foundation (NSF), the "crisis" in education and the intense interest following Sputnik increased the NSF role in secondary school reform. The NSF, established by Congress in 1950 with the aim of promoting basic research and education in the sciences, initially had little to do with the lower schools, though it did begin to sponsor science fairs and summer institutes for teachers in science and math.

The curriculum reform movement, which would eventually result in creation of the new social studies, had its seeds in the curriculum materials reform movement that began, almost unnoticed, at two universities in the 1950s. The University of Illinois Committee on School Mathematics (UICSM) was formed in 1951 out of concerns over the math deficiencies of entering freshmen at the University of Illinois. Based on similar concerns in science, Jerrold Zacharias at the Massachusetts Institute of Technology (MIT) wrote a memo in1956 that led to the creation of what was called the Physical Science Study Committee (PSSC). Each of these committees began with the intention of reforming college teaching, but quickly changed focus to the precollegiate level, concentrating on college prep students and courses in the secondary schools.

These early curriculum development programs established initial patterns for the funding of national curriculum development projects that would largely continue for the following 15 years. One pattern, represented by the University of Illinois Committee, was initial funding by private foundations (often Carnegie or Ford) followed by support from the NSF or the U.S. Office of Education (USOE). A second pattern, represented by the MIT Committee, was long-term funding by the NSF or USOE from start-up to publication. By 1956, six national projects were established and funded in science or math, five of which aimed at curriculum reform. By this time, it was apparent that several broad assumptions or guidelines were shared by virtually all these endeavors and included the need to change the content, materials, and methods of instruction; a focus on the textbook or learning materials; directors of projects being drawn from the academic disciplines; a focus on courses for the academically talented and gifted because it was seen as more critical to the national interest; overriding concern about the integrity of the academic disciplines and their "structures"; learning by discovery and inquiry; and a focus on the cognitive over affective, personal, or social action dimensions (Haas, 1977).

By the late 1950s, the curriculum reform movement developed new momentum, though the focus was still on math and science. Projects proliferated, made possible by increased funding from the NSF and the USOE following passage of the National Defense Education Act in 1958. Gradually, the directors of funded projects became the new "leadership" in American education. With the backing of the national government, these new reforms represented a sort of "official" direction for the creation and transmission of knowledge in the nation's schools, one that was built around the academic disciplines and the aim of personnel development, even if few of those involved seemed to recognize it at the time.

EMERGENCE

The aim of the new social studies movement was to "transform . . . students into junior historians and social scientists." The developments of the 1960s rested, in part, on a small, influential book, *The Process of Education*, written by Jerome Bruner, reporting on the proceedings of the Woods Hole Conference, of which he was the director.

The Woods Hole Conference, held in September 1959, at Woods Hole, Massachusetts, brought together leaders in the new reforms in science and math, and led to a concise and well-crafted formulation of the principles of curriculum development shared in the new movement. Among the 35 participants were luminaries such as Bruner, Richard Alpert, Lee Cronbach, Robert Gagne, Jerold Zacharias, and John Morton Blum. The conference was a reaction to Sputnik and the complaints of critics such as Vice Admiral Rickover and was funded by a range of federal agencies. In a sense, what was emerging was a manufactured consensus, paid for by stakeholders with an interest in education conducted on behalf of national security. It was a direct outgrowth of the cold war and of the war on social studies.

In *The Process of Education,* Bruner summarized his own "sense of the meeting" based on the reports of five working groups formed at the conference. The conference took the "structure of the disciplines" as its central theme and overriding assumption and examined in some depth "the role of structure in learning and how it may be made central in teaching." The conferees assumed the goal of "giving students an understanding of the fundamental structure of whatever subjects we choose to teach" and the "teaching and learning of structure" rather than simply the "mastery of facts and techniques" (1960, pp. 11–12).

The second theme of the conference had to do with readiness for learning and "the hypothesis that any subject can be taught effectively in some intellectually honest form to any child at any stage of development" (p. 33). A third theme involved the nature of intuition and the training of hunches. "The shrewd guess, the fertile hypothesis," Bruner asserted, "is a much-neglected and essential feature of productive thinking." These three themes, Bruner wrote, were all premised on a central conviction, "that intellectual activity anywhere is the same, whether at the frontier of knowledge or in a third-grade classroom. . . . The difference is in degree, not in kind" (pp. 13–14). A fourth theme centered on how to stimulate student motivation through interest in the material.

Not all of these ideas were new. The concept of inquiry- or discovery-oriented teaching had been around at least since the days of the scientific historians in the 19th century and was increasingly championed by many progressive educators. Motivation through student interest was also an old song. Parts of the new curriculum movement were a recapitulation of common ideas in the rhetoric of education. The focus on the "structures" of the disciplines was a reformulation, though what it actually meant in terms of classroom practice remained somewhat unclear.

Although there was no explicit acknowledgment of the cold war backdrop to which the conferees at Woods Hole owed their existence, Bruner, a cold war liberal in politics, did refer somewhat obliquely to the social mileu. He wrote: "If all students are helped to the full utilization of their intellectual powers, we will have a better chance of surviving as a democracy in an age of enormous technological and social complexity" (p. 10). A part of that "complexity" was no doubt entangled in the cold war struggle with communism in the minds of Bruner and his colleagues.

In the ensuing years, other theorists added to the mix, creating building blocks for the new reform and fleshing out the rationale. The era of the new social studies was introduced most clearly when an article by Charles

R. Keller, director of the John Hay Fellows Program, and a former college history teacher, appeared in the *Saturday Review.* Keller's article was titled "Needed: Revolution in the Social Studies," and appeared in 1961. His thesis was that social studies was "in the educational doldrums," partly traceable to the fact that "social studies" was a "federation of subjects . . . , often merged in inexact and confusing ways" (p. 60). Social studies teachers too frequently "depend on textbooks," leading to "unimaginative, unenthusiastic, pedantic teaching." The remedy, according to Keller, was "a possible revolution in social studies," beginning with "eliminating the term 'social studies,' which is vague, murky, and too all-inclusive and substitute for it the term 'history and the social sciences,' which is exact and hence meaningful" (pp. 61–62). Keller then echoed many of Bruner's recommendations, a clarion call for a social studies reform movement along the lines already begun in other subject areas.

Prior to the appearance of Keller's article, reformers were already engaged in pioneering work in a few isolated places. Lawrence Senesh, a scholar in economics at Purdue University, was busily creating an economics program for elementary-age students, drawing on the disciplines in creating a progressive-oriented program and textbook series, Our Working World. Edwin Fenton, a historian at Carnegie Institute of Technology in Pittsburgh who had been given responsibility for preservice teacher education in history, was bothered by the pat assertions found in high school history textbooks and by the boredom and loathing of his own students for many history and social science courses. In an attempt to bring history to life and rekindle student curiosity, he introduced primary-source documents as a means of stimulating students, asking them to experience the work of historians, and to make sense of raw data. Fenton's experiences with using primary source documents led to publication of a book titled *32 Problems in World History* and an eventual leadership role in the new social studies movement (1964).

The Projects

In the issue of *Social Education* of October 1962, the same month as the Cuban missile crisis, a small, two-paragraph piece, "Announcement for Project Social Studies," appeared at the bottom half of one page. The announcement read, in part, "The United States Office of Education has announced the initiation of Project Social Studies, which is designed to improve research, instruction, teacher education, and the dissemination of information in this field." The announcement stated that funds were available for research projects, curriculum study centers, and conferences and seminars (p. 300). The fact that the announcement coincided with the height

of cold war tension is not lost in hindsight, though at the time the depoliti-
cization of education made it appear as a rather innocuous research and
development notice, with exciting possibilities for scholars and teachers.

The earliest social science projects had begun to receive funding prior
to the announcement of Project Social Studies and received support from
the NSF as well as private foundations such as Ford or Carnegie. Senesh
and Fenton had already begun work on their projects in the 1950s, and had
received at least some private funding for their efforts. A similar endeavor,
the Amherst history project, had its beginnings in the 1959–1960 school
year under the leadership of Van Halsey (1963).

Three additional projects were launched in 1961, all emanating from
professional associations. All three eventually received funding from the
NSF. These included the High School Geography Project, Sociological Resources for the Secondary Schools, and the Anthropology Curriculum
Study Project.

Following up on the announcement of Project Social Studies, in July
1963, USOE reported that 7 curriculum centers, 11 research projects, and 2
developmental activities had been approved for funding (Smith, 1963).
These included Fenton's project in American history and Donald Oliver's
project at Harvard, focused on analysis of public issues. Four additional
new projects were funded in 1964. By 1965 there were some two dozen projects that made up the new social studies movement, funded by the NSF, the
USOE, or private foundations. Most notable among the new additions was
the Harvard Educational Development Center's Man: A Course of Study
(MACOS), for which Jerome Bruner served as the intellectual architect. The
vast majority of the projects fit the general theme of the "structures of the
disciplines," but there was some diversity in orientation. Perhaps the least
compatible with the discipline-based focus was the Harvard Project, with
its focus on public issues as the heart of citizenship education.

Clearly, a revolution of sorts was brewing, but what was its nature? In
April 1965, *Social Education* devoted virtually the entire issue to a "Report
on Project Social Studies," with an overview provided by Edwin Fenton
and John Good. Their report began with a bold and confident statement:
"The curriculum revolution which began in mathematics, the natural sciences, and modern foreign languages about a decade ago has at last reached
the social studies. More than 40 curriculum development projects of national significance promise to revolutionize teaching about man and society" (Fenton & Good, 1965, p. 206)

Calling the sum of the projects "the new social studies," in what appears to be the first use of this term, Fenton and Good provide a succinct
summary of some of the general themes of the activities supported by Project Social Studies and other funding sources including the emphasis on

structure, inductive teaching, the disciplines, sequential learning, new types of materials, new subjects, and emphases on evaluation. Although the article gave a concise overview of the new reform, the authors demonstrated little awareness of the contextual origins of the movement.

After 1965 another wave of projects was christened. By 1967 more than 50 national projects were in progress, though curricular materials were slow to appear and were not issued in significant amounts until 1967. The projects created after 1967 all claimed loyalty to the principles of the new social studies, but in actuality "moved off in all imaginable directions." Although there were many variations and permutations of the general themes of the new social studies, the general parameter of discipline-based inquiry appears to have held fairly constant as a working guideline for the vast majority of projects (Haas, 1977).

From a distance, it appears that the new social studies movement reached its zenith in 1967. In this year, the total number of funded projects appears to have peaked, and new social studies topics and concerns dominated both *Social Education* and the NCSS annual conference. Moreover, for many of the initial projects, funding periods were at or near their end. The years after 1967 would be spent dealing with publication, dissemination, and diffusion of materials.

A second wave of projects received initial funding from 1968 to 1972. Several of the newly funded projects added selected use of contemporary social problems as topics for study and as criteria for selection of social science content. Adding to the general ferment, nonproject social studies curriculum workers, teachers, and teacher educators labored in the field, often providing conferences and workshops and receiving funds from the USOE, state departments of education, and local school districts.

If 1967 was the zenith of enthusiasm for the new movement, the years following, through the early to mid 1970s, represented a continuing presence with activity at a lower level of intensity. As we shall see, events in the society, many of which impinged directly on schools, may have diluted teacher enthusiasm for the new social studies and its general focus on inquiry based in the disciplines, a step removed from the conflicts and dilemmas of the social world.

In retrospect, the materials produced in the era of the new social studies were among the most innovative and influential commodities ever produced for use in social studies classrooms. Despite the historical context out of which they were born, and perhaps partly because of it, projects funded by millions of grant dollars from the NSF, the USOE, and other sources contributed to creation of a rich and multifaceted explosion of curriculum development the likes of which may never be seen again. The projects and materials set a tone for an era of innovation and inquiry that spread to other curriculum materials, textbooks, and curriculum guides. Yet as in each of the previous attempts to reform social studies, this one too had its problems.

Critiques

The profession was far from united behind the new reform movement. In fact, there were many contemporary critiques of what came to be called the new social studies, and they originated from several different quarters. Perhaps the earliest published critique of the new social studies came from Donald Robinson in an article that appeared in 1963, shortly after the launch of Project Social Studies. Discussing the new "ferment" in social studies, Robinson cautioned that "everyone has a different notion of what the social studies should attempt" and predicted that "curriculum reform will continue to result from diverse, and often contradictory trends." He concluded that social studies curricular practice would continue to be fashioned by "a combination of national tradition, suggestive state programs, locally prescribed curricula, the considerable influence of textbooks, universities, and professional organizations" (pp. 360, 362). These comments suggested some of the factors that might blunt attempts at reform, regardless of its direction.

Another early caution came from James Becker, who observed, in 1965, that there was a new consensus emerging on the need for reform in social studies. Yet, ironically, he noted, "never before in our history has there been less general agreement about precisely what needs changing and how the changes should be made" (p. 20). He described a "nearly total confusion" and lack of agreement on goals plaguing attempts to define the field. Becker cautioned that prospects were slim for any kind of radical change in social studies.

Also among the earliest critiques were those voiced in a group of letters published in *Social Education*. Fred M. Newmann wrote that "we must be cautious to avoid seduction by the fashionable emphasis on 'inductive thinking' or 'discovery method'" when the major objectives of most of the projects centered on "communication of the structure of one discipline" and too frequently aimed at guiding students to predetermined generalizations. Byron G. Massialas charged that the projects "concentrate[d] on the empirical and cognitive dimensions of learning," neglecting the normative and affective components, and assumed that "what is good for the social scientist acting as a researcher is good for the child." Richard E. Gross suggested that the projects suffered from a failure to clearly delineate purposes, a tendency to concentrate on average and above average students, and development of "teacher-proof" materials that could reduce the teacher's role to that of technician ("Reactions," 1965).

Another critique of the new social studies movement came from a different perspective from that of many of the early critics. In an article titled "Bruner's New Social Studies: A Critique," Mark M. Krug (1966) charged that the new reforms had conceptual flaws, that there was no logical structure of ideas in the social sciences, and he quoted a question posed by Newmann: "Why should all children be taught to ask and answer the kinds of questions that interest historians, political scientists, economists, etc.?" (pp. 401–402). Krug argued that students need knowledge of history and the other social sciences and charged that Bruner slighted this need. Krug's preferred alternative was to restore traditional history.

James P. Shaver lamented the new social studies projects' "general failure . . . to examine the basic rationale for social studies instruction" and labeled them "scholacentric" (1967, pp. 592, 596). Albert S. Anthony, in a critique aimed specifically at the "new history," noted a "general lack of concern with objectives," an a priori commitment to the field of history, and charged that leaders of the "new history" had managed to "overlook the need for a philosophically and pedagogically defensible rationale" (1967, pp. 574–575). Moreover, Anthony charged that many historians were motivated to take up curricular reform by fears that the subject would disappear from schools. Somewhat surprisingly, another contemporary critique of the new curriculum movement was written by one of its founders, Jerome Bruner. Bruner wrote that the rational structuralism of the *Process of Education* "was based on a formula of faith: that learning was what students wanted to do, that they wanted to achieve an expertise in some particular subject matter. Their motivation was taken for granted" (1971, p. 19).

There was, in the new social studies, and in the new curriculum movement generally, much to critique and much to reflect back on. As a movement to change the curriculum, it aimed, largely, to shape the mindset of a generation into rational structuralist and scientific ways of seeing, and away from moral questions, social issues and social problems.

Unfortunately, the new social studies led to materials that frequently omitted citizen's questions and perennial social issues. Discipline-based experts were lionized as the main source of knowledge. This approach ignored or minimized student knowledge, community resources, issues, and problems. It also frequently served to undermine the possibility of interdisciplinary study and to reify education and power relationships endemic to the institution of schools.

Behind the New Social Studies

Several elements lay behind the development and rhetorical success of the new social studies. First, the new social studies was a result of a general intellectual and political drift toward the academic disciplines as paramount in determining school curricula supported by belief in a rational, structuralist paradigm for understanding the world. This paradigm had, of course, been present for many years in the natural sciences and was increasingly influential in the social sciences. Science as a model for history and social understanding was of relatively recent origins. It was a logical extension of the belief in science as the means of progress. It was a major part of the traditional history program created at the turn of the century, and it was the constant refrain of scholars in the mandarin, social science camp in pronouncements on social studies curricula from the 1920s forward.

Second, cold war fears were the dominant contextual factor of the era. The cold war had direct influence through red-baiting attacks and through CIA-sponsored manpower studies. Because of a variety of demographic and economic factors, the nation suffered a relative shortage of highly trained technical personnel during the decade of the 1950s. To a number of governmental and educational critics, in the context of the cold war, these personnel deficiencies appeared "ominously dangerous" (Burgess & Borrowman, 1969).

These concerns became a part of the educational rhetoric of the day through such critics and educational leaders as James B. Conant, Admiral Hyman Rickover, and Jerold Zacharias. These men viewed education as a "major part of the cold war manpower development process." By the late 1950s, they had become important players in the debates over education. In their thinking, the personnel studies sponsored by the CIA provided a "baseline" for the evaluation of schooling and a backdrop against which reform would be proposed (Karier, p. 313).

The new social studies was also a direct result of critiques of progressive education and social studies by intellectual critics. Arthur Bestor and others held that social studies was a poorly defined, anti-intellectual "social stew," and wanted to replace it with a curriculum based in history and the social sciences. Thus, the era of the new social studies represented a new phase of the war on social studies that had been raging, off and on, for several decades. Seen in this way, the new social studies was born of the cold war and of the war on social studies.

The increase in federal involvement was perhaps the major change of the era, influencing many aspects of schooling, and social studies curriculum, but this was federal involvement of a certain kind, emphasizing science and the black box of objective decision-making. Large amounts of money, from government and private foundations, made national educational policy an extension of foreign policy and contributed to a continuation of and official sanctioning of the war on social studies. By these steps, the disciplines were further reified as regimes of truth.

Despite the unprecedented focus of powerful groups outside education in an attempt to infiltrate and influence the direction of schooling, in social studies, it appears that the attempt at reform had only a little of the anticipated impact on classroom practice. What is clear is that while the new social studies movement dominated the discourse in social studies for a significant time in the mid to late 1960s, the impact on classroom practice was much less. Once again, powerful institutional obstacles combined with definitional dilemmas and strategic miscalculations to derail another attempt at reform.

DEFINITIONAL DILEMMAS

Despite these dilemmas and institutional obstacles, throughout the 1960s and beyond there was continuing interest and concern focused on curriculum and methods. Many concerns of earlier decades continued almost uninterrupted, including a focus on the problems approach and interdisciplinary approaches such as core, though the attempts at core and at the institution of various forms of integrated curricula were apparently on the way out and received much less attention after 1960, with the trend toward reinstitution of the disciplines.

In a noteworthy special issue of *Social Education* published in April 1963, a number of leaders in the field offered their thoughts in a piece titled "Revising the Social Studies." The new social studies movement was headed mostly in one direction, asserting the individual disciplines and abandoning the possibility of an integrated social studies. Though the articles included in the special section took Bruner's call for structure as a starting point, the kind of structure they described was much different than the discipline-based structures embraced by the majority of the new social studies projects. Instead, they discussed the possible structures for a discipline of social studies as a unified field of study. Shirley Engle's letter outlining his thoughts on the conceptual foundations for an integrated social studies served as the opening statement and focal point for the symposium. Engle argued that "the structure of the social studies curriculum should . . . emphasize general ideas or concepts and social problems" (Engle, 1963, p. 182). Byron G. Massialas also urged "the study of value conflicts in our society and alternative approaches to understanding or resolving them," and concluded that all students "should directly participate in inquiry, invention, and the act of philosophizing," and he cast the school as "a major reconstructing agent in society" (Massialas, 1963, p. 189).

Lawrence E. Metcalf outlined current deficiencies in the social studies curriculum, including an "inadequate . . . conception of problem-solving" and the continued "domination of history" and called for a curriculum "to help students examine reflectively issues in closed areas of American culture." Metcalf argued that students should be taught to think reflectively about the conflicting beliefs involved in such areas as "sex, economics, religion, race, and social class." He suggested that the content of social studies "would acquire meaning if its relevance to current problems and issues were perceived by students," and urged selection and use of the content of history and the social sciences in a process that "tests propositions and clarifies conflicts" (pp. 197–198).

All participants in the symposium agreed on "inquiry" in a general sense and argued for incorporating the social sciences and history, though not as the core of the field. Each offered an alternative to the structure-of-the-disciplines approach as advocates of the various disciplines were defining it.

Traditional History

The traditional history camp was still present and represented from time to time by articles calling for more of the "old history" taught well, as opposed to the "new history" championed by Fenton, Brown, Halsey, and others. Traditional history was a relatively minor player in the literature of the times, but remained a persistent presence in schools. Mark Krug, in his critique of Bruner's new social studies, had argued for the continuation of traditional history. Moreover, numerous authors wrote about trends in the teaching of history, including thematic approaches, structure, making history relevant, comparative history, American studies, oral history, and use of primary sources for an inquiry approach. Of course, much of classroom practice was still textbook oriented and little changed from the practice of earlier decades.

There is some evidence in support of Al Anthony's charge that historians were motivated by fears over losing their dominance of the social studies curriculum. Charles G. Sellers, at the annual meeting of the AHA, asked the question that was on many historians' minds, in his title "Is History on the Way Out of the Schools and Do Historians Care?" Sellers charged that while "historians have been sound asleep . . . the 'other' disciplines had taken a very militant stand over the past half dozen years, and they were indeed, going to preempt much of the place formerly occupied by history" (1969, pp. 513–514).

Issues-Centered Developments

Although all of the camps in the prolonged battle over social studies were present in the 1960s, the meliorist or issues-centered approach was one of two distinct reform rationales that appeared to be most popular. There were several important developments in the issues-centered tradition, both theoretical and practical, that were to have a lasting impact on the profession and on the ways in which learning would be conceptualized. In each case these authors were focused on the goal of social studies for meaningful learning.

One of the earliest significant contributions was a seminal article by Shirley H. Engle titled, "Decision Making: The Heart of Social Studies Instruction." This insightful work offered a new conceptualization of problem-centered learning and was written in readily accessible language. It became a seminal and influential piece. Engle's central point was stated succinctly: "My thesis is simply this, decision making should afford the structure around which social studies instruction should be organized." He developed several corollaries to this thesis: "Abandon . . . the ground-covering technique"; discard the "background theory of learning . . . that we must hold the facts in memory before we are ready to draw conclusions from them or to think about their meaning"; substitute decision making, which is "reflective, speculative, thought provoking, and oriented to the process of reaching conclusions"; and "recognize values formation as a central concern of social studies instruction" (1960, pp. 302–304).

This beautifully written and pithy article was destined to become one of a handful of classic works in the field. The emphasis on a values component was a significant addition to the theory of reflective teaching. Though Engle may have held implicit values that undergirded his recommendations, the lack of an explicit ideological justification and its link to "good citizenship" gave the article a broad and instant appeal.

Byron G. Massialas, Engle's protégé, made significant contributions in a similar vein. More explicitly reconstructionist in orientation, Massialas contributed an application of the concept of inquiry learning to the teaching of social issues. He was involved in a series of works applying inquiry method in social studies classrooms, both articles and books. The first and perhaps most significant of these was the Massialas and Cox volume *Inquiry in the Social Studies*, published in 1966, which described in depth the process of hypothesis formation and verification as a central part of the inquiry method.

Perhaps the most promising and imaginative application of the problems approach during the 1960s was made by Donald W. Oliver and his protégés James P. Shaver and Fred M. Newmann at Harvard. The Harvard Project, and much of the work that followed, was based on the seminal article by Oliver titled "The Selection of Content in the Social Sciences," published in 1957, in which he developed a philosophical rationale for a focus on public issues in social studies instruction at the secondary level. Growing out of their research in schools, *Teaching Public Issues in the High School* was published by Oliver and Shaver in 1966, advocating a problem-topic approach. The curriculum began with selection of a contemporary issue, then relevant data for presentation to the student was chosen. Their framework included six problem areas to which current topics and historical cases were related. Their purpose was to explore a controversial area, to encourage the student to find where he or she stood, and to defend a position. Thus, areas of controversy were explored, using what the authors termed a "jurisprudential approach."

The theoretical underpinnings of the Harvard Project rested on the assumption that a broad consensus exists in American society on a number of basic values such as human dignity, freedom of speech, sanctity of private property, majority rule, and rights of the minority. Much of our history is a story of conflicts between one of these general values and the specific value espoused by some opposing segment of society, or of conflicts over which basic value receives priority. Oliver and Shaver argued that the rational clarification of these value conflicts is the proper emphasis in the teaching of social studies, with a critical dialogue between teacher and students as the central curricular objective.

Meanwhile, concurrent with the important developments in issues-centered theory and practice of the period, Problems of Democracy seemed to be a dying course. Several observers reported its "illness" at the 1962 convention of NCSS, including one participant who blamed the "power struggle currently underway among the various disciplines (citing the . . . money, vociference, and power involved), the attacks against P.O.D. concerning the lack of agreement in its contents; and the notion of P.O.D. as a dumping ground course in which life adjustment, driver education, and what-not were too often included" (Alilunas, 1964, p. 11). Leo Alilunas argued that the course needed to be reformed but not abolished. He recommended a better organizational structure and a reduction in the number of basic issues to be explored (1964, p. 11). Unfortunately, Problems of Democracy, with its focus on "citizenship," "civic duty," and the threat of totalitarian communism now had a tarnished, old-fogey image, met declining enrollments, and never recovered.

THE NEWER SOCIAL STUDIES

The projects of the new social studies ran into problems almost immediately partly because their vocabulary and conceptual level were high, but primarily because they too frequently failed to address the pressing concerns of the 1960s: civil rights, the war in Vietnam, and campus unrest. The events of 1968 seemed the culmination of the building turmoil of the decade. The murder of the Reverend Martin Luther King, Jr., rioting in many cities, student strikes, antiwar demonstrators confronting police, and rising militancy by minorities contributed to a crisis atmosphere in the nation and calls for massive social change. The social studies response to this turmoil took shape in the code word *relevance* and peaked interest in social problems. Perhaps the most significant effect of this new trend was its impact on course offerings, contributing to a short-term flurry of expansion in which high schools suddenly offered minicourses on a cornucopia of topics: Black history, Native American history, and women's history, among others. Though the minicourse revolution was short lived, it had a significant impact on the curriculum.

The turmoil in the streets was accompanied by drastic changes in the journal *Social Education* in both content and style. Though a reflection of the times, the shift in the pages of *Social Education* was a reflection of a change of editors, from Lewis Paul Todd to Daniel Roselle. There was a crescendo toward change from the early 1960s and before. In the newer movement, the student as Little League social scientist was replaced by the student as social activist. The newer social studies had an issues-centered focus, largely presentist in orientation. Following the initial explosion, a new wave of topical interest evolved, including a focus on urbanization, environmentalism, population, futurism, women's studies, and area studies, especially concerning Africa and Asia. Concurrent with the topical focus on issues was a growing emphasis on newer methods and techniques, including simulation and values clarification. Most of the curricular innovations of the time employed new social studies terminology related to inquiry, valuing, and decision making, and were facilitated by the increased availability of a new and diverse array of classroom materials in a variety of mediums.

Not only *Social Education* but also the NCSS annual conference took on a new flavor. NCSS presidential addresses were a reflection of the newer trend; with titles such as "Activism in Social Studies Education," "The Choice Before Us," and "A Social Studies Manifesto," many presidential addresses of the time reflected the focus on issues and the challenge of the "student revolution." At the NCSS conference in 1968, attendees held an "almost spontaneous speakout" following the Friday night banquet, with nearly 100 participating. According to one observer, "Those who spoke did so out of concern for and disappointment with the vitality of the NCSS convention." One of the participants in the speakout captured the general tenor of commentary: "This meeting is supposed to have the theme of Urban Education. Does this conference have anything to do with this theme? I haven't seen . . . any real urgency about the world passing us by in the cities and beginning to go awry" (Arnoff, 1969).

Thus, during the late 1960s and early 1970s the rhetoric of social redemption through schooling experienced a brief revival. The new focus on the present dilemmas of American society had an implicit social reconstructionist orientation. The social reconstructionist camp had been largely moribund for some time, though a few scholars had kept the tradition alive. By the late 1960s there was something of a revival of social reconstructionism in social studies. In an article titled "The Year of the Non-Curriculum: A Proposal" (1968), Gerald Leinwand proposed a poststructuralist focus on social issues, an idea that appeared prophetic for a time. Deriding both the new social studies and traditional practice, Leinwand blamed the lack of improvement in classrooms on "the fact that there is such a thing as a social studies curriculum" and charged that "students learn a distorted, rather euphoric lesson in national and world events and emerge ill-equipped to wrestle with the evils that do exist and with which the revolutions of our day are involved . . . the social studies . . . remain detached and aloof, perhaps even alienated, from the throbbing events of our time as the curriculum bulletin decrees one thing but events show something quite different" (pp. 542–543).

He then proposed an NCSS conference focused on a "non-curriculum" with section meetings devoted to "major problems of our time" and with a focus on how teachers should teach and "what students should know how to do if they are to function effectively as intelligent members of a society in revolution." Leinwand then listed and discussed 11 problem topics, as the focus of the meeting including many of the most pressing issues of the late 1960s: air and water pollution, traffic and transit, urban and rural slums, adult crime and juvenile delinquency, civil rights and civil liberties, the Negro in the city, urban and rural poverty, Black Power, protest—violent and nonviolent, the draft, and war and peace (pp. 544–545).

Citing Theodore Brameld's similar call almost 2 decades earlier for schools to become active participants in the affairs of humankind, Leinwand summoned schools and social studies to "ameliorate the problems of the seventies and to restructure the social order" (p. 549). Leinwand later developed and edited a paperback anthology series titled Problems of American Society, which seemed ubiquitous for a time and contributed to the ferment for teaching social issues (1968–1969).

The development that I am labeling the newer social studies coincided with an explosion of interest in education. A veritable slew of books drew attention to the problems of the schools and proposed reform, revolution, or exit through creation of alternatives. Among the new wave were books critical of educational practice in general, and of "ghetto-school" education in particular, including Nat Hentoff's Our Children Are Dying, James Herndon's The Way It Spozed To Be, John Holt's How Children Fail and How Children Learn, and Jonathan Kozol's Death at an Early Age. Each of these authors, with the exception of Hentoff, were writing about their own experiences as teachers. They suggested greater concern with the affective aspects of schooling than with academic excellence, and called for humanizing teaching and the school bureaucracy, as well as a return to some of the best aspects of progressivism. The new-wave literature was critical of a system that too often stifled creative teaching, a curriculum that was frequently outmoded and dysfunctional, and testing that was often counterproductive. It was also critical of many teachers who behaved in an ignorant if not destructive manner toward children.

This new wave was accompanied by a host of additional titles in a similar though more radical vein, sharing, but frequently going beyond, the new-wave critique. These included Paul Goodman's *Compulsory Miseducation* (1966), Everett Reimer's *School Is Dead* (1971), and Neil Postman and Charles Weingartner's *Teaching as a Subversive Activity* (1969). At least two influential books, published earlier, became popular again, notably Paul Goodman's *Growing Up Absurd* (1960) and A. S. Neill's *Summerhill* (1960), the latter a classic seminal work on open education that proved a forerunner of the new wave. Charles Silberman's *Crisis in the Classroom* (1970) attempted to capture the new impulse toward open education. A later addition was Ivan Illich's *Deschooling Society* (1971). These works shared the new-wave disdain for traditional schooling and bore some resemblance, in many cases, to child-centered progressivism and its Rousseauan orientation. They mirrored the social trends and critiques of the time and were written partly in response to the inadequacies of American schooling for children of color, the atmosphere of racial unrest, student rebellion, and the antiwar movement.

The critique of the schools generated by the new radical literature was devastating. According to the critics, schools were institutions of conformity that destroyed the souls of children, coerced them to sit through hours of boring classes, and neglected the needs of individuals while oppressing the culture and history of students of color. The schools were attached to a boring, irrelevant curriculum and antiquated teaching methods that destroyed student curiosity. It seemed that there was no alternative but to transform the schools or abandon them (Barrow, 1978; Gross, 1971; Sobel, 1968). The new radical perspectives on schooling and the movement to create open and alternative schools exemplified the tone of the late 1960s and early 1970s and set an intellectual context for the newer social studies.

Then there were the issues. Never before in American history had a confluence of issues exploded upon the scene the way they did in the 1960s. Perhaps most prominent were the multicultural issues of race, class, and gender, with the antiwar movement equally if not more powerful in generating a growing opposition to mainstream culture. Although social studies

journals and literature had given occasional though often superficial attention to racial issues, in the late 1960s, there was a burst of activity. An article
by James A. Banks in 1969 recommended that "inquiries into black power,
poverty, racism, the black revolt, and historical reactions to oppression
should characterize social studies for black pupils" (p. 68). The April 1969
issue of *Social Education* was devoted in its entirety to what it titled "Black
Americans and Social Studies" as well as "minority groups in American society." Other special issues and articles followed, devoted to American In-
dians, and women in history. There were articles titled "Women and the
Language of Inequality," and "Clarifying Sexist Values." Later, there was a
special section called "Eliminating Sexism from the Schools."

The 1971 NCSS Curriculum Guidelines embodied the tenor of the
times, proposing an issues-centered approach to social studies. The guidelines, developed by an NCSS task force composed of Gary Manson, Gerald
Marker, Anna Ochoa, and Jan Tucker, suggested that students of social studies "should apply their knowledge, abilities, and commitments toward the
improvement of the human condition." The guidelines included recommendations that social studies should be "directly related to concerns of
students, focus on the real social world, draw from the social sciences, provide clear objectives and engaging and active learning experiences"; social
studies should "Deal with the Real Social World" and should emphasize social issues, controversial problems, study of race and cultural groups, and
participation in the real world. They suggested that "schools ought to encourage mini-courses, independent study, small group interest sections,
specially planned days or weeks focused on social problems, alternative
courses of study proposed by students, or other innovative plans for un-
freezing the frigid school year" (NCSS Task Force, 1971, pp. 860–862, 865).

What has been called the minicourse explosion may also be some indication of the possible impact of the *Guidelines*, though there were, no
doubt, many other influences contributing to this trend of the 1970s. In the
April 1973 issue of the *The Clearing House*, a proposal was presented for the
restructuring of traditional-length courses into a series of minicourses that
are more accommodating of student interests and needs. Accompanying
the proposal was a survey of minicourse offerings in schools, an indication
that the trend was well under way by that time. A survey conducted in the
mid-1970s indicated that 31% of the public high schools in Kansas had developed minicourse programs in social studies, most commonly in American history and government. The most frequently offered minicourses in
American history were on the Civil War, recent American history, the
American West, and the colonies. The most frequently offered government
courses were called State and Local Government, The Presidency, The Constitution, and Youth and the Law (Guenther & Hansen, 1977).

A listing of social studies course offerings from Tamalpais High School in Marin County, California, from 1976–1977, provides a good example of a minicourse curriculum. The school offered 44 social studies courses, grouped under American Studies, World Studies, and General Studies, with one year of study required in each area. Most were one-semester in length, though a few were quarter-length courses. The list included many interesting-sounding topical courses such as Bread and Roses, Minorities in American History, Revolutionary Movements, Is War Necessary? and Human Sexuality, as well as the more traditional survey courses (Branson, 1977). This kind of rich array of alternatives to the usual social studies curriculum persisted in some school districts into the early 1980s.

Behind the Newer Social Studies

The burst of issues-oriented materials and concerns, reflecting 1960s issues in society, had been simmering for some time. The origins of the newer social studies may be found in the burning issues of the times and in a culmination of much of the educational thought and criticism of the 1960s. The issues focus was foreshadowed by the work of Engle, of Hunt and Metcalf, and of Oliver and Shaver, though it is difficult to assess the degree to which their work influenced the turn of events.

There were several influences at work behind the explosion. First, the tradition of issues-centered education was strong in the educational rhetoric of the times and may have had some influence on the thinking in journals and schools. The approach had been in the background for some time and reflected 1960s issues and the alternative educational culture. The progressive, meliorist, and reconstructionist traditions had always been present and were in the air. In any event, the approach apparently caught the attention and imagination of both teachers and the public. Its strong appeal and meteoric rise reflected the concerns of a time when the counterculture was in vogue. In short, the issues-centered approach became something of a fad.

Unfortunately, this burst of energy was short lived. Several factors weighed against an issues-centered approach having major and lasting impact. The long-term trends in curriculum of the time were discipline based and, by the mid-1970s, toward a back-to-basics approach. The war in Vietnam ended. Optimism was replaced by cynicism, with Watergate, the perceived American failure overseas, and the specter of nuclear holocaust. All denied the possibility of social improvement.

The issues-oriented approach, as it became fashionable in the late 1960s and early 1970s, was frequently flawed and poorly conceptualized. It too frequently became a hodgepodge of topics, addressed helter-skelter.

The newer social studies reflected something closer to a simple presentism than a thoughtful issues-centered approach to the teaching of social studies. In much of the literature, it appeared that history and the social sciences were too often an afterthought, left behind in the rush to concern over today. Finally, and perhaps most tellingly, both the new and newer social studies led to attacks on teachers, textbooks, and curricular programs. Those attacks, especially when combined with a trend toward more traditional forms of schooling, may have marked the beginning of the end of a remarkable era.

AFTERMATH

In the late 1960s and early 1970s there were growing concerns over academic freedom that coincided with the growth of issues-oriented approaches in the newer social studies. A number of academic-freedom cases signaled potential problems with public reactions to the new and newer curricular approaches and likely had a chilling effect on attempts at reform. Textbook controversies recurred, stirred by conservative activists.

Academic-Freedom Cases

There were several academic freedom cases involving individual teachers during the period. In one case related to social studies, an English teacher named Luke Callaway was dismissed from his position at a suburban Atlanta high school after implementing an open-ended curriculum. Another case involved history teacher Bennie G. Thompson, a young African American teacher in Madison, Mississippi; it centered on the charge that Thompson presented for discussion and written assignments issues that were not popular with the county school board and other members of the White power structure in Mississippi (NEA DuShane Emergency Fund Division, 1970).

Another case involved Keith Sterzing, a high school political science and economics teacher in Sugarland, Texas, who frequently stressed current issues and debate and often played a devil's advocate role in his classes. Following a 7½ year fight in federal court, Sterzing was awarded a $40,000 out-of-court settlement. The case was hailed as "precedential" in giving teachers wider latitude in dealing with controversial issues, though Sterzing never returned to teaching and was effectively silenced (Hartshorn, 1972; Matthews, 1975).

Another interesting case involved Frances Ahern, who taught for 10 years at a Grand Island, Nebraska, high school prior to attending a National Defense Education Act (NDEA) summer institute. Following the institute, she used student participation in planning her classes. While Ahern was attending a follow-up conference a student in her third-period consumer politics class was struck physically by the substitute teacher, who followed a traditional method of instruction and classroom management. Subsequently, Ms. Ahern was ordered by the school principal to change her philosophy of teaching, not to discuss the incident with students, and to return to more traditional teaching methods. "Her philosophy does not fit in this school," he stated. She was later dismissed, her contract for the following school year rescinded (NEA, 1970; "Judge Denies," 1970).

Another academic-freedom case involved a gay liberation speaker who left teachers feeling "a bit gun-shy . . . in the direction of censorship" (Kochheiser, 1975). A further case involved an English teacher, John Fogarty, who planned to use Ken Kesey's *One Flew over the Cuckoo's Nest* with his students. Parents complained about "objectionable language," and the school principal ordered removal of the novel (Siegel, 1978).

There were also textbook controversies in a number of locations during the 1970s. Perhaps the most well known was the battle over adoption of more that 300 separate books from several publishers for use in language arts classes in Kanawha County, West Virginia, in 1973–1974. The battle was perhaps the most violent of any textbook controversy in the history of the nation, involving stormy meetings and several individual acts of violence and intimidation, including dynamite used against school property and bullets shot at school buses—luckily empty of students—spurred by citizens who wanted a school program "that emphasizes basic skills and patriotic indoctrination" (Clark, 1975).

A textbook controversy also occurred in Georgia over a series of new social studies textbooks on American history by Edwin Fenton. The state board of education ruled out inclusion of the Fenton texts on a motion by one member, Kenneth Kilpatrick, who charged that the book tends "to create disruption and dissension in our society. In many respects it's a biased book" (Cutts, 1972).

Censorship pressures came from a number of sources, played a role in each of these cases, and certainly contributed to the national climate (Carp, 1968). One study reported a "probable decrease in educator's optimism about the climate for innovation in the nation" (Morrissett, 1975). Censorship pressures and academic freedom cases suggest a climate of growing restraint on teacher freedom. While a number of the contestants in the cases related above received support from the NEA's DuShane Fund, the NCSS Defense Fund, the American Civil Liberties Union (ACLU), or other sympathetic groups, the damage done by the charges and the interruption of teachers' lives sent a message across the land that freedom had its limits.

The MACOS Controversy

The academic-freedom battles of the 1970s climaxed in the MACOS controversy, which signaled the virtual end of the funding period for new social studies projects. Many conservatives and traditionalists who wanted the schools to transmit the "American Way" perceived MACOS as a threat. MACOS, or Man: A Course of Study, drew from anthropological sources and focused on the middle grades (4–6) and on the question, What is human about human beings? Dramatic and graphic scenes of Netsilik Eskimo life were included, among them a film depicting senilicide and other taboos of mainstream U.S. society (Dow, 1991).

In the fall of 1970 a parent and fundamentalist minister in Florida denounced MACOS as "hippie-jippie philosophy" and linked it to "humanism, socialism, gun control, and evolution." An avalanche of hostile criticism was unleashed. Critics included the John Birch Society, the Heritage Foundation, conservative columnist James J. Kilpatrick, and the Council for Basic Education, which was, ironically, an early supporter of new social studies reform (Goetz, 1995).

The federal funding behind MACOS inflamed the situation and led to assaults on the materials in Congress led by Congressman John B. Conlan of Arizona. The congressman charged that, "thousands of parents across America view MACOS as a dangerous assault on cherished values and attitudes concerning morals, social behavior, religion, and our unique American economic and political lifestyle." Conlan quoted Peter Dow's statement that MACOS is "designed to raise questions, not to answer them," but alleged that the materials gave "the implicit view that man not only evolved from lower animals, but also derived his social behavior from them." He then charged that children are

> exposed for a full semester to the alien Netsilik Eskimo subculture, in which the following practices are rationalized and approvingly examined in free-wheeling classroom discussions:
> * Killing the elderly and female infants
> * Wife-swapping and trial marriage
> * Communal living
> * Witchcraft and the occult
> * Cannibalism

Conlan called the program a "brainwash" and heralded the congressional call for the end of federal funding for the "promotion and marketing" of classroom materials (Conlan, 1975; Dow, 1975). Subsequently, MACOS took a public relations beating. Sales of the program took a "precipitous fall" and never recovered (NCSS, 1975).

In response to the MACOS controversy, in May 1976, NCSS held a conference called "Freedom and Responsibility in the Selection and Use of Educational Materials and Learning Strategies in the Social Studies" at the Wingspread Conference Center in Racine, Wisconsin, receiving financial support from the Johnson Foundation. Congressman Conlan, invited to speak, sent his legislative assistant, George H. Archibald, whose remarks were revealing, offering a cultural conservative's critique of the new social studies. Archibald stated that since the efforts to stop federal funding to promote and market MACOS

> we have found that hundreds of thousands of parents throughout the country view the academic-bureaucracy complex—comprised of the nation's colleges of education, the NEA and its state affiliates, in league with the Federal government with its vast power and resources—as the principal national threat to their values, families, spiritual, social, economic, and political freedoms, and our national heritage itself. . . . MACOS is an obvious example of global education—now called "world order education." (1976, pp. 1, 17)

This was, in essence, the 1970s version of the "interlocking directorate" allegation against progressive education. Archibald went on to relate a partially factual history of an episode where the New Social Studies "got its start," at the Wingspread Conference in June 1968, when "40 educationists met for a week's discussion about the need to radically revamp social studies." According to Archibald, the conference theme of "survival" recommended a curricular focus on the "arms buildup," and the gulf between rich and poor in the United States, along with "alleged social and economic injustice," pollution and natural resources "threatened" by "corporations and government," and the population explosion. "The Wingspread Report declared," Archibald continued, "that traditional practices and approaches were no longer adequate," and called for a new, interdisciplinary social studies centered around "socratic dialogue, role playing, debate," with more time devoted "to inquiry, analysis, and decision, less to the acquisition of facts."

Archibald called the 1968 Wingspread Conference "a classic example of an unrepresentative minority of educationists . . . [seeking] . . . to radically alter American education for the purpose of socio-economic and political change, without the approval of the people. This call for a new nationwide social studies curriculum centered around global studies and de-emphasizing American history and our American heritage, completely disregards the wishes of local citizens and taxpayers." Archibald then made a strong case for traditional history and a return to the basics, a return "to perpetuating in their schools each community's social, religious, political, and economic way of life" (pp. 18–20, 25).

He closed his speech with the following warning:

> If you educators and the National Council for the Social Studies choose to press this ideological approach to public education, there will be a collision of major proportions between yourselves and the general public in every community throughout America. . . . Make no mistake about it: taxpayers and parents are ready to marshall every resource at their disposal to ensure that they win. And win they will. (p. 24)

Archibald's statement on behalf of Congressman Conlan sounded the ominous tone of a renewal of the war on social studies that had been going on for decades. Defenders and eloquent statements in support of academic freedom notwithstanding, the bottom line in the aftermath of the MACOS controversy was that there were profound limits on both teacher freedom and government support for curriculum materials development. Archibald gave voice to social studies reformers' worst fears.

Earlier, controversies regarding academic freedom had contributed to the decline of progressive education. In this case, the impact of conservative critics was especially ironic, because the new social studies was a discipline-based response to progressive education's excesses and seemed to match conservative preferences. The controversy over MACOS and other new social studies materials proved that even the disciplines and the new inquiry models, with students as junior social scientists, could be controversial because they frequently asked students to develop their own conclusions. Educational conservatives and many members of the public, it seems, wanted a more traditionally "American" and authoritative perspective fed to students.

The overall pattern of the era of the new and newer social studies seemed largely a replay of what had occurred during the Progressive Era: experimentation and development followed by attacks on teacher freedom and defensive statements from NCSS and various social studies spokespersons. Boom and bust, innovation and reaction, had become a now familiar cycle to many in the social studies profession. To teachers, the impact must have seemed somewhat bewildering.

CAN SOCIAL STUDIES BE CHANGED?

To what extent had social studies as a field changed as a result of the reform movements and the millions of dollars devoted to support them? American history was still the most common course, world history was second most common, and government was third. Enrollments in the social sciences, especially sociology and psychology, grew dramatically.

There were casualties as well. Community Civics and Problems of Democracy were dying courses, and enrollments fell dramatically. While the general outline of the 1916 pattern had some staying power, two of the major innovations of the Committee on Social Studies were nearing the end of their tenure (National Center for Education Statistics [NCES], 1984). By the mid-1970s, the typical overall pattern of social studies courses, grades 7–12, was as follows:

> Grade 7—World History/Culture/Geography
> Grade 8—U.S. History
> Grade 9—World Culture/History or Civics/Government
> Grade 10—World Cultures/History
> Grade 11—U.S. History
> Grade 12—American Government and Sociology/Psychology (Lengel & Superka, 1982, p. 89)

During the mid to late 1970s, reports on the status of social studies proliferated, a result of unprecedented federal funding for such research. Several surveys, based primarily on the NSF-funded studies of science, math, and social studies, came to somewhat similar and disappointing conclusions on the status of classroom practice in social studies, suggesting that recent reform efforts had made little difference. Instruction was still primarily textbook oriented, discussion was largely recitation, innovative "New Social Studies" materials were not widely used, and most students found social studies boring (Shaver, 1979; Shaver, Davis, & Helburn, 1979).

Additional studies found that recitation—a question-and-answer pattern of instruction dominated by teacher talk—was a remarkably stable and dominant form of classroom verbal behavior over the past half century or longer and that the social studies classroom had been dominated by teacher-centered instruction that includes lecture, the textbook as the solitary source of information, discussion, texts, and seatwork (Cuban, 1991).

The typical American education involved a virulent socialization process with little or no countersocialization. The educational system on the whole was clearly in step with community desires for conformity and social control, and the social studies curriculum inculcated allegiance to "God and Country" through a fairly traditional pattern of content and instruction (Peshkin, 1978).

Failure of the New and Newer Social Studies

The ultimate failure of the new social studies reform movement was the result of a complex set of conditions that make most any effort at educational reform difficult. Analysts of the NSF case studies reported that fewer than

20% of teachers had heard of or used the materials. Evidence from other sources suggests that the terminology of the movement had a wider, though more superficial, impact. So it is clear that the new social studies movement was not a complete debacle. Nonetheless, it largely disappointed the lofty expectations of its proponents, project directors, and staunch advocates. Reasons for its failure to have the expected influence relate to the sociopolitical context of the 1960s and early 1970s, the nature of the reforms proposed, and attributes of the school as an institution as well as elements of the culture in which teaching and learning are embedded.

The social, political, and cultural context of schooling profoundly influenced creation of the new social studies and largely precipitated its decline. The philosophy and materials produced were largely incompatible with the prevailing culture of schools. Moreover, many features of the new social studies were at odds with the basic sociocultural function of schooling (Anderson, 1982). The reform plan under which the new social studies programs was implemented was equally flawed. It was a top-down, hierarchical approach to reform designed by university researchers who had little experience in schools.

Critical aspects of the school as an institution also created obstacles to the success of the reform movement and made it likely that teachers would stick with the more traditional teaching approaches, or return to them after a period of experimentation (Fenton, 1991). Hard-to-change institutional factors, which Tyack and Cuban (1995) have called the grammar of schooling, made it hard for teachers to adopt new ways, even when they wanted to. Moreover, students, other teachers, and most administrators expected traditional forms of teaching. By the 1970s, many of the teachers who used new social studies materials had come to view the programs as "a parade of fads" (Nelson & Drake, 1994).

The newer social studies that emerged in the late 1960s was in many respects a revitalized, reconstructionist-oriented progressive education. With the new social studies it shared an inquiry orientation, but there the similarities ended. The newer social studies were driven by the very societal change and turmoil that had upset the new social studies. Where the earlier program focused on the structure of the disciplines, the newer trend championed valuing, relevance, and social activism. In the context of civil rights marches, antiwar protests, student sit-ins, and the sex and drug revolts, the new social studies seemed archaic. The newer movement did, however, share a similar fate to that of the new social studies. Its impact on the field was similarly limited.

Looking back, the new social studies movement and the progressive education movement, which had been put to rest in the 1950s, shared a number of important similarities. Both succeeded in capturing the imagination of a generation of scholars and a significant number of teachers; both were inquiry oriented; both challenged the traditional wisdom; and both produced a significant backlash. However, the differences between these two major reform movements were profound. The progressives favored interdisciplinary and issues-oriented approaches and materials; they elevated the child to a position of value; they encouraged education, even social action, that was relevant to community issues and concerns; the reforms they promoted had a more practicable and utilitarian side. Both movements had their day, and both ultimately failed to achieve the desired results.

CONCLUSION

Following the innovation of the new social studies, the newer social studies, and the academic-freedom battles the reforms spawned, social studies as a field, it seemed, had been cast adrift. The era of the new and newer social studies was apparently over, a conservative back-to-basics movement under way, and yet nothing had clearly taken over the mantra of reform within the field. Scope and sequence and the need for coherence in social studies programs had been neglected for much of the reform period, and both the new and newer social studies tended to create fragmentation, in part a reflection of the new social studies lack of rationale and the splintered and fragmentary nature of the dominant social issues of the 1970s. As we shall see in the following chapter, the response of social studies to the back-to-basics movement was weak and defensive.

What emerged, at least for a time, was reversion to the consensus definition of social studies that had been developed by NCSS and refined by Edgar B. Wesley: "The *social studies* are the *social sciences* simplified for pedagogical purposes" (1937, p. 4; emphasis in original). In a letter to Wesley, Shirley Engle wrote, "It is clear to me that your definition . . . has carried the day in the field of practice. People of my persuasion were never of much force in social studies practice. . . . My impression is that what we were asking was too demanding and too risky for the profession to implement" (Engle, 1979).

Upon reflection, it is difficult to estimate the impact of the turmoil taking place outside schooling on the curriculum, on the culture, and on teachers and students. The effect was undoubtedly profound and partially helps to explain the difficulties encountered by discipline-based new social studies projects and the longer-term success of some of the issues-oriented projects.

The new social studies was an exciting but wrongheaded movement.

In the final analysis, it was doomed from the start. It represents the worst of the permeability problem in school curricula, directly linking cold war fears and concerns to a curriculum reform movement. By the mid-1970s, the new social studies movement as a federally supported plan for curriculum reform was dead. Its demise left the field in a state of confusion and decline from which it still has not recovered. In most areas, the curriculum returned to the 1916 pattern, if it had ever been altered, though without Problems of Democracy or Community Civics, and thus, without the reformist, progressive bent intended by the framers of social studies in 1916. What remained was a shell of the old social studies, kind of a fallback position. The standard scope and sequence, outlined in 1916, was, it seemed, never seriously challenged by the new social studies movement.

The turf war among camps competing for social studies adherents, however, was far from settled and would continue into the 1980s and 1990s, as we shall see in the remaining chapter. Both the progressive reform movement and the new social studies reform movement demonstrated the difficulty of changing social studies, as a number of observers had warned, yet each found enough adherents to beckon with the possibility of a new day.

CHAPTER SEVEN

The Runaway Train of Standards Reform

FROM THE MID-1970s and beyond, social studies education, and in particular the progressive, issues-centered camp, experienced something of a decline, coinciding with a conservative restoration in politics, schools, and American culture. Although many of the reforms of the 1960s and 1970s were already eroding, they were subject to direct assault in the 1980s. By that time the liberal consensus on education had begun to unravel, and two related but distinct forms of educational conservatism had gained favor. The first of these came from the New Right, led by the Heritage Foundation, a Washington-based think tank consisting of several conservative scholars. The New Right called for a much smaller federal role in education, championed extremist positions against "secular humanism" and favored active censorship and teaching of creationism (Pincus, 1984a, 1984b).

In the view of the New Right, most if not all of the schools' problems could be traced to overcentralized decision making brought by increased federal control. In opposition to the mainstream, the New Right stressed educational free choice and diversity. Advocates of the New Right position believed that vested interests forced creation of a unified curriculum based on the principles of secular humanism. Through multiple and interlocking organizations, extensive mailing lists, a network of nationally circulated magazines, tabloids, and newsletters—and through the electronic church, consisting of nearly 40 television stations and more than 1,000 radio stations—the New Right sought to promote its views. Its agenda included a host of causes, among them promoting creationism, censoring textbooks, nurturing conservative ideas, fighting secular humanism, and promoting "free enterprise" (Brodinsky, 1982).

Leaders of the New Right used propaganda skillfully, making scapegoats of the NEA, the public school system, secular humanism, the Education Department, and textbook writers. Moreover, their attacks came at an opportune time, when public education was at a low point—ravaged by inflation, declines in enrollment, increasing costs, and evaporating public confidence. In fact many critics charged the schools with near total failure, citing lack of discipline, teachers unprepared in their subject matter, social promotion, subjective grading systems, and "too much pedagogical faddism" (Brodinsky, 1982).

The term *secular humanism* was used by the New Right as a code word with which to brand offenders. For hard-core Christian fundamentalists, humanism was seen as an evil so pervasive as to be at the heart of most of what was wrong with humanity. One pamphlet asked, "Is Humanism Molesting Your Child?" Another tract urged students to follow a list of commandments not to discuss values; not to take "social studies" or "future studies"; not to participate in classroom discussions that begin with "What would you do . . . ?" or "Do you think . . . ?"; and to demand defined courses in history, geography, and civics (Brodinsky, 1982, p. 90). New Right critics also engaged in a widespread movement to ban, remove, and sometimes even burn materials designed for use by students. Targets frequently involved "dirty words," but also included alternative images of family life, evolution, race relations, religion, politics, patriotism, free enterprise, communism, or other topics (pp. 91–92).

A larger and less cohesive group of neoconservative educators, politicians, and businesspeople, who could be described as "centrist conservatives," called for a shift in federal policy away from equity to an emphasis on excellence. Although the two groups overlapped on a number of issues, they had basic differences regarding the mission of schooling and the role of government in education. Centrist conservatives posited three general missions for the schools: promoting economic growth for the nation, preserving a common culture, and encouraging educational equity through improving quality and color-blind access. They agreed on the need for improved educational standards, more homework, less time on nonacademic electives, abolition of social promotion, and strengthening of graduation and admissions requirements. They also agreed on the need for traditional classroom discipline, improvement in teacher quality, a more limited and selective federal role in education, and business/education cooperation (Pincus, 1984b).

The neoconservative, centrist philosophy lay behind much of the educational agenda of the 1980s and 1990s, and it was the driving force behind many of the reports on educational reform during the time. Much of this conservative activism was a backlash against the legacy of the 1960s, for its political sins, or in some cases, against declining standards.

The heart of the neoconservative movement, combined with the New Right, found expression in the back-to-basics movement. Many of the reforms of the 1960s, including the new and newer social studies, flew in the face of the traditional teacher's content orientation and demand for order in the classroom. Public concern about declining test scores melded with complaints about lax standards and charges that students were doing less reading and writing, and led to loud calls for instruction in the basics, reading, writing, and arithmetic. In response to this demand, by 1977, 38 state legislatures had passed laws requiring minimum competency tests in the basic skills (Report, 1977).

In large part the back-to-basics movement was a media creation. Articles appeared in national publications with titles extolling the move—"Back to Basics in the Schools"—or offering complaints: "Why Johnny Can't Write." Typical was an article from 1975 that charged, "Will-nilly, the U.S. educational system is spawning a generation of semiliterates" (Sheils, p. 58). *Newsweek* reported in October 1974 that "all across the nation, parents, school boards, and often the pupils themselves are demanding that the schools stop experimenting and get back to basics—in reading, writing, arithmetic and standards of behavior to boot." Open classrooms, "relevant" course material, permissive discipline, and lax standards had been instituted at the expense of work in the traditional disciplines such as English composition, history, the sciences, and foreign languages ("Back to Basics," 1974). Professional educators were clearly to blame.

Social studies was, once again, one of the targets, as critics charged that secondary educators had stressed the "fun and the relevant" in the social sciences with the result that students were "quite conversant with local, national, and international problems, but they can't write three consecutive declarative sentences in the English language" ("Back to Basics," 1974, p. 91). By and large the response among social studies educators was to argue that instruction in basic skills and content were already a major part of the curriculum, and that infusion of work focused explicitly on reading and writing skills could help to improve student learning.

In the late 1970s, *Social Education* ran two special issues devoted to a back-to-basics theme. By 1980, NCSS had joined with a number of other leading educational organizations to support the essentials of education, acknowledging that "public concern about basic knowledge and the basic skills in education is valid." An NCSS statement titled "Essentials of Social Studies" revealed the profound influence that the conservative restoration was having on the field. The statement gave priority to the academic disciplines and implied a more traditional focus on content, along with inculcation of democratic beliefs. In hindsight, it was a curious document, melding a response to the basics movement with social efficiency and critical thinking skills, signaling the co-optation of social studies by a rising conservatism (NCSS, 1980).

Despite this flurry of activity, back-to-basics had its critics. One noted detractor, Richard Ohman, a professor of English, charged that the literacy crisis was "a fiction, if not a hoax" and wrote, "The available facts simply do not reveal whether young Americans are less literate than their counterparts in 1930 or 1960." He cited a number findings that supported his view, including an increase in the number of students taking standardized tests. Other studies found "no solid evidence of a decline in reading ability," and concluded, "anyone who says he knows that literacy is decreasing . . . is at best unscholarly and at worse dishonest" (1976, p. 32).

REFORM STORY

By the early 1980s the conservative restoration received a major boost from an unprecedented flurry of reports on the status and future of schooling. The watershed came with publication of *A Nation at Risk: The Imperative for Educational Reform,* the report of the National Commission on Excellence in Education, a blue-ribbon commission appointed by President Ronald Reagan (1983). Although the report contained no new research and was based on a compilation of findings, its timing and the language in which it was written created a heated atmosphere and attracted a great deal of media attention. The central thesis of the report was that the nation was "at risk." The commission blamed U.S. schools for the nation's decline in international economic competition, alleging that the position of the country in commerce, industry, science, and technology was overtaken by "a rising tide of mediocrity in our schools which threatens our very future as a nation and a people" (p. 1).

Several reports shared the central thesis of *A Nation at Risk* and offered similar remedies for regaining our preeminent position in global industrial competition. In clear and unabashed language one typical report called for a broadened definition of education to meet the demand for "highly skilled human capital" in the "new era of global competition" (Task Force, 1983).

Although the intent of the commissions may have been to awaken schools from encroaching "mediocrity" and tilt them toward excellence, these reports were not well received by many educators. If the nation did have an educational crisis, it was one manufactured by business and political leaders. Critics charged that the reports contained "weak arguments, poor data, and simplistic recommendations" and described them as political documents that made polemical arguments rather than offering a reasoned and well-documented case (Stedman & Smith, 1984). On the whole, the reports had a pronounced tendency to regard schools rather narrowly as instruments for training human capital and regaining U.S. dominance over world markets. The arguments in the reports were based on inaccurate, incomplete, and misleading data centered around a faulty thesis and revealed a failure to understand the broader aims of education (Tanner, 1984).

On the whole, the report of the National Commission expressed a corporate agenda for schooling, and demanded more traditional education for human capital development. This was a new version of education for social efficiency, a turn away from the progressive vision, and another step back from the potential redemptive power of schooling.

Social Studies Developments and Trends

During the early years of the conservative restoration, the back-to-basics movement, and the business-driven push for excellence, social studies appeared to be a field adrift. The era of the new social studies had come to a close, yet no similarly powerful movement for reform had taken its place. Moreover, the failure of the new and newer social studies to have the anticipated impact on classrooms led to a great deal of hand-wringing. By the late 1970s, it seemed that social studies was a field in search of itself. The journal *Social Education* and a number of other publications reflected this soul-searching. From the late 1960s, it seemed that *Social Education* had become something of a potpourri, a journal dominated by special issues with a focus on what seemed to at least one observer as "one damn thing after another." First it was an issue on Russia, then Japan, then back-to-basics, and so forth, seemingly without end. Even though there were many thoughtful articles and special issues published, the journal of the late 1970s and early 1980s seemed to lack conceptual focus. Social studies, it seemed, could be whatever one wanted it to be.

Definitional dilemmas within the field appeared to be the major feature of social studies during the late 1970s and early 1980s, making the time ripe for alternative initiatives from outside. Appropriately, given the depth of social studies malaise, a front-cover cartoon accompanied a special issue of *Social Education* in 1980, titled "Discussion and Debate on New Proposals for the Social Studies Curriculum." The cartoon depicted a group of seven social studies professionals sitting at a table considering a jigsaw puzzle with pieces labeled to reflect many of the traditional and current approaches to the social studies puzzle: social sciences, history, decision making, concepts, ethnic studies, international human rights education, generalizations, social action, global education, geography, futurism, career education, consumerism, moral education, law-related education, citizenship, drug education, geography, factual knowledge, skills, socialization. One of the participants commented, "It might help if we had a picture of what this is supposed to look like" (Editor, 1980).

Also, by the 1980s there was a growing recognition of the difficulty of changing social studies, an awareness that diffusion did not necessarily equate with curricular change, and a feeling that the theory/practice split was perhaps the central dilemma of the field. One letter to the editor lamented the paradox between the "real" and the "ideal" in social studies (Letter to Editor, 1979b). Another shared the important insight that "diffusion doesn't equal change" (Letter to Editor, 1979a). The work of Larry Cuban in *How Teachers Taught* revealed that despite repeated efforts to improve the quality of teaching in the nation's schools, traditional teaching practices relying on teacher talk, seatwork, and use of textbooks and recitation were remarkably persistent (1984).

In sum, social studies appeared to drift for a time in part because there were no new initiatives with the force or power of either the new social studies or the progressive movement. Moreover, many scholars in the field had witnessed the demise of both these movements and had increasingly begun to recognize the difficulty of large-scale change. So there emerged, for a time, a gap in reform movements, combined with a retreat in the face of the conservative restoration and the return by many teachers to more traditional means of teaching. Much of the blame for the slide in the vigor of social studies reform efforts lay in the context of the times. In the Reagan years and beyond, progressives in social studies were swimming against a rising tide.

THE REVIVAL OF TRADITIONAL HISTORY

Into this vacuum of near "directionlessness" came a new movement more in keeping with the tenor of the times: the revival of history. The origins of the revival of history may be traced to the same general concerns that motivated the back-to-basics movement. It was, in a sense, the citizenship wing of the conservative restoration. Though sentiment for traditional history had never disappeared, such predilections seemed at low ebb during the era of the new and newer social studies with their focus on inquiry and issues. At least a few critics of the new social studies had called for a return to traditional history, and by the mid-1970s an increasing number of historians were expressing alarm over the decline of history teaching in schools and the loss of students to other majors in colleges and universities.

The most well known survey of the time was issued in 1975 by a committee of the Organization of American Historians headed by Richard S. Kirkendall. The survey reviewed the status of history in the schools and colleges and reported that "history is in crisis." The committee found wide variations in the qualifications required of teachers in the secondary schools. In a number of states, requirements for the certification of "social studies" teachers were undergoing revision, with the number of required courses in history being reduced. On the whole, the situation regarding teacher certification requirements was described as "quite fluid," with the implication that history's preeminence was in danger (Kirkendall, 1975, pp. 558–561).

History's position in the curriculum was also slipping, according to the report. The committee detected a dynamic situation with most movement away from history, at least as history was "traditionally defined and taught." History was being deemphasized and incorporated into social studies units with trends favoring a "multidisciplinary approach." In many cases, the perception was that the chronological approach had been replaced by the "inquiry method," and efforts "to link courses to the issues facing society" (p. 565).

The report drew heavy criticism along several lines. Some charged that the committee was badly informed about the secondary schools. Others suggested that the report reflected a traditional approach to teaching history that should be discarded. Kirkendall and historians generally seemed to blame social studies for failures in the teaching of history. It was an attack reminiscent of those of Allan Nevins and the *New York Times* crusade of the 1940s. Moreover, the "survey" reported in the *Journal of American History* provided little in the way of hard evidence to verify a "crisis" in history teaching in the schools, and appeared to be almost entirely anecdotal.

A number of neoconservative writers contributed to a growing groundswell among historians, politicians, and more than a few teachers to support the revival of traditional history. The so-called crisis served as preface to the broader revival that was spurred by another *New York Times* involvement in the war against social studies. In the November 17, 1985, issue of the *New York Times Magazine,* an article by educational historian Diane Ravitch appeared under the title "Decline and Fall of History Teaching." Ravitch argued that history was in trouble in the schools and the culprit was social studies. In the years that followed, publications by Ravitch, Lynne Cheney, Paul Gagnon, Chester Finn, and others contributed to a growing call for the revival of history in schools and made the case for a return to history and geography as the core of citizenship education. Each of these scholars made significant contributions, Cheney in *American Memory: A Report on the Humanities in the Nation's Public Schools* (1987), Gagnon in an article titled "Why Study History?" that appeared in the *Atlantic Monthly* (1988), and Finn, as co-author with Ravitch of *What Do Our 17-Year-Olds Know? A Report on the First National Assessment of History and Literature* (Ravitch & Finn, 1987). By the late 1980s it was clear that Ravitch was the driving force.

The general thesis of Ravitch's work on the teaching of history was, first, that history was in trouble. Requirements had declined as history was forced to share curricular time with the ill-defined social studies, thus leaving students ignorant of even the most basic facts of U.S. history. Second, internal disorder within history as a discipline crowded out the idea of history as a story and replaced it with process-centered approaches through which students learn how to make investigations as if training to be historians, resulting in less attention to learning the content or facts of history. Third, she argued, "History is above all the retelling of what happened in the past," and should emphasize content knowledge, appeals to the imagination, and empathy so that students can experience a different time and place (Ravitch, 1987, 1989).

Ravitch described a "golden age" of history in schools during the early years of the 20th century and held up traditional history, centered around a textbook; chronology; and history as "a story well told" as a model curriculum; she charged that this prototype had been dislodged by a "social efficiency"–oriented social studies program focused on immediate social utility, on "relevance and student interest." In contrast, she proffered the new California Framework as "a historic step towards the national revival of the teaching and learning of history." The framework established history in virtually every grade, chronologically sequenced to develop in students a repertoire of knowledge. It stressed democratic values and principles of democratic government "throughout the curriculum" (Ravitch, 1987, pp. 12, 18). The underlying purpose, the use of history to instill American democratic values, to build a sense of national identity and a common culture, was a slightly revised version of Nevins's aims from the 1940s. If the problem was social studies, the solution, in Ravitch's view, was to turn back the clock to the 1890s and reinstitute a back-to-basics traditional history curriculum.

Ravitch, Gagnon, and a group of prominent historians formed the Bradley Commission on History in Schools. Generously funded by the Lynde and Harry Bradley Foundation, the Bradley Commission released a pamphlet outlining its program in 1988, titled *Building a History Curriculum*. The commission adopted a platform of nine resolutions calling for study of history to be required of all students; for the kindergarten through grade 6 social studies curriculum to be history-centered; and for no fewer than 4 years of history in grades 7 through 12. The platform contained many useful recommendations but took an extreme position regarding the balance of history and the other social sciences in the curriculum. Furthermore, it all but ignored one of the key problems facing history teachers in the schools—the problem of making the study of history relevant and meaningful to students.

Following publication of the guidelines, the Bradley Commission published *Historical Literacy: The Case for History in American Education* in 1989.

The book was edited by Gagnon and included contributions from many members of the Bradley Commission. Most of the chapters were authored by historians. Notably, not one educational theorist or curriculum specialist was included among the authors. The few professors of education who were included had clearly established that they favored a history curriculum. The book was a polemical argument for more and better history in schools, with little or no consideration of the place of the other social sciences in the curriculum. The argument was advanced that these would be incorporated within history.

Critiques

The response among social studies educators was rather anemic given the challenge to their leadership of the field. Richard E. Gross described the critics as "a small but vocal, highly motivated, well-funded, and very visible interest group . . . promoting the primacy of history and geography in the school curriculum." Gross argued that there was "little evidence from the past, when history and geography held sway, that the study of these subjects produced the results that today's proponents desire" (1988, p. 49).

Ronald W. Evans critiqued the revival of history and its chief proponent, Diane Ravitch. Evans argued that Ravitch was using social studies as a scapegoat and ignoring the history and purposes of the social studies movement, preferring to make facile condemnations instead. The reality, he wrote, was that "history continues to hold a dominant position among the social studies, and that one goal of the social studies movement has been to make instruction in history and the social sciences more meaningful and relevant to the average citizen." He criticized Ravitch and her colleagues for assuming that a chronological narrative, the "tell a story" approach to history teaching, was some sort of answer, when that traditional approach had continued without interruption in most classrooms and had been failing for years to interest and educate students (1989, pp. 87–88).

In his critique of the reform movement, Stephen J. Thornton asked, "Should we be teaching more history?" Thornton questioned whether the proposed reforms were well founded and whether a renewed emphasis on content acquisition would bring us back, nostalgically, to the golden age that Ravitch had identified. He argued that there was "scant support in the research literature for the reformers' views, and that the substitution of history for other social studies courses will be to little avail unless entrenched patterns of instruction and learning are also changed" (1990, p. 54).

Sid Lester, a professor at San Jose State University, wrote a critique of the California Framework in which he criticized the short shrift given to the social sciences and the failure of the Framework Committee to be more inclusive. He wrote, "There were no professors of economics, anthropology, sociology, psychology, or political science. None! Not any! Zip! Nada! . . . According to most authorities," he countered, "the 'social studies' should be comprised of the disciplines of history, geography, anthropology, economics, political science, sociology, and psychology, with some humanities, philosophy and law thrown in" (1989, p. 56). Another professor from California, Duane Campbell at Sacramento State, complained in a letter published in *Social Education* that the framework had been "railroaded through" the framework adoption process using undemocratic means, and over the strong objections of many representatives from the field (1988, p. 403). In sum, critics charged that the nascent revival of history was an attempt to turn back the clock, to overturn a decades-old attempt at a compromise position between historians and social scientists, brokered by educators with the needs and interests of students at heart.

What was behind the revival of history? The movement came to fruition because of the confluence of persons and ideas with an appropriate national climate during which conservative notions were in ascendancy, both in schools and in the nation. It received strong support from those in positions of power, and generous funding from the Bradley Foundation, a philanthropic foundation with a strong conservative bias and the goal of influencing policy (Stehle, 1997). This kind of financial support, from a private foundation leaning in a particular direction, was unprecedented in the history of social studies. Moreover, there were some elements of truth in the critiques leveled against social studies. The new social studies had placed emphasis on the social sciences and social issues. Even the 1916 report reflected a moderate, compromise position between history and the social sciences and resulted in less time being devoted to pure history instruction than was the case under the Ten and the Seven. Also, it was definitely true that social studies practice was a shadow of what was possible, regardless of its philosophical orientation.

Clearly, the movement touched a nerve among historians and the general public, who seem always susceptible to appeals to tradition, nostalgia, and a golden age, and it came at an opportune time. On the whole, the revival of history was yet another episode in the recurring war on social studies. Yet this new initiative was different in some important ways. Although polemical, its arguments were much more powerfully developed than by previous similar critics. Moreover, Ravitch and company enlisted substantial support among respected historians, had generous organizational and financial backing, and had established a firm beachhead by developing a "model" curriculum in the most populous state in the nation. Apparently, this was a movement to reform social studies that would be around for some time.

THE NATIONAL COMMISSION ON SOCIAL STUDIES

The definitional dilemma facing social studies early in the post–new social studies era led to a sense among many within the profession that social studies had reached an impasse, and that something had to be done. Major curricular change seemed impossible, wrote one former president of NCSS, "because the primary political forces affecting curricular decisions immobilize each other" (Mehlinger, 1992, p. 149). The idea for creation of a national commission to examine social studies curriculum had been floated since the late 1970s by several prominent social studies figures.

In his 1984 presidential address to the AHA, Arthur S. Link called for a "blue ribbon" committee to study the status of history in the schools. In 1985, Donald Bragaw, president of NCSS, asked the board of directors to set up a task force to examine the entire social studies program in the schools, K–12. Formation of the National Commission on Social Studies in the schools in 1985 grew out of these two recommendations, eventually emerging as a joint project of four organizations with an interest in improving social studies instruction: the American Historical Association, the Carnegie Foundation for the Advancement of Teaching, the National Council for the Social Studies, and the Organization of American Historians (OAH) (Metcalf & Jenness, 1990).

Membership on the commission, and on its curriculum task force, included a mix of historians, social scientists, social studies educators, and school personnel, but was weighted toward historians, reflecting the makeup of its sponsoring organizations. Historians in both the AHA and the OAH later endorsed the recommendations of the Bradley Commission, so there was a great deal of overlap in the philosophical orientation of the two groups.

The curriculum recommendations made in *Charting a Course: Social Studies for the 21st Century,* the report of the National Commission, were generally supportive of the goals of the traditional history camp. The report argued that "history and geography should provide the matrix or framework for social studies" and called for integration of "concepts and understandings" from the other social sciences (National Commission on Social Studies in the Schools, 1989, pp. v., 3–4).

Perhaps the most innovative aspects of the report's proposals were the notion of integrating world and U.S. history into three courses at the high school level, allowing for in-depth and global study of topics, issues, and problems from the past, and the recommendation of a middle school course focused on the local community, on local issues, and on neighborhood problems. Both these recommendations were, however, a drastic departure from current practice.

A number of critiques of the commission's work were published in *Social Education*. Shirley Engle wondered "whether changing the scope and sequence" was a "sufficient way to go about reforming social studies," and wrote that in the commission's report, "the value of history in the development of good citizens is taken for granted." He argued that the commission needed "to shift the locus of its thinking from the declarative to the hypothetical mood" (1990). Jack Nelson charged that the report was "narrow and conservative" and "anti-intellectual in its lack of concern for contemporary issues and competing ideas." Nelson concluded that the report "deserves to be forgotten quickly" (1990).

Looking behind the commission report, two of the four main sponsors were *the* major historian's interest groups in the nation. Commission members were clearly not representative of the various traditions in the field, but were apparently chosen with an eye toward furthering the revival of history. The impact of the commission may have been limited by its failure to create a more inclusive membership with a balanced representation from the various camps and stakeholders in the century-long battles over social studies. It was soon eclipsed by other developments and largely forgotten.

CROSSCURRENTS

By the mid-late 1980s the decline of issues-oriented social studies was apparent, and a renewed interest in traditional history was the trend in vogue. Progressivism in schools appeared to be dead, and dialogue on education continued as discussion of a national "crisis."

The public educational dialogues of the latter 1980s centered on a continuation of the central themes of the conservative restoration and a reaction to the leftward tilt of academia and the growing trend toward what conservatives called "political correctness." Books on education seldom become best-sellers. For two books in the same year to achieve such status was without precedent. The public success of Allan Bloom's *The Closing of the American Mind* and E. D. Hirsch's *Cultural Literacy: What Every American Needs to Know* in 1987 signaled a strong and continuing public interest in education. Bloom's thesis was that higher education was in the process of sacrificing the monuments of a great civilization on the altar of equality, that higher education, stressing openness and relativism, and seeking to overcome ethnocentrism, aimed to indoctrinate citizens who would support a democratic regime. He lamented the decline of philosophy and a liberal education, and called for a return to a classical Western canon and traditional history.

In *Cultural Literacy,* Hirsch made similar charges of decline but focused his work on the public schools. For that reason, his work is of greater interest to social studies. The thesis of Hirsch's book was stated in its first sentence: "To be culturally literate is to possess the basic information needed to thrive in the modern world" (1987, p. xiii). It was Hirsch's contention that Dewey and progressive educators "too hastily rejected 'the piling up of information'" (p. xv).

In regard to the social studies curriculum, he offered a description of a field gone astray: process oriented, fragmented, devoid of content. This was the same general argument made by Ravitch, casting social studies as scapegoat. Like Ravitch, Hirsch offered a superficial and poorly drawn interpretation driven by ideology rather than hard evidence.

The educational dialogues of the 1980s and 1990s contained multiple voices, from many different perspectives. One of the main camps in the long turf battles over the curriculum was the social reconstructionist group. In the latter 20th century, social reconstructionism was itself transcended by critical perspectives largely imported from outside, but generally sharing a similar radical orientation. Critical theorists in education were far from a monolithic group and included scholars specializing in reconceptualist curricular theory, cultural studies, feminist scholarship, and other forms. Critical pedagogy retained a strong link to the works of Dewey and forged some direct links to social reconstructionist theory. Frequently, critical pedagogues drew on the works of European theorists. Their agenda was similar in ultimate goals to that of the social reconstructionists, but their work seemed to focus on building a community of scholars critical of mainstream educational practice; conversant in critical theory; cognizant of the systemic and interwoven nature of educational, political, and social systems; and committed to resisting the dominant groups that control the bulk of wealth and power in America and whose interests the schools tend to serve.

Among the earliest and most influential was the Brazilian educational theorist Paulo Freire. In his seminal work *Pedagogy of the Oppressed,* Freire drew a distinction between traditional forms of education built around the banking theory, in which knowledge is bestowed upon ignorant students by knowledgeable teachers, mirroring the oppression of capitalist society, and problem-posing education, which breaks this hierarchical pattern. "Education," he wrote, "is suffering from narration sickness" (1970, p. 57). The narration at the heart of traditional educational practices "turns students into 'containers,' into 'receptacles' to be 'filled' by the teacher." Education then becomes "an act of depositing, in which the students are the depositories and the teacher is the depositor" (p. 58). Problem-posing education, by contrast, creates a dialogue of teacher-student with student-teacher through which both teacher and student teach and learn simultaneously.

Given its political stance, critical theory was not without opponents. Many scholars asserted that it was unrealistic, naive, or unreasonable to expect schools and teachers to act as agents of social transformation. The majority of teachers and school administrators were mainstream in their thinking and reflected the general populace. Others charged that social reconstructionism had the potential to lead toward indoctrination of students, toward proselytizing and propaganda.

Another important influence on educational dialogue in the latter 1980s and the 1990s came in the continuing discourse over multicultural education. An outgrowth of the civil rights movement, multicultural education became a major focus for growth and development in universities and schools of teacher education as well as in the public schools. The multicultural education of the late 20th century represented the evolution of a long trend—reflecting the civil rights movement—from intercultural education in the World War II period, to early multicultural education in the 1960s and 1970s, to the 1990s. There were new players in the curriculum game, and groups that had long been excluded were now among the power brokers struggling over the curriculum.

Supporters of multicultural education asserted that the perspectives of persons of color, women, and the working class had been excluded from the study of history, literature, and the humanities. They maintained that mainstream ignorance of multicultural groups, of both their contributions and their historical oppression intensified intolerance and contributed to bigotry. Multicultural education was based on the premise that the purposeful inclusion of the stories, literature, and historical perspectives of diverse groups in school curricula and textbooks could help students attain a broader perspective and contribute to creation of a more equitable society (Banks, 1999).

Critics of multicultural education, however, argued that multicultural education was divisive because it deemphasized our common heritage and culture and placed undue emphasis on conflicts and differences related to race, class, and gender and argued that it would Balkanize the nation (Schlesinger, 1991).

STANDARDS

The era of national educational reform leading to the standards movement began in earnest during a time of political conservatism and educational retrenchment heralded by publication of *A Nation at Risk* in 1983. The reform movement spawned by *A Nation at Risk* continued under the America 2000 and Goals 2000 programs with a top-down push for standards. The documents of America 2000 and Goals 2000 specifically called for the teaching of "history, geography, and civics" and made no mention of social studies.

The standards movement was launched amid a mythical national crisis in education based upon the charge that our schools were in dire condition and largely to blame for a U.S. decline in international economic competition. Many educators and the public agreed that drastic reform was required to remedy the situation. However, a lack of meaningful discourse about the mythical crisis resulted in a national obsession with fixing the schools. Proposals included returning to basic subjects such as history and geography, developing a national curriculum, and using standardized tests to assess student knowledge.

Others were less than sanguine about the basis for the new reforms. Gerald W. Bracey, a policy analyst for the NEA, charged that the assumption that our schools were not performing well constituted "The Big Lie" about education, and reported, "The evidence overwhelmingly shows that American schools have never achieved more than they currently achieve." He characterized *A Nation at Risk* as "xenophobic screed that has little to do with education" and concluded that the Bell Commission's "rising tide of mediocrity" simply did not exist (1991, pp. 105–106, 116).

Support for Bracey's claims came from the findings of a major study of education, commissioned by none other than the first Bush administration, *The Sandia Report*. The Sandia National Laboratories, in New Mexico, were a component of the U.S. Department of Energy. Major findings of the Sandia report flatly contradicted claims about education being circulated by the Bush administration, and the report was suppressed (Berliner & Biddle, 1995). Like Bracey, Sandia researchers found strong evidence that schools in the United States were performing well, with the exception of many schools serving poor and minority youth. SAT scores had declined because of the much larger number of test takers; international comparisons were inherently flawed, a case of making unfair cross-cultural comparisons. When the top students in the United States were compared with the top students in other countries, U.S. students performed as well or better. Moreover, in higher education, the United States was the unquestioned leader (Huelskamp, 1993).

In Social Studies

As for the social studies curriculum, among the six national goals for schools described in the *America 2000* report, social studies was nowhere to be found, replaced instead by history and geography (U.S. Department of Education [USDOE], 1991). This shift was a major change from the earlier reports of the excellence era, which generally included social studies as one of the core subjects. Now, in the 1990s, as the reform movement gathered steam, the inclusion of social studies as a broad field had ended.

Circumstantial evidence strongly suggests that the shift from social studies to history and geography was a result of the neoconservative revival of history and that group's alliance with other educational conservatives in positions of power. The move to reassert the dominance of traditional history combined with the human capital emphasis of national commission reports to form a powerful government line in favor of a history-geography matrix. Ravitch served as assistant secretary of education during the first Bush administration and commented in 1991 to a national meeting of state social studies supervisors that their protests and questions were to no avail because "the train has already left the station" (Judy Butler, personal communication, 1998).

The response of social studies leaders to these developments was mixed. In the early 1990s, leaders of NCSS attempted to persuade policy makers that the term *social studies* is a useful umbrella term, and that history, geography, and the other social sciences could coexist within the social studies curriculum, but to no effect (Risinger & Garcia, 1995).

While there were many critics of the developing trend, NCSS chose to respond to the revival of history and the criticism of social studies by developing a new version of the consensus definition that it had always promoted, and by participating in the standards movement by developing its own set of standards statements. The goal was to develop a set of integrated standards that would draw on content from the various social studies subjects. Apparently, the thinking among the NCSS leadership was that the move toward standards-based reform and high-stakes testing was the wave of the future and that not being involved would have dire consequences for the organization, and for the survivability of a broadly defined social studies. Development of standards would, the thinking went, place social studies in a position to have some influence over the eventual standards and testing program and provide teachers with assistance in implementing the other diverse standards statements in state and local curricula.

In the early 1990s, NCSS president Margit McGuire and the board of directors launched a process by which a new definition for social studies would be crafted. The board wanted to establish a definition that was "concise, clearly stated, and consistent with sound democratic and participatory principles and with existing NCSS position statements and other documents." The board of directors, at its meeting in January 1992, crafted a brief definition statement to be circulated for comment and review. The initial statement read: "Social studies is the integration of history, the social sciences, and the humanities to promote civic competence."

After due consideration of comments from members and affiliates, in 1992 the board of directors adopted the following, two-part definition:

> Social studies is the integrated study of the social sciences and humanities to promote civic competence.
>
> Within the school program, social studies provides coordinated, systematic study drawing upon such disciplines as anthropology, archaeology, economics, geography, history, law, philosophy, political science, psychology, religion, and sociology, as well as appropriate content from the humanities, mathematics, and natural sciences. The primary purpose of social studies is to help young people develop the ability to make informed and reasoned decisions for the public good as citizens of a culturally diverse, democratic society in an interdependent world. (McGuire, 1992)

As the board worked with the comments and suggestions in the summer of 1992, it developed the compromise above, removing mention of any particular discipline from its initial sentence, and opting for a consensus definition that would alienate as few as possible. Also, it chose not to include any reference to social issues, social problems, or reflective methods of teaching in its definition.

Despite a worthy effort to state a clear definition and purpose, the aim of "civic competence" stopped far short of the long-held potential envisioned by progressive, reconstructionist, or critical educators that supported aims of "social improvement," "social justice," or "social transformation." The consensus position had been challenged by many social studies educators over the years. Nevertheless, it appeared to have staying power. The 1992 definition adopted by the NCSS board of directors seemed but a slightly revised, softened version of the Wesleyan definition from the 1930s. An NCSS Task Force for Social Studies Standards was created by the board of directors in 1992 and charged with development of a standards statement congruent with the new definition.

With congressional approval of the 1994 Goals 2000: Educate America Act, six national educational goals agreed upon by the nation's governors and the first Bush administration were formalized into law with minor changes. Although differences with America 2000 were in evidence, continuity was the notable theme (USDOE, 1995).

Changes to Goal 3 were significant, with a broader array of subject areas now included. In the social studies arena these included "civics or government" and "economics." Moreover, the Goals 2000 Act specified that state and local school districts were responsible for creation of their own goals and standards and that nationally produced standards statements, such as those in history, geography, and civics, were voluntary. Among the social studies disciplines, standards for history, geography, and civics were specifically mentioned. The NCSS Standards for Social Studies were not mentioned, and the term *social studies* was again nowhere to be found.

A STORM OF CONTROVERSY

During the early 1990s, groups of scholars and teachers were busy completing national standards for the schools in each of the core subject areas. The 1994 National History Standards were an outgrowth of thinking among many historians, that if standards were inevitable, it was better to be involved and have some influence.

Prior to its release, the *National Standards for United States History* swirled in a storm of controversy in the media, touched off by an editorial in the *Wall Street Journal* written by Lynne Cheney, the former chairperson of the National Endowment for the Humanities. Cheney charged that the standards were a loaded document whose "authors save their unqualified admiration for people, places, and events that are politically correct," and that the standards offered heavy doses of multiculturalism and obsession with such topics as McCarthyism (19 references), racism (the Ku Klux Klan is mentioned 17 times), and mistreatment of indigenous peoples, but gave little attention to some of the core developments and figures of American history (1994).

The talk-show host Rush Limbaugh echoed Cheney's critique, and he extended it by defining his own approach to the study of history:

> What? . . . history is an exploration? Let me tell you something, folks. History is real simple. You know what history is? It's what happened. It's no more. . . . The problem you get into is when guys like this [Gary Nash, the principal author] try to skew history by, "Well, let's interpret what happened because maybe we don't like the truth as it's presented. So let's change the interpretation a little bit so that it will be the way we wished it were." Well, that's not what history is. History is what happened, and history ought to be nothing more than what happened. Now, if you want to get into why what happened, that's probably valid too, but why what happened shouldn't have much of anything to do with what happened. (1994)

The Cheney and Limbaugh commentaries were accompanied by a stream of articles and editorials in the nation's media portraying the battle over the standards largely in terms of a political debate over what history should be taught in secondary school U.S. history courses, and how those courses should be taught. Critics suggested that the standards presented young learners with a grim picture of American history that cast every-thing European and American "as evil and oppressive" (Johnson & Avery, 1999, p. 457).

The storm of controversy continued into the halls of the U.S. Senate, where Slade Gorton, a Republican from the state of Washington, intro-duced an amendment to abolish the standards. The senate, in a voice vote of 99 to 1, rejected the standards. In his speech, Gorton contended that "these standards are ideology masquerading as history," and declared, " In order to stop this perverted idea in its tracks and to ensure that it does not become, de facto, a guide for our nation's classrooms, it must be publicly and officially repudiated by this Congress."

The standards were developed at the National Center for History in the Schools at the University of California, Los Angeles (UCLA), and were in two major categories: historical thinking skills and historical under-standings. The reports placed a strong emphasis upon moving students be-yond the passive approach of absorbing dates, facts, and concepts, and to-ward analysis of historical issues and decision making. On the whole, the standards made a strong effort at developing a workable, inquiry-based approach. For example, students were asked to find evidence, identify cen-tral questions, examine major social issues, and address moral questions. Some standards focused on historical thinking skills, including chronolog-ical thinking, historical comprehension, historical analysis and interpre-tation, historical research capabilities, and historical issues-analysis and decision making. These "thinking skills" were "integrated" into various standards throughout the volumes as they related to specific historical top-ics (National Center for History, 1994).

Unfortunately, critics focused on the illustrative classroom activities as if they were intended to provide a comprehensive, detailed list of the con-tent to be included. Nash and Dunn, lead authors of two of the volumes, charged that critics, by counting names mentioned in the illustrative activ-ities, made "a deliberate attempt to mislead the public that these guide-lines are textbooks, which of course they are not." Instead, the standards themselves included few names because they focused on "big ideas, move-ments, turning points, population shifts, economic transformations, wars and revolutions, religious movements, and so forth" (Nash & Dunn, 1995, p. 6). Moreover, critics "tried to link the standards in the public mind to ex-treme, left-wing revisionism, hoisting them as a useful symbol of all things un-American." The critics had scrawled "politically correct" across the standards and conducted "campaigns of disinformation" (pp. 5, 7).

Nash and his colleagues responded as scholars often do—they pro-duced a redraft. The revised *National Standards for History* combined the standards for U.S. history, world history, and K–4 into one volume, replacing the three volumes that had stirred such controversy. In this version, the authors wisely deleted the source of so much controversy, choosing to omit most of the teaching and class activity suggestions contained in the original volumes. It was a watered-down version designed not to offend. It had the desired impact, blunting the criticism of the earlier volumes and receiving a much more positive reception (Nash, Crabtree, & Dunn, 1997; Ravitch, 1997).

A Multitude of Standards Statements

During the years in which the standards were being developed, there were three concurrent projects for the development of standards in the broader social studies arena, each receiving federal funding from the U.S. Department of Education. These projects included the development of standards for the teaching of civics/government, geography, and history. Development of the NCSS standards received neither federal funds nor the official sanctions that went with them.

The National Standards for Civics and Government were developed by the Center for Civic Education, with support from the U.S. Department of Education and the Pew Charitable Trusts, and published in 1995. This document included content standards, a rationale, and a statement of standards for each relevant content area. The standards were organized around five major questions aimed to help students inquire into several important concepts related to civic life, the American political system, and the roles of citizens.

The work of the Geography Education Standards Project, which received support from the U.S. Department of Education and several geographic education societies, was published under the title *Geography for Life: National Geography Standards*. This book identified a set of voluntary benchmarks that every school and district could use as a guideline in developing its own curricula. It detailed 18 geography standards to be included in grades K–4, 5–8, and 9–12 and addressed geographic skills and student achievement. These two sets of standards received a much more positive reception from both policy makers and the general public than had the history standards. They were fewer in number than the history standards, and they were more specific regarding assessment of student learning.

As for the social studies standards, in the fall of 1993 a draft of the NCSS Standards for Social Studies was circulated by the Task Force on Curriculum Standards, and received a mixed reaction.

While many of those who worked on the standards statement felt that it offered a strong alternative to the standards statements coming from the disciplinary organizations, a number of others were critical of the standards for presenting a weak compromise on the curriculum, for suggesting thematic strands that were clearly disciplinary, and for failing to develop a fully issues-centered and interdisciplinary approach. The NCSS standards were published the following year under the title *Expectations of Excellence: Curriculum Standards for Social Studies* (1994).

By the mid-1990s the social studies arena had a number of national statements on appropriate curriculum standards. All the major national organizations in social studies had, through their actions, purchased the standards mentality. Some believed that it was good to have a voice in the developments, while others argued against involvement in a reform with whose assumptions they did not agree. However, as several scholars observed, the multitude of different standards statements from the various associations masked a lack of general consensus on the content of the curriculum, leaving the field in what appeared to be a continuing state of "fragmentation" and disarray (Buckles & Watts, 1998; Hartoonian, 1994).

In fact, many of the recommendations made in the standards documents were in conflict. The four sets of standards available by the spring of 1995 totaled 1,292 pages. The standards in both history and geography called for separate required courses in each subject in grades 5–12: historians wanted 6 full years of history, and geographers called for 2 required years of geography, as well as a senior elective. Both groups also argued that their standards should be fully integrated into the K–4 curriculum as well. Administrators, curriculum supervisors, teachers, and curriculum committees reported feeling overwhelmed by the prospects of designing a coherent K–12 curriculum based on the mass of separatist claims on the social studies portion of the school day (Risinger & Garcia, p. 227).

Because of the storm of controversy generated by the *National Standards for United States History* in 1994, the movement for uniform national standards and one nationwide assessment was apparently dead. By and large, the focus shifted to the states. In most areas, state and local standards were developed and by the late 1990s formed the basis for state and local assessments, mainly through standardized tests, based on a traditional pattern of subject organization.

Moreover, not everyone supported the standards movement. The first argument of many who opposed standards was that schools simply didn't need this kind of broad-brush fix. Opposition began to give rise to resistance to standards-based reform among many educators, and among some social studies educators. There was a growing literature of critique from various authors that included Alfie Kohn's *The Schools Our Children Deserve* (1999) and Susan Ohanian's *One Size Fits Few* (1999). There was increasing resistance from the public, from parents and teachers organizations, and from students who began to question the wisdom of standards and the imposition of high-stakes testing. A few students even refused to take the tests.

In addition, a number of social studies educators offered critiques of the movement toward standards and high-stakes testing. C. Frederick Risinger and Jesus Garcia (1995) complained that most of the standards statements contributed to increasing fragmentation and that they provided too little guidance on assessment of student learning. E. Wayne Ross (1996) maintained that the standards had diverted democracy and were heavily influenced by a small group of conservative foundations and academics and backed by the power of the federal government. These groups, he argued, were creating an ideological consensus striving to preserve a Eurocentric culture. Murry R. Nelson (1997) charged that the standards movement neglected large issues and constructs in the search for a simple, quick fix solution. He critiqued its focus on content and general lack of attention to teachers, students, and the nature of educational change. He also noted its congruence with the work of J. Franklin Bobbitt, one of the century's most prominent advocates of education for social efficiency, and concluded that the standards movement was doomed to failure. Kevin D. Vinson (1998) discussed the nascent opposition movement growing among the pedagogical and political left.

While the standards movement was transformed from the aim of national to state standards and continued to grow, along with the increasing focus on history, geography, and civics, and a growing juggernaut of bipartisan support, a diversity of other trends continued. Among these were increased interest in the use of computers and technology, constructivism, moral and character education, continuing interest in global education, growing interest in authentic assessment, a renewal of issues-centered approaches, and an emerging focus on education for social justice.

Despite the mainstream trend toward the disciplines brought by the revival of history and geography and the standards movement, advocates of issues-centered approaches to social studies experienced a revival of their own during the late 1980s and 1990s. Shirley H. Engle and Anna S. Ochoa published a major work in the meliorist, issues-centered tradition, *Education for Democratic Citizenship: Decision Making in the Social Studies,* which appeared in 1988. The book called for an approach to teaching centered around reflective thinking and decision making and for a curriculum focused on thematic strands.

The following years witnessed a growing number of conference sessions, journal publications, and books on issues-centered education or related topics. There was Walter Parker's *Educating the Democratic Mind* (1996), Wayne Ross's *The Social Studies Curriculum* (1997), and John A. Williams's *Classroom in Conflict* (1994). The flurry of activity culminated in the publication of the *Handbook on Teaching Social Issues* as an NCSS bulletin (Evans & Saxe, 1996). Despite this renewal of sorts, it appeared that the issues-centered, meliorist approach would remain a relatively minor refrain in the battles over the field.

This renewed attention to the issues-centered, meliorist tradition developed in the late 1980s and 1990s, seemingly at a time when it was largely out of step with the mainstream trends. As with the revival of history, a few interested and dedicated individuals were at the heart of the renewal. It offered a powerful alternative vision that could improve social studies teaching. The paradox was that it hadn't received more attention. During the 1990s a related strand in the long struggles over social studies, the critical/social reconstructionist camp, also seemed to receive an emerging boost in the literature of the field under the rubric of *education for social justice*. Perhaps these camps witnessed a resurgence as a counterpoint to the conservative restoration and the revival of history and geography to which it led.

EXPLAINING THE CONSERVATIVE RESTORATION

Although the modal pattern of the 1970s and 1980s appears to be largely intact at the turn of this century, the development of state standards and assessments has meant a good deal of variation by state, amid a general narrowing of the social studies curriculum. American history remains a near universal requirement in the high school, with a yearlong course required of nearly all students. American history is also taught in the middle school, with eighth grade the most common year. Most high school students also take a semester-long course in government, usually in the 12th grade. Also, there appears to have been a substantial increase in world history course requirements.

In general, a shift toward courses in the disciplines has occurred, particularly in those areas that have received standards-based endorsement in America 2000 and Goals 2000. Student credits in history, geography, government, and economics have increased substantially. Increases in these subjects have been accompanied by declining student credits in many of the other social sciences, and a number of elective courses with smaller enrollments have disappeared with the general trend toward consolidation in fewer offerings (NCES, 2001). In sum, the national reform movements promoting the revival of history and geography and a return to the disciplines have had a significant impact on course offerings and credits.

The problem set forth at the outset of this chapter was to explain the conservative restoration in schools and society that lay behind the revival of history and declining attention to reflective, issues-centered social studies. First, the educational reforms of the era, back to basics, the pursuit of excellence, and the revival of history were driven by educational, political, and economic forces outside of education. This was largely a response to a manufactured crisis, based on a faulty thesis and flawed assumptions, driven by those in power and in control of considerable financial resources from both governmental and private sources. New Right and neoconservative reformers were well organized, highly motivated, visible, articulate, and well funded. In part, the political trends culminating in the conservative restoration originated in reaction to the perceived excesses of reforms of the 1960s and 1970s.

Second, the conservative restoration was built on pervasive myths about American schooling and on the creation of a mythical golden age. In the larger realm, this took the form of the injunction that the schools as a whole were failing. Thus, proponents argued, back to basics, reassertion of tougher standards, and a return to more conservative traditions were in order. In the revival of history, the myth of a golden age was combined with the scapegoating of social studies as *the* factor that led to the supposed decline of history in schools. A return to the golden age meant a return to the familiar "grammar of schooling" and the belief that the only real social studies was traditional history.

Third, many of the objections to the reforms of the 1960s and 1970s were based on the very real, factual assessment that the reforms were not working. The failure of reforms in the era of the new and newer social studies created an easy target for criticism from the New Right, from neoconservatives, and from historians. In large part, the earlier reforms had failed because of the reformers' neglect in accounting for organizational barriers to school change. Barriers to the promotion of higher order thinking in social studies classrooms seemed endemic to schools. Among these were the pervasive conception of instruction as knowledge transmission, a curriculum focused on coverage, teachers' low expectations of students, large numbers of students per teacher, lack of sufficient planning time, and a culture of teacher isolation (Onosko, 1991). Additional constraints on teaching such as the length of the class period, the lack of readily available materials, and the content to be taught were typically influenced, if not mandated, by those outside the classroom. While teachers did have a good deal of discretion over classroom space, student grouping, classroom discourse, tools, and activities, these decisions could not escape at least two major dictates from outside: maintain order and get students to learn the required curriculum. These constraints resulted in a remarkable pattern of persistent instruction, of constancy marked by teacher-centered forms of pedagogy, especially at the secondary level (Cuban, 1984).

Moreover, these constraints were shaped by a remarkably resilient grammar of schooling that seemed to impose structural constraints on school reform. In the high school, for example, the grammar of schooling included hourly shifts from one subject and teacher to another, teachers and subjects divided into specialized departments and instructing 150 or more students a day in five classes, and students rewarded with grades and

Carnegie units. Over time we have seen little lasting change in the way schools divide time and space, classify students, allocate them into classrooms, splinter knowledge, and award grades. This standard grammar of schooling has proved remarkably durable, persisting partly because it enables teachers to perform their duties in a predictable and efficient fashion. Such established institutional forms take on a life of their own, becoming fixed by custom, legal mandates, and cultural beliefs until they are so ingrained that they are barely noticed. As Tyack and Cuban put it, "They become just the way schools are" (1995, p. 86).

Fourth, philosophically, the conservative restoration and the revival of history both served what were perceived as the traditional purposes of education. The more conservative members of the school culture and the public rose up and reasserted, at least for a time, more traditional forms of schooling. During the era of the new social studies, a significant number of students were being asked to question social structures. Now, instead of education for social criticism and independent thinking, it was education for socialization, social control, and creation of human capital. Many Americans, it seemed, did not want education to reform American society, but simply to restore its luster. Employers wanted the education of workers who were punctual, who would follow instructions, and who would not ask too many questions. Behind this was a public education that seemed to have more to do with maintaining the class structure than with opening opportunity. As one social studies luminary, Shirley Engle, suggested, "More of our citizens than we would like to think . . . do not want the schools to teach their children to think" (1989, p. 51).

The central theme in this most recent chapter in the history of social studies is increasing government involvement at previously unheard of levels with the onset of the standards movement and, with it, the creation of a technology to enforce a neoconservative vision of schooling and American life. If the schools are thought of as a machine, then the standards movement is a runaway train, a machine in the garden of American schooling— and prospects for redirecting the movement appear to be growing dim.

The standards movement, through its imposition of a technology of testing, may freeze out the possibility of alternative approaches to social studies aimed at creating a thoughtful citizenry, in favor of a more narrowly conceived history and social science curriculum. The entire standards endeavor is predicated on the misguided notion of schooling as a lever for improving the position of the United States in international economic competition. It has been strongly influenced and enhanced by "philanthropic" conservative interest groups such as the Heritage Foundation, the Hudson Institute, the American Enterprise Institute, and the Hoover Institution, and in social studies, the Bradley Foundation. Far right and neoconservative groups have coalesced to lead development of a national consensus favoring standards-based reform built on dubious assumptions and activities: human capital ideology, unprecedented crisis rhetoric, scapegoating, the specter of self-interest, the myth of American individualism, and the misuse and abuse of evidence: lies, propaganda, suppression of evidence, simplistic analyses, premature reporting, and press irresponsibility (Berliner & Biddle, 1995).

In the continuing struggle for social studies among camps, these developments could spell the death knell for more than one opposing camp. It certainly suggests a more complex arena, one with ever more imposing obstacles to experimentation and development of thoughtful practice. It also suggests an atmosphere in which democracy is increasingly endangered. In the battles over social studies, these developments imply the continued domination of the disciplines, and a full institutionalization of the war on social studies. In terms of the range of ideological perspectives and the multiplicity of voices present in the curriculum, they indicate a strong narrowing, concentrating on what can most readily be tested. Yet other voices with a stake in the battles over social studies won't go away easily. To quote Shirley Engle, a longtime advocate of a reflective, issues-centered approach to the field, "Possibly our day will come again" (personal communication, 1988).

The Continuing Struggle for Meaningful Learning

THE PATTERN OF the history of social studies during the 20th century is one of struggles over content and approaches to teaching. Like waves, the competing camps in the struggle are all present at any given time, with one wave rising and another falling. At times, certain camps, notably the meliorist and reconstructionist, have challenged mainstream culture, institutions, or ideologies. More often than not, such challenges led to attacks on social studies by small groups of vocal critics followed by mainstream skepticism or outright condemnation of social studies as a field. What began as a struggle among interest groups evolved into a war on social studies that has strongly influenced the direction of the curriculum. Instead of a broad and interdisciplinary social studies, we now have a more narrow focus on history and the social sciences. Rather than an inquiry- and issues-centered approach to instruction, the current trend is toward an emphasis on content acquisition. In classroom practice, the dominant trend over the 20th century had been education for social efficiency and social control. Why does the pattern of conflict exist? Is it healthy? How are we to understand it?

In part, it is a cultural war. At the level of ideals, visions, beliefs, and values, social studies movements have questioned American institutions and a segment of Americans' beliefs about the good way of life. Among the challenges to the prevailing American orthodoxy were those perceived in the Problems of Democracy course, Harold Rugg's textbook series, George Counts and education for social reconstructionism, the progressive education movement, MACOS and other portions of the new social studies movement, global education, and more recently, multiculturalism and critical pedagogy. In most cases, the challenges were not as threatening as critics made out. Yet legitimate social criticism was a significant element in each of these episodes in the history of social studies. Moreover, the prob-

lems, values, and commitments that motivated Rugg, Counts, and other reform-minded educators are as pertinent as ever.

As we have seen, from the inception of social studies in the early part
of the 20th century, challenging approaches to the field have met with severe criticism. Social studies as a field also faces many other serious dilemmas. Perhaps its central conundrum is the failure of classroom practice to
live up to the potential for interesting and engaging teaching worthy of the
social issues we face as citizens. In this book I have examined this dilemma
over time, chronicling the rhetorical and practical struggles over what subject matter should be taught and how it should be presented. Far from
simply being an academic matter, controversy over the teaching of social
studies in schools represents a tangible forum through which Americans
have struggled over competing visions of the good society and the future.
At its heart, this is a struggle over the nature of social studies and the kind
of society in which we want to live.

There are many perspectives on the nature of social studies, a few of
which have been very critical. In the 1940s, Allan Nevins described social
studies as the bogey responsible for declining attention to American history. His associate Hugh Russell Fraser viewed social studies as the unfortunate product of "extremists—from NCSS and its twin brother, Teachers
College." In the 1950s, Arthur Bestor described social studies as an anti-
intellectual "social stew." More recently, Diane Ravitch described it as "tot
sociology."

Over the history of social studies various camps have emerged with
competing approaches to social studies and differing visions of the worthy
society. These camps are multiple, overlapping, and not always distinct. As
I have described them, they include traditional history; social science, the
mandarins; education for social efficiency; social meliorism, progressive
and issues-centered; critical or social reconstructionist; and a consensus or
eclectic camp. The struggles among these camps over time makes for a dramatic story full of heroes and villains, influenced by the economy, war, perceived threats from abroad, the funding of commissions, moneyed interests, media campaigns, and interest group politics. My thesis is that what
began as a struggle among interest groups gradually evolved into a war
against progressive social studies that has profoundly influenced the current and future direction of the curriculum.

There are various perspectives on these ongoing cultural struggles.
They may be characterized as heroic battles between good and evil or as
dogmatic posturing that diverts the mainstream from realization of important goals (Gaddy et al., 1996; Jacoby, 1994). Previous scholars have described the pattern and paradox of curriculum change and stability and the
ever evolving issue-attention cycle (Lowe, 1979). Despite what seem con-

tinual debates and battles over the curriculum, it appears, paradoxically, to change very slowly. For the most part, both the content and pedagogy of the curriculum retain a constancy rooted in traditional practices (Cuban, 1984; Sarason, 1982). Educational procedure is marked by continuity and routine, by the persistence of recitation and other traditional approaches (Hoetker & Ahlbrand, 1969).

In recent years the educational system has moved toward becoming a more finely tuned machine, with the unstated aim of education for social efficiency. Creation of a technology of standards and high-stakes testing threatens to freeze out alternative visions and create a one-dimensional curriculum supporting social control (Marcuse, 1964). The powerful alignment of conservative foundations, subject matter associations, and state and federal governments behind a discipline-based social studies makes this prospect more ominous and imaginable than ever.

On the whole, however, the history of social studies in schools over the past century suggests that, at least for the foreseeable future, we may be saddled with an unending dilemma, competing camps engaged in turf wars over the future of the social studies curriculum. This state of affairs reflects the inherent permeability of the field to curriculum politics and illustrates the bureaucratic nature of schools, which continue to stubbornly deflect attempts at reform. Thus, social studies is conflicted, with different visions competing for prominence in the literature of a century-long debate.

Strength or weakness, turf struggles and the severe criticism they have spawned are a way of life in social studies and have been the pattern of the 20th century. The result of the pattern is the continuing failure of curricular reform and the operation of school social studies at a low level. Nonetheless, over the history of social studies attempts at progressive reform have made some difference. The Problems of Democracy course, the Rugg social studies program, and the new social studies all made inroads in classroom practice in some schools and with some teachers. However, in each case, reforms met limited success because reformers underestimated the persistence of the grammar of schooling, basic aspects of schools, classrooms, and teaching that seem to defy change and to deflect attempts at reform.

What might make a difference in the future? A more open dialogue among the camps in the struggle over social studies could help make a difference. It could lead to a more balanced approach to reform, built around alternative conceptions of social studies with teachers and school districts encouraged to explore alternative paths. Unfortunately, much of the dialogue in the field has been clouded by cheerleading for various programs, by the unfortunate use of propaganda techniques, and by the influence of well-financed, highly visible, and vocal interest groups. Deep and sustained reflection on the purposes of social studies practice could also make a difference as teachers, administrators, curriculum supervisors, and policy makers try to sort out various reforms against the backdrop of curriculum history.

The key question haunting social studies remains the issue of its definition and its vision, and of the approaches to the field that will be practiced in schools. For meaningful resolution, the struggles over social studies deserve a full and complete airing, in a public forum—shorn of the propaganda, scapegoating, and interest group financing we have seen during the field's recent history—in an effort to advance forms of social studies practice that will contribute to the goal of meaningful learning. This might be undertaken in the hope that each educator, institution, and state curriculum task force facing decisions on this most important of its functions can reach a rational, meaningful, and democratically developed decision on the approach to social studies that it will choose to embody in curricular programs.

References

Abbott, H. E. (1941, September 16). Letter to Wilbur Murra, Executive Secretary, NCSS. File 1, Box 45, Series 4C, Executive Director Correspondence with Organizations, NCSS Archive.

Addams, J. (1907). The influence of the foreign population on the teaching of history and civics. *Proceedings of the North Central History Teachers' Association.* Chicago: North Central History Teacher's Association, pp. 3–4.

Adler, M. J. (1941, September). "Progressive education"? No! *The Rotarian,* pp. 29–30, 56–57.

Albrecht-Carrie, R. (1952). The social sciences and history. *Social Education, 16,* 315–318.

Alilunias, L. J. (1958). Bestor and the "social studies." *Social Education, 22,* 238–240.

Alilunas, L. J. (1964). Whither the Problems of Democracy course? *Social Education, 28,* 11–14.

Allen, M. L. (1956). *Education or indoctrination.* Caldwell, OH: Caxton Printers.

American Economic Association. (1924). Report of the Joint Commission on the Presentation of Social Studies in the Schools. *Papers and Proceedings of the 36th Annual Meeting of the American Economic Association, 14,* 177–182.

American Historical Association. (1899). *The study of history in schools: Report by the Committee of Seven.* New York: Macmillan.

American Historical Association. (1904). Proceedings of Chicago meeting: Conference on public school history teachers. *Annual Report, 1904,* 27–30.

American Historical Association. (1908). Proceedings. *Annual Report, 1908,* 65, 71.

American Historical Association. (1909a). Proceedings: Presidential address—William Sloane. *Annual Report, 1909,* 70.

American Historical Association. (1909b). *The study of history in elementary schools: The report of the Committee of Eight.* New York: Charles Scribner's Sons.

American Historical Association. (1910). The study of history in secondary schools: The report of the Committee of Five. *Annual Report, 1910,* 230–231.

American Historical Association. (1941). Freedom of textbooks. *Social Education, 5,* 487–488.

American history survey. (1943, April 4). Editorial. *New York Times,* p. 10 E.

American Political Science Association. (1916). *The teaching of government: Report to the American Political Science Association by the Committee on Instruction.* New York: Macmillan.

American Political Science Association. (1922). The study of civics. *Historical Out-look, 12,* 42–46.

Anderson, A. W. (1952a). The charges against American education: What is the ev-idence? *Progressive Education, 29,* 91–105.

Anderson, A. W. (1952b). The cloak of respectability: The attackers and their meth-ods. *Progressive Education, 29,* 68–81.

Anderson, H. R. (1941). The social studies, patriotism, and teaching democracy. *So-cial Education, 5,* 9–14.

Anderson, H. R. (1950). Offerings and registrations in social studies. *Social Educa-tion, 14,* 73–75.

Anderson, L. F. (1982). Barriers to change in social studies. In I. R. Morrissett, C. Hawk, & D. Superka (Eds.), *The current state of social studies: A report of project SPAN.* Boulder, CO: Social Science Education Consortium.

Announcement for Project Social Studies. (1962). *Social Education, 26,* 300.

Anthony, A. S. (1967). The role of objectives in the "new history." *Social Education, 31,* 574, 580.

Armstrong, O. K. (1940, September). Treason in the textbooks. *American Legion Magazine,* pp. 8, 9, 51, 70–72.

Arnoff, M. (1969, January 24). Letter and manuscript from Melvin Arnoff to Shirley Engle. Impromptu Speakout: NCSS Conference, 1968. Box 6, Papers of Shirley Engle, Series 4B, NCSS Archive.

Ashley, R. L. (1920). Present day tendencies in the teaching of social sciences in the high school. *Proceedings of the Mississippi Valley Historical Association, 10,* 491–505.

Association of History Teachers of Middle States and Maryland. (1904). Meeting of History Teachers' Association. *The Educational Review, 27,* 428–431.

Archibald, G. H. (1976, May 16). George H. Archibald speaking at the NCSS Wing-spread Conference. Wingspread Conference Center, Racine, Wisconsin. File: Wingspread Conference, Box 2, Accession #850625, NCSS Archive.

Atomic Information Committee. (1946). Various articles on threat of atomic bomb. File 1, Box 17, Series 4C, Director's Files, NCSS Archive.

Attacks on education [Special issue]. (1952, January). *Progressive Education, 29.*

Attacks on education [Special issue]. (1953, June). *Phi Delta Kappan, 34.*

Avery, C. K. (1957). The problem in problem solving. *Social Education, 21,* 165–166.

Back to basics in the schools. (1974, October 21). *Newsweek,* pp. 87–93.

Bagley, W. C. (1938). An essentialist platform for the advancement of American ed-ucation. *EducationalAdministration and Supervision, 24,* 241–256.

Ballou, F. W. (1934, May 21). Statement of Superintendent Frank W. Ballou concern-ing his reasons for not signing the report of the Commission on the Investiga-tion of History and the Other Social Studies of the American Historical Asso-ciation. File: Commission on Social Studies, Box 1, Accession #850001, NCSS Archive.

Banks, J. A. (1969). Relevant social studies for Black pupils. *Social Education, 33,* 66–68.

Banks, J. A. (1999). Multicultural education in the new century. *School Administra-tor, 56,* 8–10.

Barnard, J. L., et al. (1915). *The teaching of Community Civics.* Washington, D.C.: United States Bureau of Education, Bulletin No. 23.

Barnes, H. E. (1934, May 13). The liberal viewpoint. *New York World Tribune.* File: Commission on Social Studies, Box 1, NCSS Office Files, 1921–1978, NCSS Archive.

Barrow, R. (1978). *Radical education: A critique of freeschooling and deschooling.* New York: John Wiley and Sons.

Beard, C. A. (1929). The trend in social studies. *The Historical Outlook, 20,* 369–372.

Beard, C. A. (1932). *A charter for the social sciences in the schools.* New York: Charles Scribner's Sons.

Becker, J. M. (1965). Prospect for change in the social studies. *Social Education, 29,* 20–22.

Berelson, B. (Ed.). (1963). *The social sciences and the social studies.* New York: Harcourt, Brace, and World, 1962.

Berliner, D., & Biddle, B. J. (1995). *The manufactured crisis: Myths, fraud, and the attack on America's public schools.* Reading, MA: Addison-Wesley.

Bestor, A. (1953). *Educational wastelands: The retreat from learning in our public schools.* Urbana: University of Illinois Press.

Bloom, A. (1987). *The closing of the American mind: How higher education has failed democracy and impoverished the souls of today's students.* New York: Simon and Schuster.

Bobbitt, F. (1934, August 18). Questionable recommendations of the Commission on the Social Studies. *School and Society, 40,* 201–208.

Bode, B. H. (1935). Which way democracy? *The Social Studies, 25,* 343–346.

Book burnings. (1940, September 9). *Time,* 64–65.

Boozer, H. R. (1960). *The American Historical Association and the schools, 1884-1956.* Unpublished doctoral dissertation, Washington University, St. Louis.

Bowers, C. A. (1969). *The progressive educator and the depression: The radical years.* New York: Random House.

Bracey, G. W. (1991). Why can't they be like we were? *Phi Delta Kappan, 73,* 104–117.

Bradley Commission. (1988). *Building a history curriculum: Guidelines for teaching history in schools.* Washington, DC: Educational Excellence Network.

Branson, M. S. (1977). The status of social studies: Marin County. *Social Education, 41,* 591–594.

Breeding communism. (1935, September). *Philadelphia Evening Bulletin.* File 2, Comment on AHA Commission on Social Studies, Box 2, Series 10, NCSS Archive.

Broder, D. (1976). *Life adjustment education: An historical study of a program of the United States Office of Education, 1945–1954.* Unpublished doctoral dissertation, Teachers College, Columbia University, New York.

Brodinsky, B. (1982). The New Right: The movement and its impact. *Phi Delta Kappan, 64,* 87 94.

Brown, C. G. (1930). Proceedings of the Commission on Secondary Schools. *The North Central Association Quarterly, 5,* 102.

Bruner, J. (1960). *The process of education.* Cambridge: Harvard University Press.

Bruner, J. (1971). The process of education revisited. *Phi Delta Kappan, 53*, 18–21.

Buckles, S., & Watts, M. (1998). National standards in economics, history, social studies, civics, and geography: Complementarities, competition, or peaceful coexistence? *Journal of Economic Education, 29*, 157–166.

Burgess, C., & Borrowman, M. L. (1969). *What doctrines to embrace.* Glenview, IL: Scott, Foresman.

Campbell, D. (1988). California Framework, letter to editor. *Social Education, 52*, 403.

Carbone, P. F. (1977). *The social and educational thought of Harold Rugg.* Durham, NC: Duke University Press, 1977.

Carbone, P. F., Jr., & Wilson, V. S. (1995). Harold Rugg's social reconstructionism. In Michael James (Ed.), *Social reconstructionism through education* (pp. 57–88). Norwood, NJ: Ablex.

Carp, R. A. (1968). Censorship pressure on social studies teachers. *Social Education, 32*, 487, 488, 492.

Carr, W. G. (1940, November). This is not treason. *The Journal of the National Education Association.* Reprint, File 7, Box 45, Series 4C, Director's Correspondence, NCSS Archive.

Cartwright, W. H. (1957). Presidential address: The social studies—scholarship and pedagogy. File 1, Box 4, Series 4B, NCSS Archive.

Cartwright, W. H., & Watson, R. L., Jr. (Eds.). (1961). *Interpreting and teaching American history.* Washington, DC: National Council for the Social Studies.

Cheney, L. V. (1987). *American memory: A report on the humanities in the nation's public schools.* Washington, DC: National Endowment for the Humanities.

Cheney, L. V. (1994, October 20). The end of history. *The Wall Street Journal*, p. A22.

Citizenship Education Project. (1952). *Premises of American liberty.* New York: Teachers College.

Citizenship Education Project. (1955). *When men are free: Premises of American liberty.* Boston: Houghton Mifflin.

Clark, T. (1975). The West Virginia textbook controversy: A personal account. *Social Education, 9*, 216–219.

Commission on Social Studies of the American Historical Association (1934). *Conclusions and recommendations.* New York: Charles Scribner's Sons.

Commission on Wartime Policy of NCSS. (1943). The social studies mobilize for victory. *Social Education, 7*, 3–10.

Conlan, J. B. (1975). MACOS: The push for a uniform national curriculum. *Social Education, 39*, 388–392.

Counts, G. S. (1932). *Dare the school build a new social order?* New York: John Day.

Cox, P. W. L. (1922). Social studies in the secondary school curriculum. *Sixth Yearbook, National Association of Secondary School Principals, 6*, 126–132.

Cremin, L. (1961). *The transformation of the school.* New York: Knopf.

Cuban, L. (1984). *How teachers taught: Constancy and change in American classrooms, 1890–1980.* New York: Longman.

Cuban, L. (1991). History of teaching in social studies. In J. P. Shaver (Ed.), *Handbook of research on social studies teaching and learning* (pp. 197–209). New York: Macmillan.

Curti, M. (1941, October 14). Merle Curti to Wilbur Murra. File 1, Box 2, Series 7, Committee Records, Academic Freedom Correspondence, NCSS Archive.

Cutts, B. (1972, May 19). Educators won't finance textbook: But "Americans" is not Banned. *The Atlanta Constitution*, p. 6A.

Dahl, E. J. (1928). Chaos in the senior high social studies. *The High School Teacher, 1928,* 185–188.

Dannelly, C. M. (1941). Facing a major threat. *The School Executive, 60,* 32.

Dawson, E. B. (1922). Characteristic elements of the social studies. *Historical Outlook, 13,* 327, 337.

Dawson, E. B. (1924). The history inquiry. *Historical Outlook, 15,* 268.

Dawson, E. B. (1926). The social studies in grade 12. *Historical Outlook, 17,* 157–161.

Dawson, E. B. (1927). *Teaching the social studies.* New York: Macmillan.

Dawson, E. B. (1929). Efforts toward reorganization. *Historical Outlook, 20,* 372–375.

Dawson, E. B. (1940, December 22). Edgar Dawson postcard to Wilbur Murra. Box 5, Series 4B, NCSS Archive.

Dewey, J. (1897). Ethical principles underlying education. *The third yearbook of the national Herbart society for the scientific study of teaching.* Chicago: University of Chicago Press, pp. 7–34.

Dewey, J. (1899). *The school and society.* Chicago: University of Chicago Press.

Dewey, J. (1916). *Democracy and education.* New York: Macmillan.

Dewey, J. (1938). *Experience and education.* New York: Collier.

DiBona, J. (1982). The intellectual repression of the cold war. *Educational Forum, 46,* 343–355.

Dilling, E. (1934). *The red network.* Kenilworth, IL: Author.

Dow, P. B. (1975). MACOS revisited: A commentary on the most frequently asked questions about man: A course of study. *Social Education, 39,* 388, 393–398.

Dow, P. B. (1991). *Schoolhouse politics: Lessons from the Sputnik era.* Cambridge, MA: Harvard University Press.

Drafts of NCSS Constitutions. (1921–1940). File 1, Box 1, Series 1, NCSS Archive.

Drost, W. H. (1967). *David Snedden and education for social efficiency.* Madison: University of Wisconsin Press.

Editor. (1920). Notes from the historical field: N.E.A. Committee on Social Studies. *Historical Outlook, 11,* 203.

Editor. (1934). Notes and news. *The Social Studies, 25,* 84–85.

Editor. (1936). Notes and news: Portland meeting, tentative program. *The Social Studies, 27,* 349.

Editor. (1980). Discussion and debate on new proposals for the social studies curriculum. *Social Education, 44.*

Eherenreich, B. (1997). *Blood rites: Origins and history of the passions of war.* New York: Henry Holt.

Eliot, C. W. (1894). The unity of educational reform. *The Educational Review, 8,* 209–226.

Elson, R. M. (1964). *Guardians of tradition: American schoolbooks of the 19th century.* Lincoln: University of Nebraska Press.

Engle, S. H. (1947). Factors in the teaching of our persistent modern problems. *Social Education, 11*, 167–169.

Engle, S. H. (1960). Decision making: The heart of social studies instruction. *Social Education, 24*, 301–306.

Engle, S. H. (1963). Thoughts in regard to revision. *Social Education, 27*, 182.

Engle, S. H. (1979, February 15). Cited in Previte, M. A. (1997). *Shirley H. Engle: A persistent voice for social education.* Paper presented at the annual meeting of the Foundations of the Social Studies Special Interest Group, Cincinnati, OH.

Engle, S. H. (1989). Whatever happened to the social studies? *International Journal of Social Education, 4*, 51.

Engle, S. H. (1990). The Commission Report and citizenship education. *Social Education, 54*, 431–434.

Engle, S. H., & Ochoa, A. S. (1988). *Education for democratic citizenship: Decision making in the social studies.* New York: Teachers College.

Evans, R. W. (1989). Diane Ravitch and the revival of history: A critique. *The Social Studies, 80*, 85–88.

Evans, R. W., & Saxe, D. W. (Eds.). (1996). *Handbook on teaching social issues.* Washington, DC: National Council for the Social Studies, Bulletin #93.

Fenton, E. P. (1964). *32 problems in world history.* Glenview, IL: Scott, Foresman.

Fenton, E. (1991). Reflections on the "new social studies." *The Social Studies, 82*, 84–90.

Fenton, E. P., & Good, J. M. (1965). Project social studies: A progress report. *Social Education, 29*, 206–208.

Fersh, G. L., Ed. (1955). *The problems approach in the social studies.* Washington, DC: National Council for the Social Studies.

Fine, B. (1941, February 22). Un-American tone seen in textbooks on social sciences. *New York Times*, pp. 1, 6 [Late city edition].

Fine, B. (1943, April 4). Ignorance of U.S. history shown by college freshmen. *New York Times*, pp. 1, 32–33.

Fink, W. B. (1955). The split within our ranks. *Social Education, 19*, 9–10.

Finney, R. L. (1920). Tentative report of the Committee on the Teaching of Sociology in the Grade and High Schools of America. *The School Review, 28*, 255–262.

Finney, R. L. (1924). What do we mean by "Community Civics" and "Problems of Democracy?" *The School Review, 32*, 521–528.

Flynn, J. T. (1951). Who owns your child's mind? *The Reader's Digest*, pp. 23–28.

Forbes, B. C. (1939, August 15). Treacherous teaching. *Forbes*, p. 8.

Franklin, B. M. (1987). The social efficiency movement and curriculum change, 1939–1976. In T. Popkewitz (Ed.), *The formation of the school subjects: The struggle for creating an American institution.* New York: Falmer.

Fraser, D. M. (1955). The NCSS at work. *Social Education, 19*, 104.

Fraser, D. M. (1957, June 16). Dorothy Fraser to Mac, Merrill, and Howard. Box 8, Series 2B, Board of Director Minutes, Committee Reports, NCSS Archive.

Fraser quits post in history dispute. (1943, April 11). *New York Times*, p. 30.

Freire, P. (1970). *Pedagogy of the oppressed.* New York: Continuum.

Frymier, J. R. (1955). A new approach to teaching history? *The Social Studies, 46*, 255–257.

Fuller, W. D. (1941, February 24). Telegram to Wilbur Murra. File 1, Box 2, Series 7, Committee Records, Academic Freedom Correspondence, NCSS Archive.

Gaddy, B. B., et al. (1996). *School wars: Resolving our conflicts over religion and values*. San Francisco: Jossey-Bass.

Gagnon, P. (1988, November). Why study history? *Atlantic Monthly*, pp. 43–66.

Gagnon, P. (Ed.). (1989). *Historical literacy: The case for history in American education*. New York: Macmillan

Gambrill, J. M. (1921, April 19). Temporary constitution, attached. File 8, Box 7, President's Correspondence, Series 4B, NCSS Archive.

Gambrill, J. M. (1924). Some tendencies and issues in the making of social studies curricula. *Historical Outlook, 15*, 84–89.

Gell, K. (1934). Implications of the report of the Commission on Social Studies of the American Historical Association as it affects the high school teacher. *The Social Studies, 25*, 289, 291.

Get adjusted. (1947, December 15). *Time*, p. 64.

Giles, H. H., McCutchen, S. P., & Zechiel, A. N. (1942). *Exploring the curriculum: The work of the thirty schools from the viewpoint of curriculum consultants*. New York: Harper & Brothers.

Goetz, W. W. (1995). The rise and fall of MACOS: A blip on the historical screen? *Theory and Research in Social Education, 23*, 515–522.

Gold, H. M. (1917). Methods and content of courses in history in the high schools of the United States. *School Review, 25*, 88–100.

Goodier, F. T. (1926). The Rugg plan of teaching history. *High School Conference, 1926*, 323–327.

Goodman, P. (1960). *Growing up absurd: Problems of youth in the organized system*. New York: Random House.

Goodman, P. (1966). *Compulsory mis-education, and The community of scholars*. New York: Vintage Books.

Gould, K. M. (1941, Autumn). The war on social studies. *Common Ground*, pp. 83–91.

Greenawald, D. (1995). Maturation and change, 1947–1968. *Social Education, 59*, 416–428.

Griffin, A. (1942). *A philosophical approach to the subject matter preparation of teachers of history*. (Unpublished doctoral dissertation, Ohio State University, Columbus).

Gross, R. (1971). From innovations to alternatives: A decade of change in education. *Phi Delta Kappan, 70*, 22–24.

Gross, R. E. (1988). Forward to the trivia of 1890: The impending social studies program? *Phi Delta Kappan, 70*, 47–49.

Gross, R. E., & Allen, D. W. (1958). Upside down but not backwards: Beginning U.S. history with a unit on current events. *The Social Studies, 49*, 180–184.

Gross, R. E., Muessig, R., & Fersh, G. L. (Eds.). (1960). *The problems approach in the social studies*. Washington, DC: National Council for the Social Studies.

Guenther, J., & Hansen, P. (1977). Organizational change in the social studies: Mini-course subject options. *Educational Leadership, 34*, 64–68.

Gutek, G. (1986). *Education in the United States: An historical perspective*. Englewood Cliffs, NJ: Prentice-Hall.

Haas, J. D. (1977). *The era of the new social studies.* Boulder, CO: Social Science Education Consortium.

Haefner, J. H. (1942). The historical approach to controversial issues. *Social Education, 6,* 267–269.

Hall, T. L. (1953). A study of the teaching of controversial issues in the secondary schools of the state of Ohio. Unpublished doctoral dissertation, Ohio State University, Columbus.

Halsey, V. R., Jr. (1963). American history: A new high school course. *Social Education, 27,* 249–252.

Hartoonian, M. (1994). National standards: A common purpose. *Social Education, 58,* 4.

Hartshorn, M. (1947–1972). Files on communism. File 1: Communism, Box 3, Series 4D, NCSS Archive.

Hartshorn, M. (1953, February 4). Memo from Hartshorn to members of the board of directors and the Academic Freedom Committee. File 2, Academic Freedom, Box 2, Series 7, NCSS Archive.

Hartshorn, M. (1965, December 29). Letter from Merrill Hartshorn to Rose M. Brennan, Torrington, Conn. H.S. File 4, Citizenship Education Committee, 1958–1966, Box 3, Series 7, NCSS Archive.

Hartshorn, M. (1972, May 1). Memo from Merrill Hartshorn to NCSS Legal Defense Fund. File: Sterzing Case Correspondence and Clippings, Box 44, Series 4D, NCSS Archive.

Harvard Committee. (1945). *General education in a free society: Report of the Harvard Committee.* Cambridge, MA: Harvard University Press.

Harvard University. (1941, January). Statement of Harvard Graduate School of Education group. *Educational Cooperation Bulletin* (NAM), p. 1.

Harvill, H. (1954). Eight advantages of the core organization. Social Education, *18,* 4–6.

Hentoff, N. (1966). *Our children are dying.* New York: Viking Press.

Herndon, J. (1968). *The way it spozed to be.* New York: Simon and Schuster.

Hertzberg, H. W. (1981). *Social studies reform, 1880–1980.* Boulder, CO: Social Science Education Consortium.

Hill, E. H. (1901). The teaching of social sciences in secondary school. *Education, 21,* 497–502.

Hirsch, E. D., Jr. (1987). *Cultural literacy: What every American needs to know.* Boston: Houghton Mifflin.

History and "social studies." (1943, April 4). Editorial. *New York Times,* p. 24.

Hoetker, J., & Ahlbrand, W. P., Jr. (1969). The persistence of the recitation. *American Educational Research Journal, 6,* 145–167.

Hofstadter, R. (1963). *Anti-intellectualism in American life.* New York: Alfred A. Knopf.

Holt, J. (1964). *How children fail.* New York: Pitman.

Holt, J. (1967). *How children learn.* New York: Pitman.

Hook, S. (1949, February 27). Should Communists be permitted to teach? *New York Times Magazine,* pp. 7, 22, 24, 26, 28–29.

Huelskamp, R. M. (1993). Perspectives on education in America. *Phi Delta Kappan, 75,* 718–721.

Hughes, R. O. (1934). Implications of the report of the Commission on Social Studies of the American Historical Association. *The Social Studies, 25,* 285–288.

Hunt, E. M. (1941a). Dr. Robey versus the NAM? *Social Education, 5,* 288–292.

Hunt, E. M. (1941b). The manufacturers and the textbooks. *Social Education, 5,* 88–89.

Hunt, E. M. (1941c). The NAM restates its policy. *Social Education, 5,* 328.

Hunt, E. M. (1941d). Twenty-five years of Problems of Democracy. *Social Education, 5,* 507–511.

Hunt, E. M. (1942a). American history in democratic education. *Social Education, 6,* 346–353.

Hunt, E. M. (1942b, October 25). History charges called untrue. *New York Times,* p. 6D.

Hunt, E. M. (1942c). More American history? *Social Education, 6,* 250–252.

Hunt, E. M. (1942d, October 16). Reply to Nevins, Box 4, Series 4D, American History Controversy, Correspondence, 1941–1943, NCSS Archive.

Hunt, E. M. (1943). The New York Times "Test" on American history. *Social Education, 7,* 199–200, 240.

Hunt, M. P., & Metcalf, L. E. (1955). Teaching high school social studies: Problems in reflective thinking and social understanding. New York: Harper & Brothers.

Hutchins, R. M. (1953). *The conflict in education in a democratic society.* New York: Harper.

Huxley, A. (1946). *Brave new world.* New York: Harper and Brothers.

Illich, I. (1971). *Deschooling society.* New York: Harper and Row.

Jacoby, R. (1994). *Dogmatic wisdom: How the culture wars divert education and distract America.* New York: Doubleday.

Jessen, C. A., & Herlihy, L. B. (1938). *Offerings and registrations in high-school subjects, 1930–34.* Washington, DC: U. S. Office of Education, Bulletin No. 6.

Johnson, H. (1917). The school course in history: Some precedents and a possible next step. Proceedings of the Conference of Teachers of History. *Annual Report of the American Historical Association, 1917,* 219–229.

Johnson, H. (1921). Report of Committee on History and Education for Citizenship: Part II, History in the grades. *Historical Outlook, 12,* 93–95.

Johnson, H. (1940). *Teaching of history in elementary and secondary schools with application to allied studies.* New York: Macmillan.

Johnson, T., & Avery, P. G. (1999). The power of the press: A content and discourse analysis of the United States history standards as presented in selected newspapers. *Theory and Research in Social Education, 27,* 447–471.

Jones, E. (1954). Analysis of social studies requirements. *Social Education, 18,* 257–258.

Jones, K., & Olivier, R. (1956). *Progressive education is REDucation.* Boston: Meador.

Jones, T. J. (1913). *Social studies in secondary schools: Preliminary recommendation by the Committee of the National Education Association.* Washington, DC: U.S. Government Printing Office, United States Bureau of Education, Bulletin No. 41.

Jordan, P. D. (Ed.). (1942). The *New York Times* survey of United States history. *Mississippi Valley Historical Review, 29*, 238–242.

Judge denies dismissal plea. (1970, February 11). *Grand Island Independent.*

Kappan. (1935, January). Report published in *Phi Delta Kappan, 17*, 106–107.

Karl, B. D. (1974). *Charles E. Merriam and the study of politics.* Chicago: University of Chicago Press.

Karier, C. (1986). *The individual, society, and education.* Urbana: University of Illinois Press.

Keels, O. M. (1988). Herbert Baxter Adams and the influence of the American Historical Association on the early social studies. *International Journal of Social Education, 3*, 37–49.

Keller, C. R. (1961, September 16). Needed: Revolution in the social studies. *Saturday Review,* 60–62.

Kepner, T. (1940, December 12). Letter to Messrs. Anderson, Hunt, Murra, Rugg, Wesley. File 1, Box 2, Series 7, Committee Records, Academic Freedom Correspondence, NCSS Archive.

Kerrison, I. L., & Hughes, R. O. (1944). A positive philosophy for the social studies: Two interpretations. *Social Education, 8*, 79–81.

Kidd, J. W. (1953). Social science or social studies. *Social Education, 17*, 207.

King, E. J. (1930). The motivation of current events in connection with American history. *The Historical Outlook, 21*, 226–227.

Kingsley, C. (1913). *The reorganization of secondary education: Preliminary report of the Commission on the Reorganization of Secondary Education of the National Education Association.* Washington, DC: U.S. Government Printing Office, United States Bureau of Education, Bulletin No. 41.

Kirkendall, R. S. (1975). The status of history in the schools. *Journal of American History, 62*, 557–570.

Kochheiser, C. (1975). What happened when a speaker for gay liberation addressed high school students. *Social Education, 39*, 219–221.

Kliebard, H. M. (1986). *The struggle for the American curriculum, 1893–1958.* Boston: Routledge & Keegan Paul.

Kliebard, H. M. (1996). *The struggle for the American curriculum, 1893–1958.* London: Routledge.

Kohn, A. (1999). *The schools our children deserve: Moving beyond traditional classrooms and "tougher standards."* Boston: Houghton Mifflin.

Kolko, G. (1968). *The politics of war: The world and United States foreign policy, 1943–1945.* New York: Random House.

Koos, L. V. (1917). *The administration of secondary school units.* Chicago: University of Chicago Press.

Kozol, J. (1967). *Death at an early age.* Boston: Houghton Mifflin.

Krug, E. A. (1964). *The shaping of the American high school, 1880–1920.* Madison: University of Wisconsin Press.

Krug, E. A. (1972). *The shaping of the American high school: Vol. 2, 1920–1941.* Madison: University of Wisconsin Press.

Krug, M. M. (1966). Bruner's new social studies: A critique. *Social Education, 30*, 400–406.

Lansner, K. (Ed.). (1958). *Second rate brains.* New York: Doubleday News Books.

Latimer, J. (1958). *What's happened to our high schools?* Washington, DC: U.S. Office of Education.

Leinwand, G. (1968). The year of the non-curriculum: A proposal. *Social Education, 32,* 542–545, 549.

Leinwand, G. (Ed.). (1968–1969). Problems of American society [series]. New York: Washington Square Press.

Leming, J. S. (1989). The two cultures of social studies education. *Social Education, 53,* 404–408.

Lengel, J. G., & Superka, D. (1982). Curriculum organization in social studies. In I. R. Morrissett (Ed.)., *The current state of social studies: A report of Project SPAN* (pp. 26–103). Boulder, CO: Social Science Education Consortium.

Lester, S. (1989). An analytic critique of the 1987 framework. *Social Studies Review, 28,* 52–61.

Letter to Editor. (1979a). Diffusion doesn't equal change. *Social Education, 33,* 484.

Letter to Editor. (1979b). Real vs. ideal. *Social Education, 33,* 414.

Lillibridge, G. D. (1958). History in the Public Schools. *Social Education, 22,* 110–115.

Limbaugh, R. (1994, October 28). Transcript from the Rush Limbaugh television show.

Lowe, W. B. (1979). Curriculum change and stability. *Educational Researcher, 8,* 12–18.

Lybarger, M. (1981). *Origins of the social studies curriculum, 1865–1916.* Unpublished doctoral dissertation, University of Wisconsin, Madison.

Lynd, A. (1953). *Quackery in the public schools.* Boston: Little, Brown.

Lynd, H., & Lynd, R. M. (1929). *Middletown.* New York: Harcourt, Brace.

Lynd, R. S. (1927). What are "social studies." *School and Society, 25,* 216–219.

Marcuse, H. (1964). *One-dimensional man: Studies in the ideology of advanced industrial nations.* Boston: Beacon Press.

Martz, C. E. (1924). The place of history in a new social studies program. *Historical Outlook, 15,* 71–73.

Massialas, B. G. (1963). Revising the social studies: An inquiry-centered approach. *Social Education, 27,* 185–189.

Massialas, B. G., & Cox, B. (1966). *Inquiry in the social studies.* New York: McGraw-Hill.

Matthews, J. (1975, June 10). Fired teacher settles for $40,000. *Washington Star,* A2.

McAulay, J. D. (1960). Two major problems in the teaching of the social studies. *The Social Studies, 51,* 135–139.

McCutchen, S. P. (1947). The problems approach to the social studies. *Journal of Educational Sociology, 20,* 529–536.

McGrath, E. J. (1951a). *Life adjustment education for every youth.* Washington, DC: U.S. Office of Education.

McGrath, E. J. (1951b). *Vitalizing secondary education: Report of the First Commission in Life Adjustment Education for Youth.* Washington, DC: U.S. Office of Education.

McGuire, M. (1992). Definition of social studies papers submitted by Margit McGuire, NCSS president, 1991–1992. File 2, 1991–1992, Accession #960307, NCSS Archive.

Mehlinger, H. (1992). The National Commission on Social Studies in the Schools:

An example of the politics of curriculum reform in the United States. *Journal of Curriculum Studies, 23,* 449–465.

Meiklejohn, A. (1949, March 27). Should Communists be allowed to teach? *New York Times Magazine,* pp. 10, 64–66.

Metcalf, F., & Jenness, D. (1990). The National Commission on Social Studies in the Schools: An overview. *Social Education, 54,* 429–430.

Metcalf, L. E. (1963). Some guidelines for changing social studies education. *Social Education, 27,* 197–201.

Michener, J. A. Ed. (1939). *The future of the social studies.* Washington, DC: National Council for the Social Studies.

Mills, C. W. (1959). *The sociological imagination.* New York: Oxford University Press.

Minutes of Board of Directors. (1939, December 29). File 1, Box 8, Series 2B, NCSS Archive.

Minutes of Board of Directors. (1951, November 21–24). Discussion of report of the Committee on Industry-Education Cooperation, Box 8, Series 2B, NCSS Archive.

Minutes of Board of Directors. (1958). Series 2B, p. 32–33, NCSS Archive.

Missed the boat (1943, April 19). *The Sun.* Greeneville, Tennessee. File: Editorial comment by Hearst Newspapers on American history, April 1943, Box 6, Series 4D, NCSS Archive.

Morrissett, I. R. (1975). Curriculum information network, fourth report: Controversies in the classroom. *Social Education, 29,* 246–252.

Moseley, N. (1936). Content and conduct of teachers' conventions. *Progressive Education, 13,* 337–339.

Murra, W. (1941a, September 17). Reply to H. E. Abbott. File 1, Box 45, Series 4C, Executive Director Correspondence with Organizations, NCSS Archive.

Murra, W. (1941b, February 22). Telegram to Walter D. Fuller, NAM, sent from Atlantic City. File 1, Box 2, Series 7, Committee Records, Academic Freedom Correspondence, NCSS Archive.

Murra, W. F. (1943, April 15). "Social studies" defended. Letter. *New York Times,* p. 24.

Myers, A. F. (1940). The attacks on the Rugg books. *Frontiers of Democracy, 7,* 17–21.

Nash, G., Crabtree, C., & Dunn, R. E. (1997). *History on trial: Culture wars and the teaching of the past.* New York: Knopf.

Nash, G. B., & Dunn, R. E. (1995). History standards and culture wars. *Social Education, 59,* 6.

National Association of Manufacturers. (1941, January). Statement by NAM. *Educational Cooperation Bulletin (NAM),* pp. 2–3.

National Center for Education Statistics. (1984). *A trend study of high school offerings and enrollments: 1972–73 and 1981–82.* Washington, DC: U.S. Government Printing Office.

National Center for Education Statistics. (2001). *The 1998 high school transcript study tabulations: Comparative data on credits earned and demographics for 1998, 1994, 1990, 1987, and 1982.* Washington, DC: U.S. Department of Education.

National Center for History in the Schools. (1994). *National standards for United States history: Exploring the American experience, grades 5–12.* Los Angeles: National Center for History in the Schools.

National Center for History in the Schools. (1996). *National standards for history, basic edition.* Los Angeles: National Center for History in the Schools.

National Commission on Excellence in Education. (1983). *A nation at risk: The imperative for educational reform.* Washington, DC: U.S. Government Printing Office.

National Commission on Social Studies in the Schools. (1989). *Charting a course: Social studies for the 21st century.* Washington, DC: National Commission on Social Studies in the Schools.

National Council for the Social Studies. (1975, June 20). The MACOS question: Views of 'Man: A course of study,' and the roles of the National Science Foundation and the federal government in curriculum development and implementation. Box 1, Executive Director Office Files, 1974–1980, Accession #820912, NCSS Archive.

National Council for the Social Studies. (1994). *Expectations of excellence: Curriculum standards for social studies.* Washington, DC: National Council for the Social Studies.

National Council for the Social Studies Board of Directors Resolutions/Votes. (1953, November 27). Resolutions Adopted by the Board of Directors, Buffalo, New York. File 1, Box 1, Series 2D, NCSS Archive.

National Council for the Social Studies Board of Directors Resolutions/Votes. (1955). File 1, Box 1, Series 2D, NCSS Archive.

National Council for the Social Studies Essentials of Education Statement. (1980). *Essentials of social studies.* Washington, DC: National Council for the Social Studies.

National Council for the Social Studies Resolutions. (1942, November 28). Annual meeting resolutions. File 3, Box 5, Series 4D, NCSS Archive.

National Council for the Social Studies Task Force on Curriculum Guidelines. (1971). Social studies curriculum guidelines. *Social Education, 35,* 853–867.

National Education Association. (1894). *The report of the Committee of Ten on secondary school studies.* New York: American Book.

National Education Association. (1918). *Cardinal Principles of Secondary Education: A Report of the Commission on the Reorganization of Secondary Education.* Washington, DC: U.S. Government Printing Office.

National Education Association DuShane Emergency Fund Division. (1970, November). Guarding your freedom to teach, *Today's Education,* pp. 21–23.

Neill, A. S. (1960). *Summerhill: A radical approach to child rearing.* New York: Hart.

Nelson, J. L. (1990). Charting a course backwards: A response to the National Commission's 19th century social studies program. *Social Education, 54,* 434–437.

Nelson, L. R., & Drake, F. R. (1994). Secondary teachers' reactions to the new social studies. *Theory and Research in Social Education, 22,* 44–73.

Nelson, M. R. (1975). *Building a science of society: The social studies and Harold O. Rugg.* Unpublished doctoral dissertation, Stanford University, Stanford, CA.

Nelson, M. R. (1977). The development of the Rugg social studies materials. *Theory and Research in Social Education, 5,* 64–83.

Nelson, M. R. (1995). NCSS: *Directionless from birth.* (Document Reproduction Service ERIC No. ED391706).

Nelson, M. R. (1997). Are teachers stupid? Setting and meeting standards in social studies. (Document Reproduction Service ERIC No. ED426035).

Nelson, M. R., & Singleton, H. W. (1978). Governmental surveillance of three progressive educators. Paper presented at the annual meeting of the American Educational Research Association, Toronto, Canada.

Nevins, A. (1942a, May 3). American history for Americans. *New York Times Magazine*, pp. 6, 28.

Nevins, A. (1942b, October 13). Letter to Hunt. Box 4, Series 4D, American History Controversy, Correspondence, 1941–1943, NCSS Archive.

New England History Teachers Association. (1909). Modifications in the report of the Committee of Seven recommended by the N.E. [New England] Association, *The History Teachers' Magazine, 1*, 89–90.

Ohanian, S. (1999). *One size fits few: The folly of educational standards.* Portsmouth, NH: Heineman.

Ohman, R. (1976, October 25). The literacy crisis is a fiction if not a hoax. *Chronicle of Higher Education*, p. 32.

Oliver, D. (1957). The selection of content in the social sciences. *Harvard Education Review, 27*, 271–300.

Oliver, D. W., & Shaver, J. P. (1966). *Teaching public issues in the high school.* Boston: Houghton Mifflin.

Onosko, J. J. (1991). Barriers to the promotion of higher-order thinking in social studies. *Theory and Research in Social Education, 19*, 341–366.

Our American history. (1943, April). *Hearst Newspapers.* File: Editorial Comment by Hearst Newspapers on American History, April, 1943, Box 6, Series 4D, NCSS Archive.

Park, J., & Stephenson, O. W. (1940). Clarifying social studies terms. *Social Education, 4*, 311–316.

Parker, W. C. (Ed.). (1996). *Educating the democratic mind.* Albany: State University of New York Press.

Peshkin, A. (1978). *Growing up American: Schooling and the survival of community.* Chicago: University of Chicago Press.

Phillips, B. W. (1933). Some current criticisms of the teaching of history. *The Historical Outlook, 24*, 241–246.

Phinney, J. T. (1934a). The objective selection of curriculum material in the social studies. *The Social Studies, 25*, 69.

Phinney, J. T. (1934b). The scientific reconstruction of the social studies curriculum. *The Social Studies, 25*, 108–109.

Pincus, F. L. (1984a). Book banning and the New Right: Censorship in the public schools. *The Educational Forum, 49*, 7–21.

Pincus, F. L. (1984b). From equity to excellence: The rebirth of educational conservatism. *Social Policy, 14*, 50–56.

Postman, N., & Weingartner, C. (1969). *Teaching as a subversive activity.* New York: Delacorte.

Prentis, H. W. (1940, May 8). H. W. Prentis to Howard Wilson. File: Correspondence 1940–43, Box 45, Series 4C, Executive Director Correspondence with Organizations, NCSS Archive.

Price, M. E. (1983, November). *A thousand year march: The historical vision of Harold Rugg*. Paper presented at the meeting of the National Council for the Social Studies, San Francisco, CA.

Price, R. A. (Ed.). (1958). *New viewpoints in the social sciences*. Washington, DC: National Council for the Social Studies.

Propaganda in education. (1934, May 23). *New York Sun*. File: Commission on Social Studies, Box 1, Accession No. 85001, NCSS Archive.

Proposed program of social studies in the secondary schools. (1922). *American Economic Review, 12*, 66–74.

Quillen, I. J. (Ed.). (1942). *Problems in American life*. Units No. 1–5. Washington, DC: National Council for the Social Studies.

Quillen, I. J. (1944, March 18). Letter to Orlando Stephenson. File 1: Correspondence, 1940–1949, Box 2, Series 7, NCSS Archive.

Quillen, I. J., & Hanna, L. (1948). *Education for social competence: Curriculum and instruction in secondary school social studies*. Chicago: Scott, Foresman.

Ravitch, D. (1983). *The troubled crusade*. New York: Basic Books.

Ravitch, D. (1985, November 17). Decline and fall of history teaching. *New York Times Magazine*, pp. 50–53, 101, 117.

Ravitch, D. (1987). The revival of history: Problems and progress. Paper presented at the annual meeting of the American Educational Research Association, Washington, DC.

Ravitch, D. (1989). The plight of history in America's schools. In P. Gagnon (Ed.), *Historical literacy: The case for history in American education* (pp. 51–68). New York: Macmillan.

Ravitch, D. (1997). Better than alternatives. *Society, 34*, 29–31.

Ravitch, D. & Finn, C., Jr. (1987). *What do our 17-year-olds know? A report of the first national assessment of history and literature*. New York: Harper & Row.

Reactions to the reports on Project Social Studies. (1965). *Social Education, 29*, 356–360.

Read, C. (1938). Report of the executive secretary for 1936–1937. *The American Historical Review, 43*, 728–740.

Reimer, E. (1971). *School is dead: Alternatives in education*. Garden City, NJ: Doubleday.

Report of the Advisory Panel on the Scholastic Aptitude Test Score Decline. (1977). *On further examination*. New York: College Entrance Examination Board.

Rickover, H. G. (1959). *Education and freedom*. New York: E. P. Dutton.

Risinger, C. F., & Garcia, J. (1995). National assessment and the social studies. *The Clearing House, 68*, 225–228.

Robinson, D. W. (1959). What happened to our schools? *Social Education, 22*, 322.

Robinson, D. W. (1963). Ferment in the social studies. *Social Education, 27*, 360–364, 410.

Robinson, J. H. (1912). *The new history: Essays illustrating the modern historical outlook*. New York: Macmillan.

Roorbach, A. O. (1937). *The development of the social studies in American secondary education before 1861*. Unpublished doctoral dissertation, University of Pennsylvania, Philadelphia.

Root, E. M. (1958). *Brainwashing in the high schools.* New York: Devin-Adair.

Ross, E. W. (1996). Diverting democracy: The curriculum standards movement and social studies education. *International Journal of Social Education, 11,* 18–39.

Ross, E. W. (Ed.). (1997). *The social studies curriculum.* Albany: State University of New York Press.

Rudd, A. G. (1940, April). Our "reconstructed" educational system. *Nation's Business,* pp. 27–28, 93–94.

Rugg, H. O. (1921). On reconstructing the social studies: Comments on Mr. Schafer's letter. *Historical Outlook, 12,* 249–252.

Rugg, H. O. (1923). Problems of contemporary life as the basis for curriculum-making in the social studies. In H. O. Rugg (Ed.), *The social studies in the elementary and secondary school* (pp. 260–273). 22nd Yearbook of the National Society on the Study of Education, Part II. Bloomington, IL: Public School.

Rugg, H. O. (1931). *An introduction to problems of American culture.* Boston: Ginn & Company.

Rugg, H. O. (1933). *The great technology: Social chaos and the public mind.* New York: John Day.

Rugg, H. O. (1941a). A study in censorship: Good concepts and bad words. *Social Education, 5,* 176–181.

Rugg, H. O. (1941b). *That men may understand: An American in the long armistice.* New York: Doubleday, Doran.

Sarason, S. B. (1982). *The culture of the school and the problem of change.* Boston: Allyn & Bacon.

Saxe, D. W. (1991). *Social studies in schools: A history of the early years.* Albany: State University of New York Press.

Schafer, J. (1921a). The methods and aims of committee procedure: Open letters from Dr. Schafer and Mr. Rugg. *Historical Outlook, 12,* 248.

Schafer, J. (1921b). Report of Committee on History and Education for Citizenship, part I. *The Historical Outlook, 12,* 90.

Schlesinger, A. M., Jr. (1991). *The disuniting of America: Reflections on a multicultural society.* New York: W. W. Norton.

Scott, C. W., & Hill, C. M. (Eds.). (1954). *Public education under criticism.* New York: Prentice-Hall.

Sellers, C. G. (1969). Is history on the way out of the schools and do historians care? *Social Education, 33,* 509–516.

Shaver, J. P. (1967). Social studies: The need for redefinition. *Social Education, 31,* 588 592, 596.

Shaver, J. P. (1979, October 6). Status in social studies and educational innovation: Implications of the NSF and the RAND reports for the ABA Youth Education for Citizenship Committee. Summary of Comments by James P. Shaver at the meeting of the YEFC Committee.

Shaver, J. P., Davis, O. L., Jr., & Helburn, S. W. (1979). The status of social studies education: Impressions from three NSF studies. *Social Education, 42,* 150–153.

Sheils, M. (1975, December 8). Why Johnny can't write. *Newsweek,* 58.

Siegel, B. (1978, March 12). "Cuckoo" drops a bomb on private world. *Los Angeles Times,* pp. 1, 16–19, part IV.

Silberman, C. (1970). *Crisis in the classroom: The remaking of American education*. New York: Random House.

Smith, G. R. (1963). Project social studies: A report. *Social Education, 27,* 357–359, 409.

Snedden, D. (1914). Teaching of history in secondary schools. *History Teacher's Magazine, 5,* 277–282.

Sobel, H. W. (1968). The new wave of educational literature. *Phi Delta Kappan, 50,* 109–111.

Staff. (1935). Recent happenings in social studies. *The Social Studies, 26,* 482–483.

Staff. (1936). Tentative program, Portland meeting, National Council for the Social Studies, Monday, June 29, 1936. *The Social Studies, 27,* 349.

Stanley, W. B. (1982). A reinterpretation of Harold Rugg's role in the foundation of modern social education. *Journal of Thought, 17,* 85–94.

Stedman, L. C., & Smith, M. S. (1985). Weak arguments, poor data, simplistic recommendations. In R. Gross & B. Gross (Eds.), *The great school debate: Which way for American education?* (pp. 83–105). New York: Simon and Schuster.

Stehle, V. (1997, June 30). Righting philanthropy. *The Nation,* pp. 15–20.

Stewart, A. (1921). The social sciences in secondary schools. *Historical Outlook, 12,* 53–56.

Stone, K. (1985). Hartshorn remembers the NCSS past and reflects on its future. *Social Education, 49,* 656.

Streb, R. W. (1979). *A history of the citizenship education project: A model curricular study.* Unpublished doctoral dissertation, Teachers College, Columbia University, New York.

Tanner, D. (1984). The American high school at the crossroads. *Educational Leadership, 41,* 4–13.

Tanner, D. (1993). A nation truly at risk. *Phi Delta Kappan, 75,* 288–297.

Task Force on Education for Economic Growth. (1983). *Action for excellence: A comprehensive plan to improve our nation's schools.* Denver, CO: Education Commission of the States.

Taylor, W. W. (1946). The dilemma of the social studies. *Social Education, 10,* 163.

Thorndike, E. L. (1907). *The elimination of pupils from schools* (Bureau of Education Bulletin No. 4). Washington, DC: Government Printing Office.

Thornton, S. J. (1990). Should we be teaching more history? *Theory and Research in Social Education, 18,* 53–60.

Todd, L. P. (1949). Curriculum revision. *Social Education, 13,* 101.

Todd, L. P. (1956). Letter from reader! *Social Education, 20,* 149.

Todd, L. P. (1957). Juggling act. *Social Education, 21,* 245–246.

Trow, W. C. (1954). Academic utopia? An evaluation of *Educational Wastelands. Educational Theory, 3,* 1–11.

Tryon, R. M. (1922). Conference upon desirable adjustments between history and the other social studies in elementary and secondary schools. *Historical Outlook, 13,* 78–82.

Tryon, R. M. (1935). *The social sciences as school subjects.* New York: Charles Scribner's Sons.

Tyack, D. (1974). Ways of seeing: An essay on the history of compulsory education. *Harvard Education Review, 46,* 355–389.

Tyack, D., & Cuban, L. (1995). *Tinkering toward utopia: A century of public school reform*. Cambridge, MA: Harvard University Press.

Tyack, D., & Hansot, E. (1982). *Managers of virtue: Public school leadership in America, 1820–1980*. New York: Basic Books.

Tyack, D., Hansot, E., & Lowe, R. (1985). *Public schools in hard times*. Cambridge, MA: Harvard University Press.

Tyack, D., & James, T. (1985). Moral majorities and the school curriculm: Historical perspectives on the legalization of virtue. *Teachers College Record, 86*, 513–537.

U.S. Bureau of Education. (1916). *The social studies in secondary education*. Washington, DC: U.S. Government Printing Office, Bulletin No. 28.

U.S. Bureau of Education. (1924). Statistics of public high schools, 1921–1922. Washington, DC: U.S. Government Printing Office, Bulletin No. 7.

U.S. Department of Education. (1991). *America 2000: An education strategy*. Washington, DC: U.S. Department of Education.

U.S. Department of Education. (1995, Spring). *Goals 2000: A Progress Report*. Washington, DC: U.S. Department of Education.

U.S. Office of Education. (1930). *Biennial survey of education, 1926–1928*. Washington, DC: U.S. Government Printing Office, Bulletin No. 16.

U.S. Senate. (1943, April 6). Senate resolution 129. File 4, Box 5, Series 4D, NCSS Archive.

Vinson, Kevin D. (1998). National curriculum standards and social studies education: Dewey, Freire, Foucault, and the construction of a radical critique. Paper presented at the annual meeting of the National Council for the Social Studies, Anaheim, CA, November 20–22.

Washburne, C. (1941, September). Shall we have more "progressive education"? *The Rotarian*, pp. 26–28.

Watkins, W. H. (2001). *The White architects of Black education: Ideology and power in America, 1865–1954*. New York: Teachers College Press.

Watson, B. A. (1957). Social science and social studies. *Social Education, 21*, 25–26.

Wesley, E. B. (1936). A guide to the commission report. *The Social Studies, 27*, 448.

Wesley, E. B. (1937). *Teaching the social studies: Theory and practice*. Boston: D. C. Heath.

Wesley, E. B. (1943a). Early outline for E. B. Wesley. *American history in schools and colleges*. File 8, Box 5, Series 4D, NCSS Archive.

Wesley, E. B. (1943b). History in the school curriculum. *Mississippi Valley Historical Review, 9*, 565–575.

Wesley, E. B. (1944). *American history in schools and colleges*. New York: Macmillan.

Whelan, M. (1997a). A particularly lucid lens: The Committee of Ten and the Social Studies Committee in historical context. *Journal of Curriculum and Supervision, 12*, 256–268.

Whelan, M. (1997b). Social studies for social reform: Charles Beard's vision of history and social studies education. *Theory and Research in Social Education, 25*, 288–315.

White, H. (1978). *Tropics of discourse: Essays in cultural criticism*. Baltimore: Johns Hopkins University Press.

Williams, J. A. (1994). *Classrooom in conflict: Teaching controversial subjects in a diverse society.* Albany: State University of New York Press.

Wilson, H. E. (1938). *Education for Citizenship.* New York: McGraw Hill.

Wilson, H. E. (1940, December 20). Response to Kepner. File 1, Box 2, Series 7, Committee Records, Academic Freedom Correspondence, NCSS Archive.

Winters, E. A. (1967). Man and his changing society: The textbooks of Harold Rugg. *History of Education Quarterly, 7,* 509–510.

Winters, E. A. (1968). *Harold Rugg and education for social reconstruction.* Unpublished doctoral dissertation, University of Wisconsin, Madison.

Wirth, F. P. (1931). Classroom difficulties in the teaching of history. *Historical Outlook, 29,* 116–117.

Woodring, P. (1953). *Let's talk sense about our schools.* New York: McGraw-Hill.

Wright, G. S. (1950). *Core curriculum in public high schools: An inquiry into practices, 1949.* Washington, DC: U.S. Office of Education, Bulletin No. 5.

Zinn, H. (1980). *A people's history of the United States.* New York: Harper and Row.

Index

About the Author

RONALD W. EVANS is a professor in the School of Teacher Education at San Diego State University. A former middle school and high school teacher, he has authored numerous articles and book chapters and served as the first editor of the *Handbook on Teaching Social Issues* (National Council for the Social Studies, 1996). He is currently working on a biography of Harold O. Rugg.